D1534832

		DATE DUE		

Other titles in the Greenhaven Press Literary Companion series:

British Authors

Jane Austen
Joseph Conrad
Charles Dickens
J.R.R. Tolkien

British Literature

Animal Farm
Beowulf
Brave New World
The Canterbury Tales
A Christmas Carol
Great Expectations
Gulliver's Travels
Hamlet
Heart of Darkness
The Importance of Being Earnest
Jane Eyre
Julius Caesar
Lord of the Flies
Macbeth
The Merchant of Venice
A Midsummer Night's Dream
Oliver Twist
Othello
A Portrait of the Artist as a Young Man
Pride and Prejudice
Romeo and Juliet
Shakespeare: The Comedies
Shakespeare: The Histories
Shakespeare: The Sonnets
Shakespeare: The Tragedies
Silas Marner
A Tale of Two Cities
The Taming of the Shrew
Tess of the d'Urbervilles
Twelfth Night
Wuthering Heights

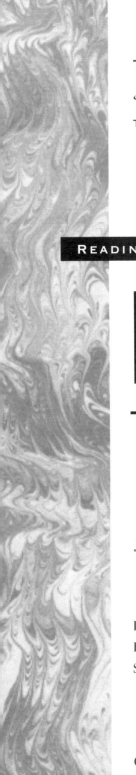

THE GREENHAVEN PRESS
Literary Companion
TO BRITISH LITERATURE

READINGS ON

HARD TIMES

Jill Karson, *Book Editor*

Daniel Leone, *President*
Bonnie Szumski, *Publisher*
Stuart Miller, *Series Editor*

Greenhaven Press, Inc., San Diego, CA

Every effort has been made to trace the owners of copyrighted material. The articles in this volume may have been edited for content, length, and/or reading level. The titles have been changed to enhance the editorial purpose. Those interested in locating the original source will find the complete citation on the first page of each article.

Library of Congress Cataloging-in-Publication Data

Readings on Hard times / Jill Karson, book editor.
        p. cm. — (Greenhaven Press literary companion to British authors)
    Includes bibliographical references and index.
    ISBN 0-7377-0436-5 (lib. bdg. : alk. paper) —
ISBN 0-7377-0435-7 (pbk. : alk. paper)
    1. Dickens, Charles, 1812–1870. Hard Times. I. Karson, Jill. II. Series.

PR4561 .R43   2002
823'.8—dc21   2001040607
                                                      CIP

Cover photo: © Stock Montage, Inc.
Library of Congress, 14

Copyright © 2002 by Greenhaven Press, Inc.
10911 Technology Place
San Diego, CA 92127
Printed in the U.S.A.

> *People mutht be amuthed. They can't be alwayth a-learning, nor yet they can't be alwayth a-working, they an't made for it. You mutht have uth [both], Thquire. Do the withe thing and the kind thing too, and make the beth of uth [life], not the wirtht [worst].*

—Mr. Sleary in *Hard Times*

CONTENTS

FOREWORD

*"'Tis the good reader that
makes the good book."*

Ralph Waldo Emerson

The story's bare facts are simple: The captain, an old and scarred seafarer, walks with a peg leg made of whale ivory. He relentlessly drives his crew to hunt the world's oceans for the great white whale that crippled him. After a long search, the ship encounters the whale and a fierce battle ensues. Finally the captain drives his harpoon into the whale, but the harpoon line catches the captain about the neck and drags him to his death.

A simple story, a straightforward plot—yet, since the 1851 publication of Herman Melville's *Moby-Dick*, readers and critics have found many meanings in the struggle between Captain Ahab and the whale. To some, the novel is a cautionary tale that depicts how Ahab's obsession with revenge leads to his insanity and death. Others believe that the whale represents the unknowable secrets of the universe and that Ahab is a tragic hero who dares to challenge fate by attempting to discover this knowledge. Perhaps Melville intended Ahab as a criticism of Americans' tendency to become involved in well-intentioned but irrational causes. Or did Melville model Ahab after himself, letting his fictional character express his anger at what he perceived as a cruel and distant god?

Although literary critics disagree over the meaning of *Moby-Dick*, readers do not need to choose one particular interpretation in order to gain an understanding of Melville's novel. Instead, by examining various analyses, they can gain numerous insights into the issues that lie under the surface of the basic plot. Studying the writings of literary critics can also aid readers in making their own assessments of *Moby-Dick* and other literary works and in developing analytical thinking skills.

The Greenhaven Literary Companion Series was created with these goals in mind. Designed for young adults, this unique anthology series provides an engaging and comprehensive introduction to literary analysis and criticism. The essays included in the Literary Companion Series are chosen for their accessibility to a young adult audience and are expertly edited in consideration of both the reading and comprehension levels of this audience. In addition, each essay is introduced by a concise summation that presents the contributing writer's main themes and insights. Every anthology in the Literary Companion Series contains a varied selection of critical essays that cover a wide time span and express diverse views. Wherever possible, primary sources are represented through excerpts from authors' notebooks, letters, and journals and through contemporary criticism.

Each title in the Literary Companion Series pays careful consideration to the historical context of the particular author or literary work. In-depth biographies and detailed chronologies reveal important aspects of authors' lives and emphasize the historical events and social milieu that influenced their writings. To facilitate further research, every anthology includes primary and secondary source bibliographies of articles and/or books selected for their suitability for young adults. These engaging features make the Greenhaven Literary Companion Series ideal for introducing students to literary analysis in the classroom or as a library resource for young adults researching the world's great authors and literature.

Exceptional in its focus on young adults, the Greenhaven Literary Companion Series strives to present literary criticism in a compelling and accessible format. Every title in the series is intended to spark readers' interest in leading American and world authors, to help them broaden their understanding of literature, and to encourage them to formulate their own analyses of the literary works that they read. It is the editors' hope that young adult readers will find these anthologies to be true companions in their study of literature.

INTRODUCTION

Written at the midpoint of his illustrious career, *Hard Times* is Dickens's scathing commentary on industrial conditions in England, on the "hard times" the author witnessed around him. Just as widely divergent opinions mark Dickensian criticism in general, *Hard Times*—and perhaps more than any other Dickensian novel—has endured a particularly checkered literary history.

On the one hand, *Hard Times* has had its share of prominent admirers—most notably John Ruskin and George Bernard Shaw, both of whom unabashedly praised the novel's power and social message. Other advocates have called it Dickens's most clear-cut novel—*Hard Times* is relatively short, bereft of elaborate subplots and changes of scenery, and thoroughly unencumbered by a myriad of minor characters. Other critics, interestingly, charge that these very same qualities cripple the novel, finding it not concise but rather crudely plotted and heavily caricatured and lacking in the colorful detail and exuberant humor that seem so central to Dickens's work. Also noteworthy is that many critics—especially in the late part of the nineteenth and early part of the twentieth century—simply ignored the novel.

These various points of view are represented in *Readings on "Hard Times."* Essays in this volume represent not only a variety of scholarly approaches and a wide range of sources but also include critics from different generations. Some focus specifically on Dickens's literary technique and identify influences—the effects of serialization, for instance—in the genesis of *Hard Times.* Several pieces consider the novel's recurring themes, highlighting Dickens's deep and abiding concern for the weak and disadvantaged. Other selections debate the artistic merit of *Hard Times* and discuss reasons why the novel remained, for many years, one of Dickens's least-read books. Also included is the famous, laudatory essay by British critic F.R. Leavis that resulted in a marked upsurge of critical attention. In addition, this volume includes several features to aid the reader of *Hard Times:* A biography of Charles Dickens lends historical background to the novel, and a chronology places the novel in broader context. A detailed plot synopsis and bibliography further aid readers as they discover the art and ideas that render *Hard Times* an ultimately provocative and enduring work.

CHARLES DICKENS: A BIOGRAPHY

Charles Dickens exuded an energy and determination that awed friends and overwhelmed relatives. His temper flared at slights to himself and his work; his generosity and compassion extended to children and the working poor. He was a pessimist who doubted that government and the upper class would ever pass reforms to help poor people, but who optimistically believed in the goodness of the lower class and championed their cause throughout his life. He made his mark in nineteenth-century England with humor, creating a cast of characters that exemplified all that he loved and satirized all that he hated about his society. Biographer Edgar Johnson says in the preface to his biography of Dickens:

> Dickens was himself a Dickens character, bursting with an inordinate and fantastic vitality. The world in which his spirit dwelt was identical with the world of his novels, brilliant in hue, violent in movement, crammed with people all furiously alive and with places as alive as his people. "The Dickens world" was his everyday world.

Scholars attribute much of the formation of Dickens's personality and, consequently, his achievements to two phases in his boyhood years. The first, happy phase gave him hope and optimism; the second, sad phase instilled his spirit for social reform.

Charles John Huffman Dickens was born on February 7, 1812, in the southwestern English town of Landport in Portsea, the second of eight children born to John and Elizabeth Barrow Dickens. John Dickens, a clerk in the Navy Payoffice, and Elizabeth, a pretty, educated woman, belonged to the middle class but were not prosperous enough to withstand the extravagant spending and entertainment they enjoyed. John Dickens enjoyed a house full of party guests and rehearsed little Charles and his sister to entertain them. In *Charles Dickens: A Critical Study*, G.K. Chesterton says:

> Some of the earliest glimpses we have of Charles Dickens show him to us perched on some chair or table singing comic

songs in an atmosphere of perpetual applause. So, almost as soon as he can toddle, he steps into the glare of the footlights. He never stepped out of it until he died.

In 1814 John was temporarily sent to the London office before being transferred to the naval dockyards in the southeastern town of Chatham in 1817, when Charles was five. There John rented a large house for his family, two servants, and Aunt Fanny, his wife's widowed sister, but soon found it beyond his means and moved his family to a smaller Chatham home.

A HAPPY AND SAD CHILDHOOD

In a family that felt financially secure, Charles enjoyed his years in Chatham, five years that permanently affected his outlook on life. He played games with friends, put on magic-lantern shows (an early form of slide projector), and continued to sing duets with his sister Fanny. Mary Weller, the maid who cared for the children, told bedtime stories and hummed evensong, or evening worship, hymns. Dickens investigated the town, recording in his mind the sights of its shipwrights, convict laborers, guild hall, cathedral, and castle on the hill and the smells of rope and wood and canvas down by the docks. Because he was often sick, Charles never played sports well, but he loved to read, saying later, "When I think of it, the picture always arises in my mind of a summer evening, the boys at play in the churchyard, and I sitting on my bed, reading as if for life." In addition to reading the family books, such as *Peregrine Pickle, Don Quixote,* and *Robinson Crusoe,* Aunt Fanny's suitor, Dr. Matthew Lamert, and his son James took Charles to farces, melodramas, and to *Richard II* and *Macbeth.*

Dickens attended the school of William Giles, a Baptist minister in Chatham. A precocious child, Charles fully expected to attend both school and college and enter a profession. These early, happy years laid the groundwork for his lifelong hope and vitality.

His hopes for a bright future were dashed, however, when his father, now heavily in debt, was transferred back to London in 1822, when Charles was ten. John Dickens settled his family in Camden Town, a poor section of London, in a four-room house that held Dickens's parents as well as six children, one maid, and James Lamert, who lived with them. No arrangement was made for Charles to go to school, though

Fanny had won a scholarship to the Royal Academy of Music. Charles did chores at home, and just as curiously as he had done in Chatham, he wandered the streets of Camden Town, observing its noisy vehicles, small factories, taverns, cooked-food stalls, and rubbish dumps and watching chimney sweeps, muffin-boys, and apprentices at work—all sounds, sights, and smells that imprinted themselves on his mind.

Not long after moving to London, Charles learned what it meant to be poor. One sad day his family sold his beloved books from Chatham days to pay debts, after which he borrowed copies of the newspapers *Spectator* and *Tatler* for his reading. His mother rented a room and started a school, but not one pupil came. James Lamert, who managed a boot-blacking factory, suggested that Charles work there to help with the deteriorating family finances. At twelve, Charles worked from eight A.M. to eight P.M. for six shillings a week in the tumbledown warehouse tying and labeling pots of blacking. Two weeks after Charles started at the blacking factory, John Dickens was arrested for not paying his debts and sent to Marshalsea, a debtors prison, or workhouse for the poor, with meager food and hard labor. Charles was sent out to pawn household goods, and when only beds, chairs, and the kitchen table were left, the rest of the family moved to Marshalsea (which admitted groups in family quarters) with the father.

Charles Dickens

John Dickens, who still drew a small naval salary, paid for lodgings so that Charles could continue his job at the blacking factory. Now that he had to feed himself on six shillings a week, he divided his money into packages, one for each day, occasionally splurging the whole day's allotment on a sweet or a good ale; when he had no money, he walked to the Covent Garden market and stared at food. Alone in the lodging house with no companion but the boys from the blacking factory, who mocked him because he was small and shy and different, Charles suffered greatly. In an unpublished autobiography, he later wrote of this time in his life:

No words can express the secret agony of my soul, as I sunk into this companionship; compared these everyday associates with those of my happier childhood; and felt my early hopes of growing up to be a learned and distinguished man, crushed in my breast.

The deep remembrance of the sense I had of being utterly neglected and hopeless; of the shame I felt in my position; of the misery it was to my young heart to believe that, day by day, what I had learned, and thought, and delighted in, and raised my fancy and my emulation up by, was passing away from me, never to be brought back any more; . . . even now, famous and caressed and happy, I . . . wander desolately back to that time of my life. . . . That I suffered in secret, and that I suffered exquisitely, no one ever knew but I.

Following a quarrel with John Dickens, Lamert fired Charles after twenty weeks that seemed to Charles like twenty years. The experience of the blacking factory made an indelible impression on him, setting in him a hard determination, but through his suffering he developed an equally permanent sensitivity from which he created in his novels a host of suffering children and other innocent victims of injustice and pain.

After three months in Marshalsea, John Dickens's mother died and John inherited £450, enough to get him out of prison, and John went back to his job with the navy. From 1824 to 1826, he sent Charles to Wellington House Academy, where Charles studied English, French, Latin, writing, mathematics, and dancing. When John lost his job and took work as a reporter for the *British Press*, he was again deep in debt, and Charles had to drop out of school. He took a job at the law office of Ellis and Blackmore, which he found so boring that he determined never to be a lawyer who spent his life "splitting hairs slowly and growing rich on the distress of others." Dickens then set out to educate himself. He taught himself shorthand in eighteen months, went to acting school, and procured a pass to the Reading Room in the British Museum (the national library) where he spent hours reading, the "usefullest [days] of my life."

While working at the law office, Dickens had met and fallen in love with Maria Beadnell, a banker's daughter a year older than he. Dickens pursued her diligently, but her parents disapproved. The disappointment of losing Maria renewed old feelings of despair and shame felt so vividly during the days of the blacking factory. At his twenty-first birthday party, Maria rejected him, after which Charles returned her letters, but she kept up a teasing relationship that fed his hopes. When Maria's parents sent her to Paris to finishing school, Charles realized he had no chance to win her love after four years of trying. He vowed he would never again be anyone's plaything. Lacking family wealth or prestige, he would need independent success, and from then on he was determined to have his way.

DICKENS BEGINS AS A JOURNALIST

Four years after taking a law-clerk job, Dickens began his writing career as a reporter. Once he had mastered shorthand, he set himself up as a freelance reporter near the law courts and waited to be hired as a recorder of court cases. He acquired a job on the *Mirror of Parliament,* a paper that reported the daily transactions of the lawmakers, and worked his way to an advanced position hiring and supervising other reporters. He earned a reputation for accuracy and speed in recording speeches of members of Parliament, and was invited to join the staff of another paper, the *True Sun.* As a reporter observing the workings of Parliament, he was unimpressed with its red tape; he saw that a few reforms benefited the middle class, but that lawmakers did nothing for the masses of poor whose lives were, as he described, "misery, starvation, unemployment and cholera." Of particular interest to Dickens, Parliament, in 1832, appointed a Royal Commission to examine legislation concerning the poor—and reform the system of providing relief. The events centering on these poor laws—and the history that led to them—made an indelible impression on Dickens.

THE POOR LAWS

For many years, England had grappled with supporting its swelling class of paupers. Since the time of Queen Elizabeth, direct relief alleviated some of the problem. As the number of paupers continued to increase, however, so, too, did the cost of public relief, which reached staggering heights. Parish taxes were imposed, not only to provide direct relief but also to supplement starvation wages. This system, inevitably, invited widespread abuse. In response, Parliament passed the Poor Law of 1834, which required that all ablebodied paupers enter a workhouse. To discourage people from living at public expense, living conditions in the workhouse were deliberately made intolerable: Workhouses were usually overcrowded, filthy facilities where food was meager and medical aid almost nonexistent. As one of Dickens's contemporaries observed: "The principle upon which relief is administered under the law appears to be to make the help rendered so distasteful, that they must be far gone indeed in wretchedness who will apply for it; and the high-hearted poor will starve rather than take it, will die instead of coming on the rates."

Dickens found the Poor Law of 1834 reprehensible. Though Dickens himself had acquired some professional and economic success, he still remembered the days in the blacking factory and had compassion for those who worked hard and had almost nothing. Several years later, when Dickens embarked on the serial that was to become *Oliver Twist*, he lashed out at the pitiable condition of the poor and, even more specifically, the harsh tenets of the Poor Law of 1834. Indeed, the treatment of the poor was to become a common—and passionate—theme in Dickens's writing.

THE ROAD TO SUCCESS

After 1833 Dickens's determination and hard work brought results. The *Morning Chronicle* hired him as a full-time reporter and soon after added him to the staff of its affiliate, the *Evening Chronicle*. When the *Monthly Magazine* printed, without his name and without paying him, a sketch Dickens had submitted, he was thrilled to see his writing in print. The editors asked for more sketches, which he signed "Boz" for the first time in 1834. Dickens took the name Boz from his family; his little brother Augustus, nicknamed Moses but unable to pronounce the word, called himself Boz. When Dickens was covering plays for the *Evening Chronicle*, he discovered that some of the Boz sketches had been adapted for the stage. Dickens's "sketches" were entertainingly written anecdotes about London people and places. Since the *Monthly Magazine* did not pay him, he quit and wrote street sketches for the *Evening Chronicle*. In addition, he wrote twelve sketches for *Bell's Life in London*. His new success brought him to the attention of writer William Harrison Ainsworth, who introduced Dickens to artist George Cruikshank and publisher John Macrone. In 1836, on Dickens's twenty-fourth birthday, Macrone published *Sketches by Boz*, a two-volume collection of sketches illustrated by Cruikshank.

George Hogarth, Dickens's editor on the *Evening Chronicle*, often invited Dickens to join family gatherings and introduced Dickens to his daughters, all of whom Dickens found charming. On April 2, 1836, he married the oldest daughter, Catherine, called Kate, at St. Luke's Church, Chelsea. When the couple was settled, Catherine's sixteen-year-old sister, Mary, came to live with them; unmarried sisters or brothers living with a married couple was common practice in Dickens's day. Later, Dickens's brother Fred also lived in their home. Charles and Mary, who had a sweeter disposition than Catherine, developed a close friendship with more understanding than existed between Charles and his wife, who nevertheless bore ten children, seven boys and three girls, between 1837 and 1852.

FROM SKETCHES TO NOVELS

When *Sketches by Boz* brought good reviews, publishers Chapman and Hall invited Dickens to write, for £14 a month, twenty monthly installments about an imaginary sports club, the Nemrod Club, sketches to be illustrated by Robert Seymour. Dickens, knowing nothing about sports, renegotiated the proposal to focus instead on the travels and investigations of Mr. Pickwick and the imaginary Pickwick Club, illustrated by Hablôt Knight Browne, called Phiz, who became Dickens's illustrator for other works. The first installments from the Pickwick Club were poorly received, until Dickens added the character of Sam Weller in the fourth installment. The addition changed the fortunes of the series from sales of four thousand to forty thousand copies. Biographer Wolf Mankowitz describes the popularity of Pickwick:

> It was read upstairs and downstairs [by all classes], by judges on the bench and the cleaners after them.... Critics spoke of Dickens as another Cervantes, poor people shared a shilling copy and read it aloud in groups. A clergyman, having consoled a sick man, heard him mutter behind his back, "Well, thank God, Pickwick will be out in ten days anyway!"

Chapman and Hall sold back issues by the thousands, and they more than doubled Dickens's salary. The installments were published as a book, entitled *Pickwick Papers,* in 1837. Dickens was "the sudden lion of the town," and offers poured in for children's books, novels, and more sketches.

Dickens accepted an offer to edit the monthly *Bentley's Miscellany* and include in it installments of *Oliver Twist,* to be illustrated by Cruikshank, the illustrator of Boz. The first February 1837 installment garnered great reviews and sold many copies even though it had a more serious tone than *Pickwick.* In *Pickwick,* Dickens presented prison with humor and a mild view; in *Oliver Twist,* he wrote about prison in grave, realistic language. While he was writing the installments for the novel, Mary Hogarth died suddenly. Because Dickens loved Mary as a close friend, he felt such grief he had to take time off. He coped with the loss by taking long walks and horseback rides with John Forster, who had become his friend and agent. Dickens's sadness over Mary's death further strained his relationship with Catherine, who, though she mourned the loss of her sister, was jealous of her husband's affection for Mary. Determined to continue writing, he finished the installments, after which Bentley published *Oliver Twist* in a three-volume book in 1838, the first book to have Dickens's name, not the anonymous "Boz," on the title page.

Before Dickens completed *Oliver Twist* he was already thinking of his next novel, and he traveled with his illustrator Phiz to Yorkshire to research the conditions of boarding schools there. He found maggots, fleas, beatings, and ignorance, schools where illegitimate children were hidden for low fees. At Bowes Academy, run by one-eyed William Shaw, boys were sick, some went blind, and on average one died each year. These schools became the model for Dotheboys Hall in *Nicholas Nickleby,* whose first installment was published in April 1838 while Dickens was still drawing praise from critics for *Oliver Twist.* Of *Nicholas Nickleby,* biographer Edgar Johnson says, "it mingles the sunlight of *Pickwick* with the darkness of *Oliver,*" and "fuses the inexhaustible laughter of *Pickwick* with the somber themes of *Oliver Twist.*" These two books, *Oliver Twist* and *Nicholas Nickleby,* Johnson says, "were clarion peals announcing to the world that in Charles Dickens the rejected and forgotten and misused of the world had a champion." The first installment of *Nicholas Nickleby* sold fifty thousand copies on the first day.

The success of Dickens's books brought him enough earnings to move up in social class. He bought a house with a gate on Doughty Street in London and traveled within England and abroad. He was invited to join social clubs and literary societies and met other writers—essayist Leigh Hunt and novelists William Thackeray and Edward Bulwer-Lytton. Invitations came to Dickens from the city's cultured elite on the west end of town, but not to Kate, not known for charm or wit. Dickens was greeted by footmen and led up grand staircases to attend breakfasts and dinners at which the educated and famous displayed their skills and amused one another. Mankowitz describes Dickens's reaction to this social class:

> It was a strictly mannered, often cruel world, but Dickens had already learned self-assurance, was a practised mimic of any tone, and felt confident in his intelligence and great gifts: gifts, he soon came to realize, that few of these privileged people had even a tiny part of. That awareness defended him against their insolence or patronization. He was acute enough to see behind the social masks.

As Mankowitz says, Dickens's novels harshly satirize the "masters of material gain and the parasites of materialism, in law courts, the factories and workhouses," but they seldom attack the aristocratic and intellectual elite. He became adviser to one of its members, Angela Burdett Coutts, an heiress who wanted to use money from her two fortunes for social improvement. She took Dickens's advice to fund slum clearance and homes for "fallen women."

Though Dickens's social relations went smoothly, his relations with critics and publishers were often rancorous. Writing about *Oliver Twist,* one critic said that Dickens wrote so much and so fast that he was likely to decline in quality and popularity unless he slowed down. Dickens, angered, vowed, "They shall eat their words." G.K. Chesterton thought perhaps the critics misunderstood Dickens and said, "Dickens has greatly suffered with the critics precisely through this stunning simplicity in his best work," but his disputes with publishers usually involved money and contracts, not the quality of his work. Dickens was inclined to sign a contract that seemed good at the time, then demand more money than the original contract stipulated when sales and the publisher's profits were much larger than expected. In one dispute with the publisher Bentley, Dickens wanted both money and a change in the work contract. Bentley had published *Oliver Twist* and contracted with Dickens for two additional novels. Dickens wanted to consider *Oliver Twist* one of the two and then jump to the publishers Chapman and Hall. When the dispute reached a stalemate, Dickens's friend and agent Forster negotiated for him. The determination Dickens had learned from the days at the blacking factory got him what he wanted but left hard feelings with the publisher that Forster was unable to smooth over.

LITTLE NELL SAVES A WEEKLY

Dickens wanted to be free of the contract with Bentley because he had an idea for a weekly that he wanted Chapman and Hall to fund. Dickens intended *Master Humphrey's Clock* to include a variety of short sketches written by a number of contributors. Responding to the sale of seventy thousand copies of the first issue, Dickens said, "What will the wiseacres say to weekly issues *now?* And what will they say to any of those ten thousand things we shall do together to make 'em writhe and stagger in their shoes." Sales, however, dropped markedly when the public discovered the weekly had no installments by Dickens. Within two weeks, Dickens was serializing *The Old Curiosity Shop,* a travel story about an odd collection of characters. In *The World of Charles Dickens,* Angus Wilson says that this novel

> shows up alarmingly to modern readers the degree of oddity then accepted in a supposedly realistic story—a devilish, fire-drinking dwarf, a little child, an undersized servant maid, a woman (Sally Brass), who is reported as having enlisted as a guardsman or gone down to the docks in male attire, a small boy who stands on his head in mudflats.

It was, however, sweet Little Nell, persecuted by the dwarf Quilp and loved by the honest boy Kit Nubbles, who captured readers' hearts and sent weekly sales above a hundred thousand copies. When Nell neared death, readers deluged the paper with letters pleading that Dickens not let her die. Die she did, nonetheless, in an installment that prompted an outpouring of emotion, as Mankowitz describes:

> Scottish critic Lord Jeffrey was found weeping in his library. 'I'm a great goose to have given way so', he sobbed, 'but I couldn't help it.' [Actor William] Macready, [playwright and poet Walter] Landor, Thomas Carlyle and Edgar Allan Poe were all moved to a similar plight. So was [member of Parliament] Daniel O'Connell, reading on a train journey; he groaned, 'He should not have killed her', and threw the story out of the window.

Dickens's hold on the attention and sentiment of the public loosened with the weekly installments of his next novel written for *Master Humphrey's Clock.* A historical novel, *Barnaby Rudge* recounts the riots of the poor against Parliament, but Dickens gives the story a more anti-Catholic than anti-Parliament emphasis. The strain of producing weekly installments of two books took a toll on Dickens's health, and he took a year's rest, which publishers Chapman and Hall funded with a salary.

DICKENS'S VISIT TO AMERICA

During his year off, Dickens and Catherine visited America. They sailed on January 2, 1842, and arrived in Boston to huge crowds wanting to know why Little Nell had to die. He and Catherine visited Boston, Niagara, Philadelphia, St. Louis, and New York City. Wherever he went, crowds surrounded him, cheered, stared, wrung his hand, and clipped fur souvenirs from his coat. He had invitations from every state, from universities, Congress, and all kinds of public and private bodies. He visited orphanages, schools for the blind, reform schools, prisons, and industrial mills. New York published a special edition, the *Extra Boz Herald,* and held a Boz Ball in a ballroom decorated with characters from his books. In a letter to Forster, Dickens wrote:

> I can do nothing that I want to do, go nowhere where I want to go, and see nothing that I want to see. If I turn into the street, I am followed by a multitude. If I stay at home, the house becomes, with callers, like a fair. . . . If I go to a party in the evening, and am so enclosed and hedged about by people, stand where I will, that I am exhausted for want of air. I go to church for quiet, and there is a violent rush to the neighbourhood of the pew I sit in, and the clergyman preaches at *me.* I take my seat in a railroad car, and the very conductor won't leave me alone. I get out at a station, and can't drink a glass of water, without having a hundred people looking down my throat when I open my mouth to swallow. . . . I have no peace, and am in a perpetual worry.

In Washington, D.C., Dickens attended a session of Congress and visited President Tyler, who said little and sat beside a spitoon. To Dickens's amazement, people everywhere—in offices of the state, in courts of law, at parties, in bars, on trains—chewed large wads of tobacco and spit everywhere, "all squirted forth upon the carpet a yellow saliva which quite altered the pattern." Dickens's patience gradually ran out. At one dinner in his honor, after being introduced as a moral reformer and a champion of the downtrodden, Dickens began speaking in the manner expected of him, but midway in his remarks, he switched to the topic of American copyright laws and railed against the unfairness of Americans who made a profit from his works and those of Sir Walter Scott without paying the authors anything. The audience applauded politely, but the next day's papers criticized him for insulting those who had come to honor him. American authors remained silent on the subject, a situation that baffled and rankled Dickens. G.K. Chesterton comments on the English misunderstanding of Americans:

> America is a mystery to any good Englishman; but I think Dickens managed somehow to touch it on a queer nerve. There is one thing, at any rate, . . . that while there is no materialism so crude or so material as American materialism, there is also no idealism so crude or so ideal as American idealism. America will always affect an Englishman as being soft in the wrong place and hard in the wrong place. . . . Some beautiful ideal runs through this people, but it runs aslant.

After four months of tours, crowds, and little privacy, Dickens left New York harbor on June 7, 1842, to sail for home, his children and friends, and his writing.

Before beginning his next novel, Dickens recorded his impressions of his American visit in *American Notes*. In polite tones, he praised many features of American life (and remained silent about copyright laws). America had, however, failed to live up to Dickens's expectations; its slavery, its business practices, its sensational journalism, and the manners of its people offended him. The book brought Dickens £1,000 toward the cost of the trip, but it brought him an array of adjectives in American newspapers—"coarse, vulgar, impudent, superficial, narrow-minded, conceited cockney, flimsy, childish, trashy, contemptible." He was less polite in his next book. After several installments of *Martin Chuzzlewit* sold poorly, Dickens hoped to increase sales by sending Martin to America. With none of the polite restraint shown in *American Notes,* Dickens expressed his impatience with America in harsh humor through the character of Mrs. Gamp, a brutalized victim of the society in which Mr. Pecksniff rules with unctuous hypocrisy. The Americans were angry, the British disappointed by its bitter tone, and Dickens's publishers reduced his year-off salary.

RESTLESSNESS AND TRAVEL

The year following his American visit, 1843, began a period of restlessness for Dickens. In a row with Chapman and Hall over salary, Dickens lost his temper and threatened to find a new publisher, but Christmas was coming soon and he did not act. Instead, with financial pressures mounting— *Chuzzlewit* sales had been disappointing and household expenses were growing—Dickens threw himself into writing a Christmas story. Working at a feverish pace, he completed the manuscript, originally titled *A Christmas Carol, In Prose, Being a Ghost Story of Christmas,* by the end of November. It was published shortly before Christmas 1843. With its attractive gold-lettered cover and hand-colored interior illustrations, six thousand copies were sold the first day. It was not just the physical beauty of the book that drew praise. Like readers today, Dickens's contemporaries were deeply moved by the story's message that Christmas can and should spread love and brotherhood among humanity.

Dickens was exceedingly pleased with his Christmas story and its huge sales. Yet the book didn't generate as substantial an income for Dickens as he had hoped. With its colored plates, the book was costly to produce. At the same time, the selling price was fixed at only five shillings, leaving little profit for the author. Dickens was incensed. Although he never used color plates again, he would go on to write in the new genre that he had created: the Christmas book.

During this time, Georgina Hogarth, daughter of George Hogarth, who was as sweet as Mary had been, came to live in the Dickens home. After the holidays, Dickens took his family and servants to Italy, stopping first in Genoa and renting a house from which he could hear Genoa's constantly chiming bells. He used the opportunity to write another Christmas story, entitled "The Chimes," which became the second in a series of annual Christmas stories. In the following years, he wrote "The Cricket on the Hearth," "The Battle of Life," and "The Haunted Man" for publication just before the holidays. Before returning to England, he and Kate toured southern Italy, where he came to appreciate the manners and language of the Italians but grew to dislike the Catholic Church, which was, he thought, "a political arm against the poor and ignorant." Unlike his American trip, this trip was private and much more satisfying. When he returned to England in 1846, he started a new liberal paper, *Daily News,* during a political turmoil over the Corn Laws. When the first issue came off the press, ten thousand Londoners wanted to see what Dickens had said, as did thousands around the rest of the country. But once the paper was successfully established, Dickens lost patience with the details of publication and turned it over to Forster after seventeen issues.

Dickens became a familiar figure in London and a comic

but difficult character in his home. A man of medium height who appeared small, he had thick brown hair, a mustache and beard, a large expressive mouth, and bright, active eyes that darted back and forth, taking in the details around him. His nervous and delicate manner belied a rather steely personality. He wore flashy waistcoats and velvet coats in public and liked to be looked at if the looks were admiring. Personally, he fussed over little things and directed his whims to be acted on instantly: If the house was too quiet at night, everyone had to get up; if it was too noisy, all had to be quiet. G.K. Chesterton said of Dickens, "His private life consisted of one tragedy and ten thousand comedies." His marriage was a failure, but he loved his children, and he filled their home with energy, daily pranks, and practical jokes.

PERSONAL AND PROFESSIONAL TURNING POINTS

The mid-1840s marked a turning point both in Dickens's personal life and in his novels. Unhappy in his marriage, he developed undisciplined and unhealthy habits in his daily routines. His discontent spurred him to go to Lausanne, Switzerland, to start a new novel, *Dombey and Son*, his last farce. Like all of Dickens's first novels, which are primarily farces, *Dombey* is filled with caricatures who could not exist anywhere; the novels that followed have more realistic characters who could live everywhere. *Dombey* attacks the class system and moral pestilence that Dickens believed corrupted English society. He believed that the aristocracy perpetuated itself by taking advantage of "the pure, weak good nature" of the people.

If *Dombey* is the last of the first novels, *David Copperfield* is the transition novel. Dickens got the idea for the title by reversing his initials. It is his most autobiographical book and his favorite, about which he said, "I really think I have done it ingeniously and with a very complicated interweaving of truth and fiction." He tells the story of David in the first person and makes memory an important part of the theme, memories so personal that at one point he temporarily stopped writing because he felt sick and weak and shed tears for days. Writing *David Copperfield* helped to heal some of Dickens's wounds: "I can never approach the book with perfect composure, it had such perfect possession of me when I wrote it." From the first installment in May 1849, the book was a success with the public. Novelist William Thackeray said, "By jingo it's beautiful. . . . Those inimitable Dickens touches which make such a great man of him. . . . There are little words and phrases in his book that are like personal benefits to his readers. . . . Bravo Dickens." And yet after the successful completion of this novel, Dickens was still restless and filled with nervous energy, which he directed toward production of plays.

As early as 1836, Dickens was interested in plays, but he had little success as a dramatist. His interest continued, however, in the form of amateur theatricals, farces Dickens and his family performed for friends at annual Twelfth Night celebrations in his home. Each year these productions became more elaborate until he offered them publicly and used the profits for charity. In 1847 he organized a theatrical company for his charity plays, arranged a benefit tour of the play *Every Man in His Humour,* and gave the profits to a budding but poor playwright. The next year the company produced *The Merry Wives of Windsor* to buy Shakespeare's birthplace in Stratford-on-Avon as a national monument. As the production of charity plays grew and audiences increased, Dickens hired professional actresses Mary Boyle and Ellen Ternan. In 1852 the company performed in thirteen cities and put on a performance for Queen Victoria, all profits going to the Guild of Literature and Art.

Amid his busy schedule of writing books and producing plays, Dickens leased a larger house in Tavistock Square in a more fashionable area of London, but first contracted to reconstruct, redecorate, and refurnish it before the family moved in. While waiting for the work to be done, he was too agitated to work; he said, "I sit down between whiles to think of a new story, and, as it begins to grow, such a torment of desire to be anywhere but where I am . . . takes hold of me, that it is like being *driven away.*" He settled down, however, after he had moved into the Tavistock home and started *Bleak House.* The first novel of the second, more realistic phase, *Bleak House* centers around a legal issue that typified the way the courts handled cases for prisoners of Chancery. Dickens parallels the slow pace of the courts to the coming and going of the indifferent political parties, satirically called Boodle and Coodle. From the first chapter, fog covers the whole London world of Chancery, the dark, murky atmosphere in which Dickens exposes the corruptions and ineptitudes of government and the courts. The first issue of *Bleak House* exceeded the sales of *David Copperfield* by ten thousand copies.

In 1850 Dickens started and edited a weekly called *Household Words*, a publication of short articles and tidbits written by a variety of contributors. Though Dickens exercised firm control over the editing of contributors' work, he gave many young writers an opportunity for valuable training. Subject matter covered a wide range: public education, campaigns against social abuses, entertainment, fiction, and humor. Two weeks after its first issue, a monthly news supplement was added, the *Household Narrative of Current Events*. The weekly carried explanations of scientific and technological discoveries, brief biographies of many historical figures, reviews of new and old books, travel tips, and Dickens's installments of *A Child's History of England*. Since three out of four people in England could read, Dickens wanted the weekly to appeal to all social classes. When circulation began to decline after more than two years of regular publication, Dickens propped up sales with a new book, *Hard Times*, in which he uses places to portray two opposing views. Coketown represents cold, rational industrialism, and the Circus represents warmth, intuition, and humanity; in the end, the natural world of Sissy Jupe and the Circus people is the only hope. Before writing this book about the materialistic laws of supply and demand, the system of high profits and cheap labor preached by utilitarians, Dickens toured the cotton mills of Lancashire and interviewed striking cotton workers in Preston.

PUBLIC SUCCESS AND PRIVATE SADNESS

As a result of the reforms Dickens advocated in *Household Words*, he was sought as a public speaker and lecturer; out of these appearances he developed public readings from his works. He began with readings of "A Christmas Carol" and donated the proceeds to poor workers. He added other works, cut the excerpts and wrote stage directions, and took his readings throughout England, Scotland, and Ireland to audiences up to two thousand. Though he did not need the money and the exertion of performance strained his health, he liked the stimulation he received from the audiences. The next year, he hired a personal valet and an agent to help him with forty-two performances in Birmingham and Ireland. In 1867 he planned a hundred readings for an American tour. He had large, sell-out audiences in Boston,

New York, Philadelphia, Baltimore, and Washington. But after seventy-six performances, Dickens's health was failing and he had to go home. In 1868 he went on a farewell reading tour in London, Ireland, and Scotland but grew more and more exhausted with each performance. His agent Dolby, who urged him to quit, described Dickens as a man with "the iron will of a demon and the tender pity of an angel." At every reading, Dickens insisted that a certain number of good seats be sold for a small amount to the poor, believing that those he had spent his life championing should be able to hear what he said.

For many years, Dickens's public life had been a series of successes, but his private life was marked by numerous sad events. In 1848 his sister Fanny died of tuberculosis, followed by the death of her crippled son. Following the birth of their third daughter, Kate had a nervous breakdown. Shortly after Kate recovered, Dickens's father, John, died, and the baby, Dora Annie, became ill and died before she was a year old. Over the years, Dickens's relationship with Kate had continued to deteriorate, and when Dickens flirted with other women and gave them his attention, Kate, cowed by her famous and brilliant husband, withdrew further. During one of the public-reading tours, Kate left him. Dickens blamed himself:

> It is not only that she makes me uneasy and unhappy, but that I make her so too—and much more so . . . but we are strangely ill-assorted for the bond there is between us. God knows she would have been a thousand times happier if she had married another kind of man, and that her avoidance of this destiny would have been at least equally good for us both. I am often cut to the heart by thinking what a pity it is, for her own sake, that I ever fell in her way.

When Kate left with one of the children, Georgina Hogarth stayed on and ran the household as she had been doing for some years. In addition to his other problems, several of Dickens's brothers, who managed money as irresponsibly as their father had done, asked Dickens for financial help. While personal problems made him impatient and irritable, they never depleted his energy and enthusiasm for his work.

Dickens's whirlwind of plays, readings, serials, family, friends, travels, and new houses never seemed to die down. By chance, Dickens learned that he could buy Gad's Hill, the "castle" from his childhood, when he discovered that one of the contributors to *Household Words,* Eliza Lynn, owned it and wanted to sell. "I used to look at it [Gad's Hill] as a wonderful Mansion (which God knows it is not), when I was a very odd little child with the first faint shadows of all my books in my head," he said. He had it renovated and enlarged and brought his family there for the summer of 1857. Dickens was spending more of his time with younger people now—his children, the staff of *Household Words,* and actors from the charity plays. He particularly enjoyed a friendship with Wilkie Collins, a young writer on the staff, and traveled with him to the Lake District and Paris. And his attraction to young Ellen Ternan, with whom he had acted in many plays, grew to serious infatuation.

NEW NOVELS FOR THE MAGAZINES

In January 1854, at about the same time that he began writing *Hard Times,* Dickens visited Preston, a textile-manufacturing town in Lancashire, England. At Preston, workers were embroiled in a strike for higher wages. Although the union was ultimately defeated, trade unions in general were gaining power in the 1850s, and many journalists, like Dickens, closely monitored events as they unfolded. Dickens recorded his own observations in the article "On Strike," which appeared on February 11, 1854. Six weeks later, *Household Words* published the first installment of *Hard Times,* a novel that indicts utilitarian principles and the callous industrial order of nineteenth-century England. While the extent that Dickens's experiences in Preston influenced *Hard Times* is uncertain, there are clear parallels between descriptions of Coketown—indeed some of the most famous passages in the novel—and Preston.

Dickens's major accomplishment in the last two decades of his life was the writing of six novels and part of a seventh that constitute the second phase of his career. After *Bleak House* and *Hard Times* came *Little Dorrit,* a serial novel in which Dickens attacks the cynicism, despair, and victim attitude that existed in all levels of society. It has few saints and few villains but many gray characters—bad people with redeeming qualities and good people with sinister motives. Little Dorrit, whose girlhood is affected, as Dickens's was, by a father imprisoned for debts, grows up to lead a useful, happy life. Before writing another novel, Dickens had a fight with his publisher of fourteen years, Bradbury and Evans. In the outcome, Dickens took *Household Words,* renamed it *All the Year Round,* and went back to publishers Chapman and

Hall. The first serial novel published in the renamed weekly was *A Tale of Two Cities,* Dickens's story version of Thomas Carlyle's account of the French Revolution and the last book illustrated by Phiz. In this book, Dickens explores the theme of renunciation, redemption, and resurrection through the character of Sydney Carton, who offers to die in a convicted man's place.

A year later, Dickens explores the same theme of renunciation, redemption, and resurrection in *Great Expectations.* The main character, Pip, goes from the country to London and back, during which he meets eccentric characters and discovers that multiple strands of his life are interwoven. During the interim between *Great Expectations* and Dickens's next novel, Chapman and Hall published a collection of pieces from *All the Year Round* entitled *The Uncommercial Traveller,* the same title used for a second collection four years later. The next novel, *Our Mutual Friend,* appeared in monthly installments for a year and a half, beginning in May 1864. It is a modern novel, set in Dickens's mid-Victorian England, in which he anticipates the nature of declining Victorianism. He portrays a society so corrupt that money, which Dickens symbolizes as huge dustheaps, has become the measure of human worth. Angus Wilson says of *Our Mutual Friend,* "What is so extraordinary is that the tired Dickens should so nearly capture this world of the future, this world only glimpsed by a few beneath the seeming-solid surface of the sixties." The last novel, *The Mystery of Edwin Drood,* set in a small cathedral town, involves the upper-middle, professional class. In the six parts that Dickens wrote before he died, there is an unsolved murder, and critics have argued that its theme involves the forces of law against evil.

DECLINING HEALTH AND DEATH

Dickens's health was in decline for the last five years of his life. After a mild stroke in 1865, he drove himself to exhaustion on his reading tours. In March 1870, he gave his final public reading at St. James Hall. At the end, when his voice weakened, two thousand people rose to their feet, and he returned to the stage. Tears falling down his cheeks, he said, "From these garish lights I now vanish for ever more, with a heartfelt, grateful, respectful, affectionate farewell," and he kissed his hands to the audience and was gone. In late spring, he went to Gad's Hill to work on *Edwin Drood*, but he seemed to know the end was near when he told his daughter Katey on her last visit that he had high hopes for the book if he lived to finish it. On June 8, he worked all day rather than following his usual routine of working only in the morning. When he stood up from the dinner table that evening, he collapsed and was put on the sofa. He lay quietly, breathing heavily, until six o'clock the next evening, June 9, 1870, when he died at the age of fifty-eight. On June 14, his body was brought to Westminster Abbey, and after a simple service, he was laid to rest in Poet's Corner, a section of the church where honored writers are buried. Thousands of people filed past the grave left open for the public until it was full to overflowing with flowers.

Characters and Plot

The Characters

Bitzer: A hardened and self-centered, yet well-learned, product of Gradgrind's educational philosophy that advocates knowledge of facts and figures alone.

Stephen Blackpool: A struggling power-loom weaver who is shunned by his peers because he refuses to join the union; he seeks a divorce from his drunken, errant wife so that he can marry Rachael.

Josiah Bounderby: Coketown's bragging, fraudulent factory owner who persuades Louisa into a loveless marriage.

Louisa Gradgrind Bounderby: Gradgrind's dutiful daughter who has been raised never to entertain wonder or fancy; in keeping with her father's wishes, she marries the braggart Bounderby, whom she does not love.

Thomas Gradgrind: The stringent father of five children; he rears them to believe only in facts, figures, and statistics.

Tom Gradgrind: Gradgrind's errant son, who, upon leaving home, rebels against his strict upbringing.

James Harthouse: An egotistical young aristocrat who tries to persuade Louisa to elope with him.

Cecilia "Sissy" Jupe: A loving, compassionate circus girl who is abandoned by her father; when taken in by the Gradgrinds, she brings warmth and love to their austere home.

Mr. M'Choakumchild: A teacher in Gradgrind's school; he espouses Gradgrind's educational philosophy.

Mrs. Pegler: An old woman who, shrouded in mystery, often lurks outside Mr. Bounderby's home.

Slackbridge: The trade-union agitator.

Mrs. Sparsit: A spiteful and scheming old lady who performs housekeeping duties for Mr. Bounderby.

THE PLOT

Book One—"Sowing." In a bare, austere schoolroom filled with pupils, Thomas Gradgrind proclaims to the schoolmaster, Mr. M'Choakumchild, and a school inspector,

> Now what I want is, Facts. Teach these boys and girls nothing but Facts. Facts alone are wanted in life. Plant nothing else, and root out everything else. You can only form the minds of reasoning animals on Facts: nothing else will ever be of any service to them. This is the principle on which I bring up my own children, and this is the principle on which I bring up these children. Stick to Facts, sir!

As they examine the students, or "little pitchers" who are numbered and not named, "girl number twenty," Sissy Jupe, who has lived among the circus people, demonstrates that she cannot be filled with facts. She is unable, for example, to describe a horse in purely statistical terms, a task that another student, a colorless boy named Bitzer, performs perfectly.

The teacher, Mr. M'Choakumchild, proceeds to teach a lesson while the inspector and Gradgrind observe the class. Dickens describes the teacher as learned in "orthography, etymology, syntax, and prosody, biography, astronomy, geography, and general cosmography, the sciences of compound proportion, algebra, land-surveying and levelling, vocal music, and drawing from models," commenting that, "if he had only learnt a little less, how infinitely better he might have taught much more!"

After the "successful" lesson, Gradgrind walks home and muses over his own children, in whom he has sown, from an early age, the seeds of Fact. Under his practical tutelage, for example, a cow was not a creature that jumped over the moon but rather a "graminivorous ruminating quadruped with several stomachs." As Gradgrind approaches Sleary's horse-riding establishment at the circus, he comes upon his own children, Tom Jr. and Louisa, a pretty girl with a face in which "there was a light with nothing to rest upon, a fire with nothing to burn." Gradgrind is horrified to see that his children are peeping at the circus people through a hole in the tent. As he admonishes the children, they tell him that they wanted to learn more than they had at the "lecturing castle."

Next, Dickens describes the influential Mr. Bounderby, "the Bully of Humility": He is a rich banker, merchant, and factory owner, who looks much older than his forty-seven or forty-eight years of age. A braggart by nature, Bounderby is talking to Mrs. Gradgrind, "a little, thin, white, pink-eyed bundle of shawls, of surpassing feebleness, mental and bodily." He boasts about how, after he had been abandoned by his mother and left to a drunken grandmother, he had pulled himself up from the gutter to his present lofty position. From her reaction, it is clear that Mrs. Gradgrind has been bored by Bounderby's "self-made man" story before. Later, when Bounderby learns that Tom and Louisa were spying on the circus people, he blames Sissy Jupe for stimulating "fancy" in the children and suggests that she should be expelled from the school. As Bounderby leaves, he kisses Louisa's cheek. When he is gone, she rubs a handkerchief across her face as if to rub away the kiss.

While looking for Sissy's father to tell him to remove his daughter from the school, Bounderby and Gradgrind walk through Coketown, a typical mid–nineteenth century industrial city. Dickens presents an appalling picture of Coketown as a "town of bricks that would have been red if the smoke and ashes had allowed it," with a huge steam engine that "worked monotonously up and down, like the head of an elephant in a state of melancholy madness." Like the steam engine at the heart of Coketown, the people too "worked long and monotonously."

As the men continue on to Pod's End, a poor section of town, they encounter Sissy. She is fleeing from Bitzer, who had been mocking her definition of a horse. Sissy, Gradgrind, and Bounderby proceed to "the door of a mean little public house" that is the Jupes' home. When Sissy notices that her father's belongings are gone, she sets out to find him. Meanwhile, Gradgrind and Bounderby converse with Mr. Sleary, the good-natured proprietor of the circus, and other circus performers. Although Dickens describes these circus people as haphazard in appearance and domestic arrangement, he goes on to say that "there was a remarkable gentleness and childishness about these people, a special inaptitude for any kind of sharp practise, and an untiring readiness to help and pity one another, deserving, often of as much respect, and always of as much generous construction, as the every-day virtues of any class of people in the world."

When Sissy reappears and learns that her father has not returned, she becomes clearly upset. Gradgrind informs Sissy and the others that he will educate and take charge of the deserted child, on the condition that she sever all ties with anyone from the circus. After a tender farewell, Sissy leaves her circus "family."

At the home of Bounderby, the reader meets Mrs. Sparsit, Bounderby's widowed housekeeper. She is an elderly lady with dense black eyebrows. Though left penniless by her former husband, Sparsit loves to remind people that she bears relations with local aristocracy. Bounderby delights in having this once highly-connected lady as his servant.

Gradgrind and his daughter arrive at Bounderby's to take Sissy to their home. Gradgrind tells Sissy that she must forget "Fairies" and "Fancy," continuing that "from this time you begin your history. You will be reclaimed and formed."

Tom and Louisa talk about the admonition to "never wonder"—as Dickens writes, the keynote of the Gradgrind educational system. Tom is disgusted with his education; indeed, he wishes that he could use gunpowder to blow up the doctrine of "Facts and Figures," but he says instead that when he leaves home to work for Bounderby, he will take revenge by enjoying life. Louisa, too, feels that there is something missing from her life. Then, recognizing Bounderby's obvious fondness for Louisa, Tom muses that he will use this influence to his advantage.

Next, Dickens introduces Stephen Blackpool, a poor-but-honest and hardworking power-loom weaver in Bounderby's factory. One night after work, Blackpool waits for Rachael, the woman whom he loves. The two walk home and converse about the laws of the land, which Blackpool calls a "muddle," commenting that "I come to the muddle many times and agen, and I never get beyond it." Although the forty-year-old Blackpool had been married, his degenerate wife had left him long ago. When he arrives home on this night, however, he finds a "disabled, drunken creature, barely able to preserve her sitting posture." The filthy, tattered woman falls toward the bed and is soon in a drunken slumber.

The next morning Blackpool is back at work. During his lunch hour he goes to see Bounderby. Blackpool tells his employer that his drunken wife has returned and inquires how he can be freed from his marriage so that he might marry his beloved Rachael. Bounderby replies that if Blackpool leaves his wife, he will be punished according to the laws. When Blackpool persists, Bounderby cites a rigid divorce law that favors only the wealthy. Blackpool, completely demoralized, replies, "Tis just a muddle a'toogether, an' the sooner I am dead, the better." As Blackpool leaves his employer's house, he meets an old woman who asks about Bounderby. Blackpool, overly distraught as he considers his problems, answers her questions but does not wonder about her identity.

The thoroughly dejected Blackpool arrives home to find Rachael present. Summoned by the landlady, Rachael is tending to his sick and derelict wife, dressing the woman's sores with a lotion that is deadly if swallowed. Later that night, Blackpool wakes up and sits unmoving as he watches his wife inadvertently pour the poisonous lotion into a drinking cup. Just as she is about to drink the fatal liquid, Rachael awakes and seizes the cup. Ashamed that he did not intervene on his wife's behalf, Blackpool blesses Rachael, calling her an angel who has saved his soul.

Several years pass. Louisa has grown into a young woman, Tom has gone to work in Bounderby's bank, and Sissy—although accepted by Gradgrind for her earnest and kind nature—has proven a totally inept student. One night Bounderby tells Louisa that he must talk to her the next morning. Tom guesses that Bounderby—thirty years Louisa's senior—will propose marriage to his sister, and he encourages her to accept—only because it will further his own interests.

The following morning Gradgrind presents Louisa with Bounderby's proposal. Louisa asks, "Do you think I love Mr. Bounderby?" Her father replies that he cannot say so, but asks her to look at the "Facts" and remain practical as she makes her decision. Devoid of emotion, Louisa tells her father that she will accept the proposal, adding that she has had no experiences of the heart, that she knows nothing of "tastes and fancies, of aspirations and affections."

Bounderby tells Sparsit of his impending nuptials. She replies that she hopes he is happy, but she says it with great condescension and compassion, as though he is a victim. Bounderby makes arrangements for Sparsit to live in an apartment over the bank. As the wedding is planned dresses and cakes are made, jewelry is ordered—the business is "all Facts, from first to last." The ceremony itself is unemotional, and Louisa breaks down slightly only when she parts from her brother, who calls her "a first-rate sister."

Book Two—"Reaping." It is a hot summer day in Coketown, so hot that the "whole town seemed to be frying in oil." The mill owners complain that they are being ruined by be-

ing "required to send labouring children to school; they
were ruined when inspectors were appointed to look into
their works; they were ruined, when such inspectors considered it doubtful whether they were quite justified in chopping people up with their machinery; they were utterly undone, when it was hinted that perhaps they need not always
make so much smoke."

Sparsit resides "on the shadier side of the frying street," in
an apartment over the bank. One night, after the bank has
closed, Sparsit talks to Bitzer, who now works for the bank.
He relates news that the workers are uniting, to which Sparsit replies, "These people must be conquered." A spy and in-
former for Bounderby, Bitzer goes on to describe Tom—also
a bank employee—as a "dissipated, extravagant idler." As the
two continue to chat, a haughty visitor arrives. He is handsome and well bred yet carries "a certain air of exhaustion
upon him."

The gentleman turns out to be James Harthouse, a young
man who, bored with his education and travels, has been re-
cruited by the Coketown establishment. Bounderby proudly
lectures Harthouse on Coketown: Its smoke is "the healthiest thing in the world" and "the meat and drink" of the town.

When Bounderby takes Harthouse to his home to meet
Louisa, the bachelor is struck with the stark bareness of the
rooms, in which "no graceful little adornment, no fanciful
little device, however trivial, anywhere expressed her influence." Louisa's obvious detachment piques Harthouse's interest. Later in the evening, Harthouse observes that Louisa
shows emotion only in the presence of her brother, Tom—
the "whelp" as Harthouse calls him.

Harthouse proceeds to befriend Tom, who is flattered by
the attention. Led by Harthouse's questions, Tom admits that
he does not like Bounderby and brags that he persuaded his
sister into the loveless marriage to further his own interests.
As Harthouse listens, he becomes increasingly intrigued by
the challenge of breaking down Louisa's emotional barriers.

Meanwhile, at the mill, the workers—hoping to improve
the deplorable conditions forced on them—listen attentively
to the labor union organizer, Slackbridge, who calls the mill
workers "the slaves of an iron-handed and grinding despotism." Yet Dickens's comments reveal that Slackbridge himself "was not so honest, he was not so manly, he was not so
good-humoured; he substituted cunning for their simplicity,

and passion for their safe and solid sense." Only Stephen Blackpool refuses to join the strike. Ostracized by the other workers, he falls into "the loneliest of lives, the life of solitude among a familiar crowd." One day soon after, Bitzer summons Blackpool to Bounderby's home. At Bounderby's home, in the presence of Harthouse, Tom Gradgrind, and Louisa, Bounderby questions Blackpool about the strike. Blackpool infuriates Bounderby when he defends the workers, making it clear that his refusal to join the union had nothing to do with loyalty to Bounderby. After Blackpool is fired, he departs with the words, "Heaven help us awl in this world!"

Upon leaving Bounderby's house, Blackpool meets Rachael and the mysterious woman he had met outside the house earlier in the novel. She asks about Louisa. Blackpool, still preoccupied with his own problems, tells Rachael he must seek employment outside of Coketown. The trio departs and later, in Blackpool's room where they are talking over tea, the woman reveals that her name is Mrs. Pegler, adding that she has a son but that he is "not to be spoken of."

Louisa and Tom arrive at Blackpool's home. Louisa, who has had little previous contact with Coketown's workers, is deeply impressed by Blackpool's travails. She offers him money but he accepts only a few pounds. As the brother and sister depart, Tom, hinting at a job prospect, tells Blackpool to wait outside the bank for an hour or two each night. Blackpool obliges, but when nothing happens after three nights of loitering outside the bank, Blackpool packs his belongings and leaves Coketown.

As time passes, Harthouse gains the confidence of Gradgrind and Bounderby, both of whom are unaware of his pursuit of Louisa. In the meantime, the Bounderbys have moved to a large estate about fifteen miles from Coketown. Here, Bounderby, "with demonstrative humility," plants cabbages in the flower garden and denigrates the home's elegant interior. One evening Harthouse finds Louisa in the garden and convinces her that he is worried about her brother's gambling problem. Preying on Louisa's weakness for Tom, he offers his assistance. Tom appears and is openly rude to Louisa, who has refused him money. Later, when Tom apologizes to Louisa, she believes that Harthouse has had a positive influence on her wayward brother. Harthouse is happy when, later, he sees that Louisa has a smile for him.

The next morning Harthouse reflects on Louisa's growing

fondness for him. Dickens notes that "the end to which it led was before him, pretty plainly; but he troubled himself with no calculations about it. What will be, will be." Later the same day, Harthouse learns that Bounderby's bank had been robbed the previous night. Other details unfold: The thief entered the bank with a false key and took £150. Bitzer and Sparsit join Harthouse and Bounderby, and they continue talking about the robbery. Stephen Blackpool is accused of the crime; he had been seen lurking about the bank for several nights before the robbery. They also implicate an old woman, Pegler, who had been seen watching the bank.

Because Sparsit is unnerved by these events, Bounderby invites her to stay at the house for several days. Plotting to get her position in the household back, Sparsit does her best to undermine the marriage between Louisa and Bounderby. Meanwhile, Louisa nervously awaits Tom's arrival, for she suspects that it is he, not Blackpool, who is responsible for the crime at the bank. When Tom arrives after midnight, he denies any involvement in the robbery. When Louisa leaves, Tom bursts into tears.

Sparsit's stay continues, as does her scheming against Louisa, and indeed, "the Sparsit action upon Mr. Bounderby threw Louisa and James Harthouse more together, and strengthened the dangerous alienation from her husband." Later, Louisa is summoned to see her dying mother. Since her marriage, Louisa had rarely visited her old home because "her remembrances of home and childhood were remembrances of the drying up of every spring and fountain in her young heart as is gushed out." She returns to her old home just in time to visit her mother one last time.

Back at the Bounderbys, Sparsit continues to lavish attention on her benefactor, but she treats him derisively when not in his presence. At the same time, Sparsit pictures in her mind Louisa standing on a giant staircase with "a dark pit of shame and ruin at the bottom; and down those stairs, from day to day, hour to hour, she saw Louisa coming." The old housekeeper continues to observe Louisa and Harthouse, hoping for evidence of an adulterous relationship—of Louisa's "descent" down the staircase. Meanwhile, Gradgrind, who has been away in London, returns for his wife's funeral.

One weekend, Bounderby is called away for several days to tend to business. Hearing this, Sparsit suspects that Harthouse will go to see Louisa while Bounderby is away. Eagerly awaiting Louisa's final descent to the "dark pit of shame," Sparsit schemes to make sure that Louisa and Harthouse will be alone. As expected, Harthouse, under the ruse of meeting Tom, goes to see Louisa. Sparsit, gloating from her hiding place behind a tree, observes the two lovers in the garden. She hears Harthouse declare his love for Louisa. When Louisa later leaves the house wearing a cloak, Sparsit—certain that the two are about to elope—follows Louisa to the railroad station. She is bitterly upset when, amidst a thunderous storm, she loses sight of the young woman.

At the Gradgrind house, a soaked and distraught Louisa appears before her father. In a fit of passion and grief, she curses the day of her birth. She continues to reproach her father for an upbringing that propelled her into a loveless marriage and left her unprepared to deal with the onslaught of emotions that now overwhelm her. "Your philosophy and your teaching will not save me," she cries. As she sinks to the floor, Gradgrind sees "the pride of his heart, and the triumph of his system, lying, an insensible heap, at his feet."

Book Three—"Garnering." Louisa awakes in her old room. She notices that Jane, her younger sister, looks happy and radiant. The young girl explains that it is "Sissy's doing." Gradgrind enters. In contrast to his usual stern and authoritative demeanor, his manner is tender and caring. He admits to Louisa that his educational system is flawed and blames himself for its failures. He tells Louisa that he now realizes that "there is a wisdom of the Head, and that there is a wisdom of the Heart." Later, in Sissy's presence, Louisa again breaks down in tears. She pleads with Sissy to "have compassion on my great need, and let me lay this head of mine upon a loving heart." The warm and sympathetic Sissy resolves to help Louisa.

Meanwhile, Harthouse grows apprehensive as he waits for Louisa. He is surprised when a young woman, Sissy, meets him in Louisa's stead. She tells Harthouse that Louisa will never see him again and asks him to leave Coketown. Although Harthouse is at first argumentative, he is taken aback by Sissy's "child-like ingenuousness" and "modest fearlessness." He bows to her request.

Sparsit, unaware that Louisa fled to her father's home for protection, rushes to London to find Bounderby. There, she reports the overheard conversation between Harthouse and Louisa. Sparsit and Bounderby rush back to Stone Lodge to confront Gradgrind. There, Bounderby learns that Louisa did not elope with Harthouse and is staying with her father. After unleashing a tirade against Sparsit, who collapses in tears, he furiously berates Louisa and demands that she return to his home by noon the next day. When Louisa fails to abide by the terms of his ultimatum, Bounderby returns her belongings to Stone Lodge and resumes his life as a bachelor.

Bounderby—eager to show the town that he is not bothered by the dissolution of his marriage—throws himself into his work and resumes efforts to apprehend the perpetrator of the bank robbery. He prints placards offering a reward for Stephen Blackpool. At a union meeting, Slackbridge, using the placards to his advantage, denounces the "fugitive" who had once disagreed with him.

Later, Bounderby brings Tom and Rachael to Louisa to confirm that she and Tom visited Blackpool's home the night after he had been fired. Tom is bitterly upset when Louisa admits that they did indeed visit Blackpool and offer him financial aid, of which he only accepted a small portion. Although uncertain, Rachael believes that Louisa may have plotted to implicate her friend in the robbery. She then reveals that Blackpool, in order to get a job, is living in another town under an assumed name. Rachael confides also that she wrote to Blackpool, asking him to return to clear his name. Bounderby, with what he sees as further evidence against Blackpool, sends assistants to apprehend the "thief," but Blackpool cannot be located.

Days pass. Blackpool fails to appear, and the townspeople speculate about his involvement in the robbery. Sissy befriends Rachael, who is growing increasingly worried about Blackpool.

One night Rachael and Sissy run into Sparsit as she detains Pegler, the mysterious old woman whom many assume to be Blackpool's accomplice in the bank robbery. They take the woman before Bounderby, who blasts Sparsit for poking her "officious nose" into his family affairs. The following exchange between Bounderby and Pegler reveal that she, in fact, is his mother. She recounts events that not only refute Bounderby's story of a miserable childhood, but also reveal that he pensioned her off on thirty pounds a year with orders to stay out of his life. Pegler, thus, has been lingering around Coketown to observe her son from afar—and not because of any complicity in the bank robbery. Even though Bounderby's face grows red and swollen, he refuses to offer any explanation to counter the woman's testimony.

Over a week has passed since Blackpool's disappearance. While out walking, Sissy and Rachael discover him—alive but fatally injured—in an old mine shaft. They summon a group of workmen, and together they retrieve Blackpool's wasted body. He survives just long enough to ask that his name be cleared, telling Gradgrind—who is now part of the crowd gathered at the mine shaft—that his son, Tom, had talked to him the night of the robbery. With Rachael by his side, Blackpool then dies.

Tom disappears. Gradgrind, who now realizes that his son is the thief, retires to his study. He later tells Louisa how Tom had cast suspicion on Blackpool by setting him up to loiter outside the bank. Then, Gradgrind learns that Sissy sent Tom to the circus. There, Gradgrind, Sissy, and Louisa find Tom disguised as a black-face clown. He admits to his broken-hearted father that he committed the robbery, but he fails to take any responsibility for his actions. Instead, Tom blames his criminal conduct on statistics—claiming that the law of averages dictate that a certain number of people will be dishonest. Although he is bitterly disappointed in his son, Grandgrind tells Tom he will help him to get out of the country. Just as Tom is about to leave, Bitzer appears and foils the escape plans.

Desperate to save his son, Gradgrind asks Bitzer if he has a heart. Bitzer—the prize pupil educated on Gradgrind's very own principles—replies, "The circulation, sir, couldn't be carried on without one. No man, sir, acquainted with the facts established by Harvey relating to the circulation of the blood can doubt that I have a heart." Remaining steadfast, Bitzer refuses a bribe to allow Tom to escape. He reasons that he will make more money when—with Tom out of the way—he is promoted to Tom's former position at the bank. Dickens comments on the Gradgrind philosophy that produced citizens like Bitzer: "It was a fundamental principle . . . [that] nobody was ever on any account to give anybody anything, or render anybody help without purchase. Gratitude was to be abolished, and the virtues springing from it were not to be. Every inch of the existence of mankind, from birth to death, was to be a bargain across a counter."

Sleary feigns a sympathetic rapport with Bitzer, but at the same time uses his dancing horse and trained dog to occupy the young man's attention. Under this ruse, Tom is able to escape to safety. Gradgrind is grateful for Sleary's help. As the two talk, Sleary speculates that Sissy's father is dead, but he wants to shield Sissy from that news. As Gradgrind leaves the circus, the lisping Sleary comments, "People mutht be amuthed. They can't be alwayth a-learning, nor yet they can't be alwayth a-working, they an't made for it. You *mutht* have uth, Thquire. Do the withe thing and the kind thing too, and make the betht of uth, not the wurtht!"

Bounderby discharges Sparsit, who is sent to live with her relative Lady Scadgers. Dickens goes on to foretell Bounderby's death in the streets of Coketown, Tom's death thousands of miles away, and Gradgrind's being scorned by his associates for "bending his hitherto inflexible theories . . . and making his facts and figures subservient to Faith, Hope and Charity." Although Sissy goes on to enjoy a happy marriage and children of her own, Louisa—never to marry again—will spend her life trying to help others.

CHAPTER 1

Themes and Style

The Black and White Motif in *Hard Times*

Juliet McMaster

In the following critical excerpt from her book *Dickens the Designer*, Juliet McMaster asserts that Dickens uses a pattern of black and white—and the modulation between the two—to reinforce thematic material in *Hard Times*. Dickens's use of black and white, however, does not carry traditional moral connotations: Black is not a symbol of evil but rather represents social degradation, and white suggests an absence of imagination or passion. In this scheme, for example, the albino Bitzer is the totally colorless product of the Gradgrind educational system—a heartless and seemingly bloodless utilitarian. Mc-Master is a professor of English at the University of Alberta. She has written a number of books on Victorian literature, including *Jane Austen on Love* and *Thackeray: The Major Novels.*

In *Hard Times* Dickens made colour a major feature of design. One of the titles he considered for it was 'Black and white'. The novel is patterned on a progression between the two most powerful scenes: the first in the 'intensely white-washed' schoolroom at the beginning, with its albino star pupil, Bitzer, so pale that he looks as though he would 'bleed white', and the second set in Sleary's darkened circus ring at the end, with Tom Gradgrind disguised as a blackamoor clown, his face 'daubed all over' with a 'greasy composition' of black make-up.

But the world of *Hard Times* is not all just black and white, and that tentative title, like 'Two and two are four', 'Stubborn things', and 'Fact', which appear in the same working list, was intended to indicate what was wrong with the world according to Gradgrind, and how much was miss-

Excerpted from *Dickens the Designer*, by Juliet McMaster. Copyright © Juliet McMaster 1987. Reprinted by permission of Macmillan Ltd.

ing in it. As it is a novel that treats of imagination, grace, instinct, and feeling, as well as of the utilitarian system that tries to reject them, so it is concerned with the modulation *between* black and white, the various tones of grey, and with brighter colours. Pigmentation is one of Dickens's recurring images, and he uses it consistently to furnish incidents for his fable and to reinforce his theme. . . .

Black and white in *Hard Times* do not represent polar opposites in a moral scale: so much is clear from the fact that Bitzer, 'the colourless boy', and Tom Gradgrind, whom we last see appropriately besmeared with black, are products of the same educational system. Dickens is in fact explicitly rejecting the light-dark moral contrast that he had exploited, say, in *Oliver Twist*, and he gives us a villain not a Fagin or a Quilp or a Carker, who all have feet more or less cloven, but a James Harthouse, 'aweary of vice, and aweary of virtue, used up as to brimstone, and used up as to bliss'. Black, as with Tom in blackamoor make-up, does have some of its customary associations with evil; but it is characteristically a pigmentation applied from without, and connotes a social degradation rather than innate evil. And white is not a positive attribute of virtue, but rather a negative quantity, an absence of imagination or passion, an absence of colour.

Dickens develops a number of unpleasant associations for whiteness and pallor. The earliest remembrance of the Gradgrind children is of 'a large black board with a dry Ogre chalking ghastly white figures on it'. Similarly—another parallel between the schoolroom and the town at large—the signs and public inscriptions in Coketown are all painted alike, 'in severe characters of black and white'. Black and white are like facts and figures, unaccommodating, undifferentiating, inhumane. The schoolroom in Mr. Gradgrind's school is bare and undecorated and 'intensely whitewashed', and his children's playroom looks like 'a room devoted to hair-cutting'—that is, presumably, hygienic and sterile, and probably whitewashed too.

But it is in Bitzer that Dickens most memorably depicts whiteness, or lack of pigmentation, as repellent:

> The boy was so light-eyed and light-haired that the self-same rays [of the sun] appeared to draw out of him what little colour he ever possessed. His cold eyes would hardly have been eyes, but for the short ends of lashes which, by bringing them into immediate contrast with something paler than

themselves, expressed their form. His short-cropped hair might have been a mere continuation of the sandy freckles on his forehead and face. His skin was so unwholesomely deficient in the natural tinge, that he looked as though, if he were cut, he would bleed white.

Dickens's bad characters in other novels, and Bounderby in this one, are apt to be all too 'colourful'—that is, they tend to make the good characters such as Oliver and Nell seem by contrast pale and vapid. But in Bitzer for once he produced a thoroughly nasty character with no colour at all, and his nastiness resides in his colourlessness. 'I [hate] that white chap', Tom Gradgrind complains of him; 'he's always got his blinking eyes upon a fellow'. The whiteness is like the lean and hungry look of Cassius, Jingle and Stiggins—it expresses the beholder's sense of evil and danger. Even when Bitzer exerts himself, as in pursuit of Tom, he gathers no colour: 'For, there was Bitzer, out of breath, his thin lips parted, his thin nostrils distended, his white eyelashes quivering, his colourless face more colourless than ever, as if he ran himself into a white heat, when other people ran themselves into a glow'. A fit profession for the grown Bitzer is as the 'light porter' at the bank—'a very light porter indeed'. Dickens seems to have considered this avocation something of an inspiration, for in his working-plan for the number he noted, 'Bitzer light porter? *Yes.*' He may, I think, have been playing on the catch-phrase of Utilitarianism, 'enlightened self-interest', for Bitzer is the supremely successful product of the Gradgrind educational system. His self-interest is complete, and enlightened—besides the light colouring— strictly to the extent that he will avoid breaking the law because breaking the law would get him into trouble. It is not surprising that F.R. Leavis should have admired the characterization of Bitzer, for he is a very Lawrentian conception— one of the effete and bloodless products, like Clifford Chatterley, of a civilization that has lost contact with the physical and instinctual sources of life. Bitzer is a successful utilitarian, but at the price of losing his humanity. His blood is white, and he has no heart—none, that is, except for the physiological organ that pumps his corpuscles around his bodily frame after the manner described by Harvey.

Mrs. Gradgrind

The other colourless product of utilitarian principles is Mrs. Gradgrind, though she is by no means so successful in the pursuit of self-interest as Bitzer. Rather she seems the result of the enlightened self-interest of others, her husband's in particular. Mrs. Gradgrind is 'a little, thin, white, pink-eyed bundle of shawls, of surpassing feebleness, mental and bodily; who was always taking physic without any effect, and who, whenever she showed a symptom of coming to life, was invariably stunned by some weighty piece of fact tumbling on her'. Again, her colourlessness is an essential aspect of Dickens's conception of her. As for Bitzer he had noted in his working-plan 'Pale winking boy', so he saw in advance Mrs. Gradgrind as a 'badly done transparency without enough light behind'. This very precise visual image, with its suggestion of the latest in the audiovisual-aids market, is one he maintains consistently for poor insipid Mrs. Gradgrind. Bitzer is unwholesomely pale and white, but at least he is opaque. She is even more washed-out in colour than he. The image, when worked up into the text of the novel, becomes, 'Mrs. Gradgrind, weakly smiling, and giving no other sign of vitality, looked (as she always did) like an indifferently executed transparency of a small female figure, without enough light behind it'. We are to understand that she has been so crushed and ground by Gradgrind facts that she is scarcely alive, and Dickens has never so successfully depicted a low ebb of life: a starved amoeba would be a dynamo to her. . . .

MRS. SPARSIT

The lady who is most fully opposed to Mrs. Gradgrind in the colour-scheme of the book (and it is a one-way opposition, for Mrs. Gradgrind wouldn't oppose anybody) is Mrs. Sparsit. Here there is no shortage of pigment infusion. With her definite views and her no-nonsense attitudes, she is rather like the black-and-white inscriptions in Coketown. Bounderby imagines her when young as dressed 'in white satin and jewels, a blaze of splendour', but at the time of life in which we meet her the black predominates in her colouring. She wears white stockings, but, as a widow, presumably a black dress. Much is made of her 'dense black eyebrows', and subsequently of her 'black eyes'. As befits her character as witch, her black eyes are black in more than their own blackness: they see evil, and, to the extent of their power, determine it. In her jealousy of Louisa she wills her into an affair with Harthouse: 'she kept her black eyes wide open, with no touch of pity, with no touch of compunction, all absorbed in interest. In the interest of seeing [Louisa], ever drawing, with no hand to stay her, nearer and nearer to the bottom of this new Giant's Staircase'. She watches eagerly, with 'gratified malice', as Louisa proceeds to compromise herself, and draw nearer to the dark abyss that her imagination has prepared for her. . . .

MR. GRADGRIND

In the colouring of Mr. Gradgrind, Dickens suggests the need for some modulation between the stark blacks and whites that prevail in the signs of Coketown and in his children's education. For the most part he is dissociated from colour, just as he outlaws fancy, and spends his life 'annihilating the flowers of existence'. The one colour that is briefly associated with him is blue, but it is not a very vivid blue, and is cleared immediately from any romantic associations: 'Although Mr. Gradgrind did not take after Blue Beard, his room was quite a blue chamber in its abundance of blue books'. This library of the dismal science is itself sufficiently dismal, being 'a stern room, with a deadly statistical clock in it, which measured every second with a beat like a rap upon a coffin-lid'. Gradgrind is to be changed by the disasters that his educational system causes in his children's lives; and his reform, and movement towards increased humanity and understanding, is marked by his going grey. After Louisa's marriage is shattered, and he begins to suspect Tom's responsibility for the bank robbery, we hear, 'His hair had latterly begun to change its colour. . . . He leaned upon his hand again, looking grey and old'. The touch might be only a passing one, but Dickens gives it weight by including 'grey' in the final image of the book—words which he had again thought out in advance. The narrator connects humane endeavour with the effort 'to beautify . . . lives of machinery and reality with those imaginative graces and delights, without which . . . the plainest national prosperity figures can show, will be the Writing on the Wall'. This is the lesson that the Gradgrinds of the world, with their tabulation of black and white facts and figures, need to learn. Then there is a final apostrophe to the reader:

> Dear reader! It rests with you and are, whether, in our two fields of action, similar things shall be or not. Let them be! We shall sit with lighter bosoms on the hearth, to see the ashes of our fires turn grey and cold.

The fire imagery has been consistent, and this ending connects it with the colour motif, and suggests a consonance between the imaginative endeavour and modulation between the uncompromising extremes of black and white.

It is characteristic of Dickens's presentation of colour here, and in keeping with movements in painting, that he should differentiate between colour that is innate in the object or person, and colour that is the effect of external context, like lighting, or the kind of deposits caused by contaminated air, as in *Bleak House*. Although, in the colourless world as projected by Gradgrind, any infusion of colour might be seen as good, the pigment imposed from without, as on Tom's face or on the cinder-blackened buildings of Coketown, is nearly always seen as evil. . . .

STEPHEN BLACKPOOL

Stephen's name, and the place of his death, associate him with the blackness of Coketown. In the street where he lies, we hear, the undertaker keeps, as a timely convenience, 'a black ladder, in order that those who had done their daily groping up and down the narrow stairs might slide out of this working world by the windows'. This black ladder, the grim *memento mori* of the working-class neighbourhood, receives some emphasis. Stephen's face, as compassionately described by Rachael, is 'so white and tired'. He belongs, then, to the prevailing black-and-white colour scheme of the tentative title, but he is not judged as responsible for this joyless pattern, as Gradgrind is, and he already has the 'iron-grey hair', the sign of his ability to accept modulation and shades of difference, which Gradgrind must painfully acquire. The dark colours associated with him suggest rather that his life has been shadowed and darkened by inescapable suffering than that he is smeared and soiled, or morally tainted. His dipsomaniac wife, however, is another matter. She is one member of the working classes for whom the narrator has no compassion, and her degradation is again signalled by external application of dirt. Her hands are 'begrimed', and she is 'a creature so foul to look at, in her tatters, stains and splashes, but so much fouler than that in her moral infamy, that it was a shameful thing even to see her'.

TOM GRADGRIND

But the character who is the most memorable instance of externally applied pigmentation as a signal of moral infamy is of course Tom Gradgrind. Tom, like the colourless Bitzer, is a product of his education, but, whereas the system makes of Bitzer a successful machine, it makes of Tom an unsuccessful brute. Both are less than human, but Bitzer has no passions and no physical temptations, whereas Tom has both, without any training in how to control them. . . .

His grovelling sensualities lead him to pander his sister to a man she finds repulsive, to embezzle funds from the bank, and to throw suspicion on an innocent man. When these crimes have caught up with him, and Sleary has disguised him as a blackamoor clown to help him to escape the law, Tom is at least shown, so to speak, in his true colours. This is a passage that most critics quote, for it is one of the most powerful in the book. But much of its force derives from the build-up that Dickens has provided, in marking the contrast as well as the parallel between Bitzer and Tom, and in training the reader in the moral infamy of externally applied pigmentation.

> In a preposterous coat, like a beadle's, . . . with seams in his black face, where fear and heat had started through the greasy composition daubed all over it; anything so grimly, detestably, ridiculously shameful as the whelp in his comic livery, Mr. Gradgrind never could . . . have believed in.

As Tom proves to his father over again that his teaching is responsible for his downfall—the statistical probabilities decree that 'so many people, out of so many, will be dishonest. . . . How can *I* help laws?'—the degrading blackening receives more emphasis still. Dickens rubs in the effect:

> The father buried his face in his hands, and the son stood in his disgraceful grotesqueness, biting straw: his hands, with the black partly worn away inside, looking like the hands of a monkey. . . . From time to time, he turned the whites of his eyes restlessly and impatiently towards his father. They were the only parts of his face that showed any life or expression, the pigment upon it was so thick.

The passage is one of Dickens's triumphs in rendering a moral condition visible. And, to complete the pattern of black and white, he now produces Gradgrind's pupil, the 'colourless' Bitzer in a 'white heat', eager to break his educator's heart by preventing his son's escape. Gradgrind is to be punished, crucified, by the black and white, the unmodulated declaration of facts that he had always advocated. . . .

Brighter colours than the black and white of the Gradgrind and Bounderby world also have their place in the design of *Hard Times.* Colour, as in Sissy Jupe and the circus, generally suggests feeling, imagination and vitality; but there are some expectations to this rule, which need considering first. For, though one would expect Bounderby to be mainly black, as he rejoices in the smoke of Coketown— 'That's meat and drink to us. It's the healthiest thing in the world in all respects, and particularly for the lungs', he boasts—he is actually vividly coloured. He is always talking about the workers' propensity to 'expect to be set up in a coach and six, and to be fed on turtle soup and venison, with a gold spoon', and in his own complexion he is as gaudy as anyone in the novel: at his final rage at the end of his marriage we see him 'with his very ears a bright purple shot with crimson', a veritable mandrill. But the coloration is not so inappropriate after all. For one thing the explosive pressure signalled by his crimson and purple features completes the main terms of his characterization as windy, inflated, explosive—a Braggadocio. But, besides this, the colourful imagery that differentiates him from the black-and-white world of Gradgrind is an early signal of his true nature as a creator of fiction. For, however he may disapprove of 'idle imagination' in others, he has fancifully invented a past for himself as romantic Dick Whittington's. Colour erupts in him, in spite of his Utilitarian principles, as fire erupts in Louisa and in the factory hands, for 'all closely imprisoned forces rend and destroy'. As Warrington Winters shows, Bounderby and his fictional past belong to Dickens's major theme in serving 'to demonstrate that we cannot live by facts alone, that the imagination must have an outlet'.

All the same, as Bounderby is differentiated from the black-and-white Gradgrind world on the one hand, so is his livid coloration distinct from the colour of Sissy Jupe's world, which symbolizes feeling and the power of the imagination. Bounderby's fiction is not a saving myth, but a self-aggrandizing lie. Likewise his colouring is crude and forced. He lives 'in a red house with black outside shutters, green inside blinds, a black street door, up two white steps, BOUNDERBY (in letters very like himself) upon a brazen plate, and a round brazen door-handle underneath it, like a brazen full-stop'. This loudly declarative arrangement of rectangles, squares and circles recalls the 'third gentleman's' disquisition on taste in the schoolroom scene. In confounding Sissy, who says she would enjoy representations of flowers in carpets as 'pretty and pleasant, and I would fancy—', he cuts her off with the command that she must never fancy, but must be regulated in all things by tact:

> 'You don't walk upon flowers in fact; you cannot be allowed to walk upon flowers in carpets. You don't find that foreign birds and butterflies come and perch upon your crockery; you cannot be permitted to paint foreign birds and butterflies upon your crockery. . . . You must see', said the gentleman, 'for all these purposes, combinations and modifications (in primary colours) of mathematical figures which are susceptible of proof and demonstration. . . . This is fact. This is taste.'

Bounderby's domestic décor would live up to these standards. For him colour is best regimented, separated, and arranged in hard-edged shapes. It is no surprise to find that his bank has exactly the same exterior as his house—red brick, black shutters, green blinds, and so forth, all 'strictly according to pattern'. These colours become, in fact, not very different from the Gradgrind black and white, inasmuch as their tendency is to eliminate differences and shades, to confound the individual with the aggregate, and so to dehumanize.

SISSY JUPE

Sissy Jupe, with her allegiance to flowers, butterflies and fancy, is the representative of both colour and goodness. In the definitive schoolroom scene, she is contrasted with the colourless Bitzer, who sits in the same ray of sunshine: 'But, whereas the girl was so dark-eyed and dark-haired, that she seemed to receive a deeper and more lustrous colour from the sun, when it shone upon her, the boy was so light-eyed and light-haired that the self-same rays appeared to draw out of him what little colour he ever possessed'. Leavis has memorably pointed out 'the force . . . with which the moral and spiritual differences are rendered here in terms of sensation', but he has not noticed how this contrast is part of a dominant visual pattern in the novel at large. The scene continues to emphasize her colour, particularly that which comes from within. She 'would have blushed deeper, if she could have blushed deeper than she had blushed all this time'. When she is grown we are reminded of her 'rich dark hair' and of her propensity to blush: 'Her colour rose', and 'Sissy flushed and started'. Such are the gestures which keep her colouring before us. Her fondness for flowers distinguishes her from Gradgrind, who annihilates the flowers of existence, from M'Choakumchild, who 'had taken the bloom of the higher branches' of science, and from Tom, whom we see literally tearing roses to pieces in one scene.

Her place of origin, Sleary's circus, is more colourful still. The circus people too cherish flowers, and the 'graceful equestrian Tyrolean flower-act' is one of their recurring numbers. They foregather at the Pegasus's Arms, where there is a theatrical Pegasus 'with real gauze let in for his wings, golden stars stuck on all over him, and his ethereal harness made of red silk'. Her father the clown wears as part of his clown's outfit a 'white night-cap, embellished with two peacock's feathers', and the diminutive Master Kidderminster, who aspires to her hand, plays the role of Cupid made up with 'white bismuth, and carmine'. (Make-up, incidentally, is not degrading to the circus people as to Tom, for impersonation and clowning are their immemorial and legitimate business.)

LOUISA

Louisa Gradgrind's moral evolution, in gravitating from Gradgrind's world to Sissy's, is also signalled by the colour scheme. Her father intends to bring her up according to the colourless Bitzer pattern, quelling all fancy and feeling in her and devoting her entirely to fact. But the young Gradgrinds are not as bloodless and passionless as Bitzer. We have seen what happens to Tom. His inability to control his 'grovelling sensualities' causes him to become besmeared with pigment from the outside. Even little Jane Gradgrind, who is to be saved for humanity by Sissy, must have her native fancy and childish cheeks daubed over by the prevailing white—she falls asleep over vulgar fractions with a composition of white clay on her features, manufactured from 'slate-pencil and tears'.

Louisa, in spite of being a docile child, early shows signs of not belonging in the Gradgrind world. She is caught, 'red and disconcerted', peeping through a loophole at the 'graceful equestrian Tyrolean flower-act!' In her face 'there was a light with nothing to rest upon, a fire with nothing to burn, a starved imagination keeping life in itself somehow'. The redness recurs, and in her it is the signal of feeling and passion, though she is not even aware of them in herself, nor can she give them a name. There is a poignant little incident of her adolescence, when the fifty-year-old Bounderby, stirred with lust, kisses her cheek.

> He went his way, but she stood on the same spot, rubbing the cheek he had kissed, with her handkerchief, until it was burning red. . . .
>
> 'What are you about, Loo?' her brother sulkily remonstrated. 'You'll rub a hole in your face.'
>
> 'You may cut the piece out with your penknife if you like, Tom. I wouldn't cry!'

The incident sharply suggests the appalling violation—though one that she could not explain or analyse—that is practised on her in giving her to Bounderby in marriage. Having no access to her own instincts and feelings, and no knowledge that she has them, she makes no strong objection. But Bounderby's polluting kiss, so fiercely disgusting to her, is the preview of her wedding-night. And the knowledge that Tom gains of her feelings in this kiss scene shows him as doubly depraved in hushing her into the marriage.

Her father's transfer of her to Bounderby, the progress from the theory to the practice of Utilitarianism, sets her on the same path as Tom, and there is the same suggestion of denigration from without. Louisa's state of mind has been consistently associated with the fires and fumes of Coketown, and as Gradgrind proposes the match we hear of 'The distant smoke very black and heavy'. She is on her way to becoming grimed over, like the red brick of Coketown and the painted face of her brother. But her symptomatic interest in fires and the light of imagination prevails over the smoke, and the more vivid colouring asserts itself. As she warns her father, 'when the night comes, Fire bursts out'.

It is Harthouse's sensual mission to awaken the dormant passion in Louisa; and he goes a long way towards succeeding. Harthouse, though not moved by strong passion himself, takes a connoisseur's delight in being the object of passion. That is, as his name implies, having no heart (he has a 'nest of addled eggs' in 'the cavity where his heart should have been') he wants to become the home for Louisa's. He specialises in arousing passion, not feeling it. Or, to use Dickens's colour metaphor, he is 'the very Devil' at 'the kindling of red fire'. As we have seen, Dickens was to develop the association of red with unleashed passion further still in *A Tale of Two Cities*, with the prominent red caps of the revolutionaries, and the red wine spilled in the streets that is the preview of the bloodbath of the Reign of Terror. Colour is Dickens's shorthand for aroused emotion in Louisa. Her love for

Tom, the one feeling she is conscious of, first signals to Harthouse her capacity for passion, and he covets it. He sees that
'Her colour brightened' for Tom, and he begins to think 'it
would be a new sensation, if the face which changed so
beautifully for the whelp, would change for him'. Presently,
by pretending interest in Tom, he has inveigled himself into
her confidence, and proceeds on the assumption not only of
her love for Tom but also of her absence of love for her husband. The signals are encouraging. She is 'flushing', and
then 'She flushed deeper and deeper, and was burning red'.
Next, when she betrays that she has sold her husband's gifts
to pay her brother's debts, 'She stopped, and reddened again'.
Now she varies her normally numb response to her husband's blustering by facing him 'with a proud colour in her
face that was a new change'. Harthouse has indeed been successful in kindling the red fire.

Louisa goes so far as to hear his urgent proposal that she
should elope with him, and to be tempted by it. So much we
may infer from her flight in the tempest on the train, amidst
'Fire and steam, and smoke, and red light'. But she flees not
to her lover but to her father, and by the time she gets to
him she is appropriately purged of pigment: 'so colourless,
so dishevelled, so defiant and despairing, that he was afraid
of her'.

Within the bounds of a brief fable, Louisa undergoes an
emotional education. Though we are not to approve of Harthouse, he provides the means by which she discovers her
own heart. Out of touch with her instincts and emotions, like
her mother, and alienated from her self, she is not fully
alive, and allows herself to be handed over to Bounderby like
a parcel of goods, hardly even knowing that it matters. Harthouse causes an awakening of passion and consciousness;
but her newly vivid colouring, like Tom's, is not integrated
with moral imagination, and must be exorcised, leaving her
torpid and colourless again. It is only the deep-hued Sissy
(who has meanwhile changed little Jane's chalk-smeared
countenance to 'a beaming face') who can reconcile her to
her self. Under her influence Louisa, at the conclusion of the
novel, is 'trying hard to know her humbler fellow-creatures,
and to beautify their lives of machinery and reality with
those imaginative graces and delights, without which the
heart of infancy will wither up'. Leaving behind the black-
and-white Gradgrind world, she has come to the Jupe phi-

losophy that rejoices in flowers, butterflies and circuses, the 'imaginative graces and delights'.

Hard Times is not a complex novel, and its colour motif is simple too. The directive we receive on the appropriate colouring of imagination and pleasure in our lives is the adage, *Not too little* (like the absence of pigment in Bitzer and Mrs. Gradgrind), *not too much* (like the artificially applied coloration of Tom, Coketown and Mrs. Sparsit), *but just right* (like the organic colouring of Sissy Jupe and, eventually, Louisa). This essentially simple and consistent scheme serves Dickens well, and furnishes some memorable scenes and characterizations. Artistically, he has been most successful in the negative extremes, the black and white of his tentative title: in the slug-like pallor of Bitzer and the daubed-over blackness of Coketown and Tom, who wear their pigment like tar and feathers. These are memorable figures, and for good reason commentators keep coming back to them. Sissy Jupe, once she has left behind the schoolroom and her childhood, is only intermittently successful. But Louisa, cut off from access to her own feelings and instincts and a stranger to her self, is a figure of considerable psychological interest, and Dickens has made the colour-scheme tell in the development of her character too. Though its design is less elaborately developed than that of *Bleak House*, *Hard Times* equally gains in impact and coherence from a dominant visual motif.

Characterization in *Hard Times*

J. Miriam Benn

J. Miriam Benn analyzes Dickens's allegorical approach to characterization in *Hard Times*. In Benn's view, the characters who are consistently allegorical—such as Bounderby—are fictionally successful. In contrast, when Dickens mixes allegory with humanism or psychological realism—as when the allegorical figure of Gradgrind becomes a humanized father—the result is an unsatisfactory character. Benn is the author of *Predicaments of Love,* a study of Victorian counterculture.

The weekly serialization of *Hard Times* set Dickens new problems; he chafed against the restrictiveness of the form:

> The difficulty of the space is CRUSHING. Nobody can have an idea of it who has not had an experience of patient fiction-writing with some elbow-room always, and open places in perspective.

Some critics blame the faults of *Hard Times* on its brevity, finding it thin, cramped, too purposeful, too scrupulous, too little pleasing to the imagination—the last a serious indictment of a book which pleads for imaginative pleasures. Others praise its power, coherence, concise logic, speed or clarity. F.R. Leavis was among the most influential of these; as early as 1947 he stressed the consistency of its effects, the relevance of its detail, and the concentration which resulted from its symbolic method.

We know that, because his novel was so short, Dickens was forced to discipline his natural tendency to multiply characters and symbols in searching for a wider frame of reference. He wished to make observations about Utilitarianism in schools and in the home; about a social anomaly in the divorce laws; about the reasons for defective relations between capital and labor; about conditions in industry, and

Excerpted from "Landscape with Figures: Characterization and Expression in *Hard Times*," by J. Miriam Benn, *Dickens Studies Annual*, vol. 1 (1970). Reprinted by permission of AMS Press. Notes in the original have been omitted in this reprint.

about safety regulations. His technical problem was to integrate his themes, and extract from them generalizations which would combine into a unified moral picture.

Occasionally Dickens himself takes on the task of generalization, but relates his observations closely to plot or fable. Thus, his comments on Harthouse imply the wider defects of dilettantism, which he represents.

> And yet he had not, even now, any earnest wickedness of purpose in him. Publicly and privately, it were much better for the age in which he lived, that he and the legion of whom he was one were designedly bad, than indifferent and purposeless. It is the drifting icebergs setting with any current anywhere, that wreck the ships.

More commonly, it is metaphor which widens the scope of his particular criticisms and helps Dickens make his generalizations. Leavis in *The Great Tradition* noted that "the symbolic intention emerges out of metaphor and the vivid evocation of the concrete." However vividly evoked, concrete detail is strictly limited to what is both characteristic and typical; there is little room in *Hard Times* for the idiosyncratic or unique. Dickens insisted that his novel was not narrowly based on affairs in Preston; even without his disclaimer, his techniques would have made this clear. He has produced an allegorical "landscape with figures": men of stone or brass in a town of machinery and tall chimneys. The OED tells us that allegory is a "description of a subject under the guise of some other subject of aptly suggestive resemblance; . . . a figurative . . . narrative, in which properties and circumstances attributed to the apparent subject really refer to the subject they are meant to suggest; an extended or continued metaphor." We can see that the definition comes very close to describing Dickens' techniques in his fable of Utilitarianism.

His method is to create a character (or characters) whose primary quality of mind is expressible through a metaphor; this metaphor is then translated into a concrete environmental parallel, and given further expression in Dickens' own narrative, in the speeches he puts into his characters' mouths, and in his ironic additions to those speeches, or echoes of them. Subsidiary qualities cluster round the primary quality of mind; each has its own metaphorical analogues to demonstrate what is wrong with it—what it lacks aesthetically, let us say, or morally; where it goes on psychological or educational grounds.

DICKENS'S METAPHORICAL METHOD

Thus, Dickens evokes the aridity of Gradgrind's Utilitarianism by the metaphor of a sterile garden or the spoiling of a fruitful one. "Plant nothing else, and root out everything else," says Mr. Gradgrind of facts—and chooses for this, Dickens notes sardonically, a teacher who has "taken the bloom off the higher branches of mathematics." The name of Gradgrind's house, the suggestions in his own name, and the children's rock specimens "broken from the parent substances by those tremendously hard instruments their own names," are all metaphorical parallels for the children's arid lives and the hardness of their parents' own substance. Mr. Gradgrind and his stony environment coalesce from the start; of the terms "square wall," "vault," "cellarage," "two dark caves," "warehouse-room," some images relate to his environment, some to his person. They are secondary metaphors, adding the ideas of passivity and storage to the main metaphor of stony hardness. They combine to condemn a system which makes the brain a storehouse for facts and children as passively receptive as stone jars.

Helpless passivity implies aggressive opposing forces: Gradgrind is a "galvanising apparatus" or a cannon "loaded to the muzzle with facts" prepared to blow the children "clean out of the region of childhood at one discharge." The description of the third gentleman's educational methods relies heavily on the language of the prize ring. Both men are ready to take childhood captive and drag it into statistical dens by the hair, yet neither is really cruel. They simply fail to understand human nature: Gradgrind uses the reproach "you are childish" to a child.

Gradgrind's other friend, Bounderby, uses aggressive and violent language even when he speaks of himself:

> You may force him to swallow boiling fat, but you shall never force him to suppress the facts of his life.

Naturally enough, these two aggressively self-opinionated men undervalue the rest of creation. Gradgrind's System teaches him to consider men "reasoning animals"; his children are lectured at, "coursed, like little hares"—the pun is a comment on the System and on the wretchedness of children under it. The two men group individuals into denigratory categories: noisy insects, vagabonds, young rabble—not circus-folk or children.

Such expressions demonstrate a tendency in Gradgrind and Bounderby which makes their friendship less incomprehensible. Both ignore individuals: to Gradgrind, men are statistical data; to Bounderby, they are Hands, or Power, or just machines. Dickens satirizes Bounderby's attitude when he echoes the metaphor: "The Hands were all out of gear." As with the address, Pod's End, Dickens is suggesting that to both men people are as alike as peas and as soulless as numbers or as machines. They become objects, to be used and classified.

THE LANGUAGE OF STATISTICS

Statistics is a powerful weapon for obliterating the differences between individuals; the metaphor of statistics shows how Gradgrind and Bounderby can voluntarily blind themselves to realities: rather than consider marital incompatibility nearer home, Gradgrind buries himself in marriage statistics about the Calmucks of Tartary. The related metaphor of calculation is centrally placed in the novel in order to link Bounderby, Gradgrind, and the various elements in their public and private worlds. Tom, "that not unprecedented triumph of calculation which is usually at work on number one," connects the two households; he is totally allegorized, being based on a single character trait expressed through a metaphor. Similarly, the attempted seduction of Louisa by her father's political ally, Harthouse, is told in the language of the countinghouse. At their first meeting they assess each other's value. Louisa hardy takes him at his own valuation, but, like a bookkeeper, she casts him up, so much on the debit side, so much to his credit: "Mr. Harthouse, I give you credit for being interested in my brother." Harthouse profits from Louisa's love for Tom, and casts up his own progress with her like a balance sheet, "so much the more . . . so much the less"; he reckons up his advantages as a winner might count his gains. Yet in the end he errs in his calculations, for Louisa's real personality, unique and incalculable, evades his arithmetical process.

Within the allegory, the logical person to oppose Harthouse is Sissy, for she is totally uncalculating. Sissy loves her father loyally and selflessly; her undiminished hope of his return prevents her running away from Stone Lodge, and is "the result of no arithmetical process," being "self-imposed in defiance of all calculation." It is her disinterestedness which helps her to rout Harthouse; besides, she speaks in language he can understand, of "compensation," or "reparation," of whether these will be "much" or "enough," in short, as if he is a moral bankrupt or has engaged in some damaging business dealings. Calculation, which entered the ninth chapter as a metaphor, has now become an allegorical way of life, which Sissy is there to overthrow.

Such a mode of expression does more than link Dickens' themes and characters. It provides lines of demarcation between those for whom the System—in whatever sphere it operates—is infallible, and those who are its unwilling victims, like Louisa or Stephen. When they appeal against the System's obliterating statistical techniques, it is as individuals. They do not want to be made into machines, like Bitzers. Bitzer, the System's star pupil, has lost his humanity: insect-like, he can respond "correctly" to the stimuli of questions, but cannot evaluate them. The allegorical approach clarifies certain values, or moral issues (like the limits of arbitrary power, the rights of individuals, or the nature of responsibility); but it also tends to simplify them, until the resolutions offered appear naïve (Sissy's routing of Harthouse) or insufficient (Stephen's promise).

Not all Dickens' characters in this novel are allegories, whether wholly or in part. Not all his characters are successful. Yet it would be completely wrong to say that it is the allegorical treatment of character which makes the novel, however interesting, so unsatisfactory. A character may be successful precisely because it is consistently and satisfyingly allegorical; it may fail either because Dickens mixed some humanity in with the allegory, or some unfortunate allegorizing in with his psychological realism. It is also possible that a wholly allegorical character fails, not because at every point of the action he is symbolizing something, but for some quite different reason, such as the poor integration of his role in the plot or the fable, or for some defect in his manner of expressing himself. In two characters, Dickens is trying, at particular places in the story, to achieve some point of balance between the human and the allegorical; in a third, he wishes human nature and allegorical significance to stand out equally throughout.

BOUNDERBY

One of the simplest and most effective characters in the novel, and one who is at the same time the most allegorical, is

Bounderby. His first metaphor is metal; more particularly, as he is a north-country banker, brass. He also represents the bullying bluster of the master-class; his second, more strongly developed metaphor, is wind. He is just coarse material stretched by much air: a windbag. He is a puffed-up boaster, his early poverty a windy lie, his final defeat a deflation.

It is no criticism to say that Bounderby is a static character based on a humor; there is no need for him to be subtle, to change or repent—it would be out of character and unnecessary. His traits are constants; his pretence about his origins adds a pseudo-rationality to his abuse of the poor and weak, and is therefore functional throughout the plot. His rejection of refinement and imagination provides a marital environment in which Louisa will suffer enough to turn gratefully to Harthouse's supposed kindness. Bounderby's home is a suitable setting for Mrs. Sparsit, because her exaggerated claims to breeding are complementary to his pretensions to none. His qualities are given: he is always hostile to Stephen, always attracting toadyism, always repelling love. They state as a datum the impossibility of communication between such masters and men. Bounderby's fiction of turtle soup and gold plate expresses metaphorically the barrier of suspicion which he deliberately erects; it is there, whether a Hand comes to get advice, or to complain; Bounderby never varies.

Certainly Bounderby is a caricature, if by that we mean that he shows exaggerated consistency, a patterned coherence of major and minor character traits. He is fictionally successful, however, because he is adequate for all that he is required to be and do in both plot and fable, and because he is active, energetic, and racy in his speech. When Stephen, fasting save for a piece of bread, stands before him while he sits lunching off chops and sherry, Dickens is successfully using a political cartoonist's technique: the broad, simple outline; the few telling, clearly visualized details; successfully, because Bounderby's part in the plot calls for no greater subtlety than does his allegorical role in the fable.

The scene of his deflation particularly illustrates the range and scope of this wholly allegorical treatment. In it, he acts strictly in character, blustering, blaming others, trying to carry off a hopeless situation. The crowd, real enough in itself, supports him in his allegorical role: it goes off, like Rumour with a thousand tongues, to publish his humiliation to the four winds. In organizing so poetic a justice, Dickens is harking back to his first description of Bounderby as a windbag; so neat a scheme cannot be despised, for if Bounderby is static, he is static as a setting, a climate, or an atmosphere is static.

A static character rarely in himself surprises the reader; Dickens achieves the unexpected by making it happen to Bounderby. When he goes to break the news of his engagement to Mrs. Sparsit, he expects her to faint, and comes prepared with a harsh restorative. Her sympathy utterly confounds him, for there is nothing in his character which tells him what to do with sympathy. The scene is comic precisely because it finds him at a loss; deprived of the one role he knows how to play, he can call on no other. What is surprising in the scene belongs not to him, but to Mrs. Sparsit's psychological ingenuity; his rigidity can feel only bewilderment and irritability when confronted with the unexpected. It is a brilliant example of the possibilities of static characterization.

In Bitzer, static, unrealistic, devoid of simple humanity, we have a case parallel to Bounderby's: an allegorical character who never steps outside his role. As with Bounderby and Gradgrind, his allegorical nature is immediately indicated through metaphor. The perfect product of the System is dehumanized, drained of color, cold, looking "as though, if he were cut, he would bleed white." So formal is Dickens' treatment of Bitzer that we need only two characteristics to recognize him next time: absence of color and an insectlike knuckling of the forehead. He does not develop, save that the cunning child grows into a cunning adult with enough psychological subtlety to flatter Mrs. Sparsit. Always a toady, he becomes a place-seeker and spy. Logically enough, his cunning operates through the technique Gradgrind taught him: simple calculation. Thus, he tries to arrest Tom not through animosity or an outraged moral sense, but simply from a calculation regarding the profit to himself. Such a character neither demands nor receives naturalistic treatment. Apart from his plot-function, which requires certain characteristic actions from him, he has no purpose save that served by his allegorical role, i.e., to show the ultimate logic of the calculus and to act as foil to Sissy's uncalculating, loving kindness.

Dickens shows clearly, by the farcical manner of their defeats, that we are not to feel for Bounderby or Bitzer as if they were human. Bounderby's public deflating and Bitzer's de-

feat by a dancing horse are suitably absurd ends to preten-
sion and cunning, maintaining the tone at a level where
there is no danger of the reader's involvement through sympathy. They are not equally successful portraits, for Bounderby's energy and liveliness of speech amuse us more, despite Dickens' exaggeration of his foibles.

THE ALLEGORICAL GRADGRIND

Gradgrind presents Dickens with a more difficult technical
problem, for he plays a double role, the human father and
the allegorical Utilitarian. Unhappily, *Hard Times* had to
open with Gradgrind in his allegorical role. After that, Dickens had insufficient space to wipe out the first deep impression made upon the reader by his metaphorical "commentary" which associated the idea of hardness with the man as
well as with the doctrine.

Dickens launches Gradgrind as if he were to be as static
and allegorical as Bounderby. His business is to crush the
imaginative side of a child's nature in order to develop its
reason. It is not an agreeable part to play, and it puts him ir-
remediably in the wrong. Even his appearance is allegorical:
his square finger and forehead, square coat, legs, and shoul-
ders do not combine to make a human being, but are merely
attributes. Gradgrind remains curiously formless, a statue
still imprisoned in stone. It becomes difficult for Dickens to
develop in him a capacity for tragedy and disillusionment,
for these are only appropriate to human beings.

Dickens saw the allegorical Gradgrind in terms of blind-
ness, and his human role as the recovery of sight, through
revelation. At first he is wilfully blind: "We don't want to
know about that here," he says, and his prejudices manipulate the truth to suit themselves; a circus clown becomes "a
veterinary surgeon, a farrier and horse-breaker." His eye
rests on the surface when that is safer, so that he does not
see Louisa's uncomfortable ironies in the proposal scene.
Because Bounderby appears to embody certain of his own
ideals—he is self-made, hardheaded, industrious; a pro-
ducer, not merely an owner of wealth—Gradgrind does not
look beneath the surface, and readily accepts his friend's autobiographical boasting.

Just as he is blind to defect where his System allows him
to approve, so also is he unable to see virtue in people whose
way of life finds no place in it. If they are entertainers, they

must be idle; if itinerant, vagabonds; yet the first great hope for Gradgrind as a human being is that he is patient with the circus folk in order to help Sissy.

When Gradgrind communicates Bounderby's proposal to Louisa, he is still almost entirely allegorical. His fatherliness is dormant, and he is the mere embodiment of a doctrine. Louisa's ironic questions cannot make him throw off his role, though they make him uncomfortable and drive him to evasions among facts and statistics. He is not entirely blind to her problem, but can shut his eyes to it until disaster opens them finally. In the meantime he gropingly accepts certain insights, though remaining blind to their full significance. Seeing that Sissy is not a shining credit to his System, he comments: "You are an affectionate, earnest, good young woman—and—and we must make that do." His vision is clearing, but his values are unchanged, and he has yet to find a place for a kind heart in his System. He finds qualities in Sissy, however, which cannot be comprehended in a tabular statement or Parliamentary return, and through this crack a little light begins to shine.

GRADGRIND AS FATHER FIGURE

Given more of this, the allegorical might have modulated successfully into the fatherly, but in II, xii, Dickens ruins a whole scene by adopting a wrong tone for Louisa. Her mannered speeches mar the simplicity and directness of Gradgrind's response to her misery; her part is too heavy, his too light, to achieve Dickens' purpose. A little later, Dickens obliterates Gradgrind's new humanity with a group of metaphors too reminiscent of the old allegorical character, which starts up before us just when we should be forgetting it:

> In gauging fathomless deeps with his little mean excise-rod, and in staggering over the universe with his rusty stiff-legged compasses, he had meant to do great things. . . . He had tumbled about, annihilating the flowers of existence.

It is, perhaps, an echo of Carlyle's "deeper than any of our Logic-plummets hitherto will sound"; if so, it comes at an inopportune time. It intrudes, spoiling the effect of some genuinely moving moments, as when Gradgrind finds for the first time that he can express love and compassion: "he softly moved her scattered hair from her forehead with his hand." His slow and painful acceptance of the flaws in his System, of the new facts of instinct, imagination, love, and

gratitude, is in fact finely done; unhappily, Dickens irrevo-
cably mars the effect by rubbing in the moral.

Gradgrind's own words, though formal, are not stilted; his
mental turmoil shows through his metaphors, which suggest
collapse, stunning shock, a blow at the foundations of his
world. He shows patience with Bounderby and a tentative
uncertainty about himself that sits better on him than his old
strident didacticism; he even shows the ghost a sense of humor. He wants to mend, if he can, what he has "perverted" in
Louisa, and the depth of his bitter disillusionment with his
System is revealed in his use of the word. The scene prepares
us to pity him as a father in his scene with Tom at the circus;
we will feel for him as we would not have done earlier.

Dickens returns to his allegory with the entrance of
Bitzer, and Gradgrind's new humanity is overshadowed by
Bitzer's cold logic, a caricature of the System's own teaching.
Discrediting Gradgrind at this late stage, and by his own
logic, puts him back in his old schoolroom role. Although
the confrontation provides a dramatic turn in the plot, it
throws out the program of a gradual development of humanity in Gradgrind. As allegory gains control, his humanity dwindles; we are back to the moral fable, and stay there
while Sleary sees that the rewards that Gradgrind gives for
services rendered shall be allegorically appropriate.

On the whole, Gradgrind is a failure. Bounderby is a success because he is not asked to step outside his allegorical
role; Gradgrind fails because of the uneasy tension between
his allegorical and his human selves. The shifts between
them are uncomfortable, and are hampered by defects in
other characters. We can feel, perhaps, that suffering and re-
formation came to the second Gradgrind, but we can hardly
envisage any change which would bring them to the first.

Gender and Paradox in *Hard Times*

David L. Cowles

In the following essay, David L. Cowles closely examines Dickens's treatment of gender issues in
Hard Times. Dickens's presentation of women,
Cowles concludes, reveals the author's own irreconcilable contradictory beliefs. For example, Louisa
exhibits many of the standard Victorian feminine
virtues that Dickens idealized, yet Dickens continually renders her unable to perform her womanly duties. Louisa can exhibit loving loyalty to her father
only by rejecting everything he—and his educational system—represents. Cowles is a professor of
English at Brigham Young University.

Hearing that her husband has apprehended Tom and Louisa
peeping into Sleary's circus, Mrs. Gradgrind exclaims: "'I declare you're enough to make one regret ever having had a
family at all. I have a great mind to say I wish I hadn't. *Then*
what would you have done, I should like to know'". Dickens
obviously intends us to laugh at this obvious paradox: Mrs.
Gradgrind could only prove her suffering *to* her wayward
children if they did not exist. Yet such self-contradiction typifies Dickens's own dependence on paradox in *Hard Times*,
particularly regarding gender issues.

Throughout Dickens's works, treatments of women probably engender more unintentional self-contradiction than
any other topic. Like all great artists, Dickens typifies as
much as he transcends the conceptual languages of his age,
and for the mid-Victorians "the woman question" was a linguistic Tower of Babel. Examining aspects of gender in *Hard
Times*, especially as they relate to Louisa Gradgrind/Bound-
erby, reveals irreconcilable contradictions in Dickens's
treatment of women and suggests other crucial ways in
which the text differs from itself.

Reprinted from "Having It Both Ways: Gender and Paradox in *Hard Times*," by David
L. Cowles, *Dickens Quarterly*, June 1991, by permission of the Dickens Society of
America.

IDEALIZED WOMEN

Hard Times provides two portraits of idealized Dickensian women: Sissy Jupe and Rachael. Both characters exhibit standard Victorian feminine virtues: extraordinary devotion (especially to a needy male), remarkable love-based powers of intuition, firm but modest assertion of heart-felt values, great spiritual strength and endurance. Throughout his novels, Dickens identifies these traits as inherently feminine, natural to all good-hearted women. The sensitive male gratefully admires a woman's natural devotion to him, and does not stand between her and self-sacrificing feminine fulfillment. This obvious projection of male desire, of course, conveniently excuses men for using the women who love them. The man's own worthiness in the formula is largely irrelevant—especially if he is a father or brother. Indeed, as with Nancy, Florence Dombey, Little Dorrit, and Lizzie Hexam, the worse the man, the more admirable the woman's loyalty. Such devotion is a sure sign of inner goodness, even in otherwise wicked or insensitive female character like Nancy and Pleasant Riderhood. Sissy and Rachael, sensitive to their own hearts and to others' needs, clearly exhibit all these characteristics.

Louisa, too, feels intimations of these "natural" womanly traits, especially as she functions as daughter, sister, and wife—roles that always call for selfless devotion in Dickens. Yet Louisa's Utilitarian education—normally reserved for boys and particularly hostile to the traditional female virtues so essential to her "real" nature—has largely incapacitated her for these all-important relationships. Moreover, in Louisa's cast these roles require simultaneous loyalty and disloyalty to the particular males involved. She can exhibit "natural" loving loyalty to her father only by rejecting everything he sincerely stands for. Sacrificing herself for Tom means marrying a man to whom she cannot offer loving devotion. And wifely loyalty to Bounderby—a man embodying the opposite of all her inner yearnings—is unthinkable. Indeed, Dickens places Louisa in an impossible position, and in the end he punishes her for her inability to bridge gaps inherent in his own contradictory beliefs about women.

These contradictions reveal themselves whenever gender issues arise. Consider, for example, Tom's attitude about his sister's female duty toward him. In an early conversation with Tom, Louisa laments that she cannot make his life comfortable in traditionally feminine ways. Clearly Tom considers this desire perfectly natural. After all, he points out, "'You are a girl, too, and a girl comes out of it better than a boy does'"). But Tom selfishly trades on Louisa's devotion without proper appreciation for her sacrifices. He later calls her a "capital girl", indicating the economic (mis)use to which he puts her. Tom explains to Harthouse why Louisa married Bounderby: "'Not that it was altogether so important to her as it was to me, . . . because my liberty and comfort, and perhaps my getting on, depended on it. . . . A girl can get on anywhere. . . . Girls can always get on, somehow'".

THE BROTHER-SISTER RELATIONSHIP

Daniel P. Deneau points out the sexual overtones apparent in the private final conversation between Tom and Louisa.

The details of the scene are so telling that a long quotation must be supplied; in what follows I omit the brief and unresponsive replies of Tom.

> Then she arose, put on a loose robe, and went out of her room in the dark, and up the staircase to her brother's room. His door being shut, she softly opened it and spoke to him, approaching his bed with a noiseless step.
>
> She kneeled down beside it, passed her arm over his neck, and drew his face to her. . . .
>
> "Tom, have you anything to tell me? If ever you loved me in your life, and have anything concealed from every one besides, tell it to me.". . .
>
> "My dear brother," she laid her head down on his pillow, and her hair flowed over him as if she would hide him from every one but herself, "is there nothing that you have to tell me? . . . You can tell me nothing that will change me. O Tom, tell me the truth!". . .
>
> "As you lie here alone, my dear, in the melancholy night, so you must lie somewhere one night, when even I, if I am living then, shall have left you. As I am here beside you, barefoot, unclothed, undistinguishable in darkness, so must I lie through all the night of my decay, until I am dust. In the name of that time, Tom, tell me the truth now!". . .
>
> "You may be certain," in the energy of her love she took him to her bosom as if he were a child, "that I will not reproach you. You may be certain that I will he compassionate and true to you. You may be certain that I will save you at whatever cost. O Tom, have you nothing to tell me? Whisper very softly. Say only 'yes,'

Dickens unquestionably condemns Tom for his insensitive, gender-based demands on Louisa's devoted service as his natural male right, as well as for his repeated statements that her loving sensitivity is just "another of the advantages . . . of being a girl". In fact, Dickens blames Tom for not being more like Louisa. On the other hand, Dickens has taken pains to show that Tom and Louisa have had identical educational and family experiences, and that the primary differences between the siblings are gender-determined. Further, though he shows disdain for Tom's attitude, Dickens clearly approves of Louisa's desire to serve Tom in the ways

and I shall understand you!"

She turned her ear to his lips, but he remained doggedly silent. . . .

"You are tired," she whispered presently, more in her usual way.

In spite of Tom's insistence that he has nothing to tell Louisa, she presses the matter with a peculiar urgency, even passionately. A "yes," as I read the scene, is really the answer Louisa desires; she seems intent on establishing a type of mental intimacy her brother—on sharing a secret about a dark matter, a not-to-be-revealed chime. Moreover, Dickens's reference to "a loose robe" and Louisa's more pointed reference to her state of undress—"'barefoot, unclothed'"—are pretty insistent details. I suggest, in fact, that sexual overtones hover over the scene, or, more plainly, that the scene has the atmosphere of a seduction. And still another emotional current is established when we are told that Louisa takes Tom "to her bosom as if he were a child." For a moment at least (notice that after a time she returns to speaking "more in her usual way") Tom seems to become for Louisa an object of both sexual and maternal love. Though writing obliquely enough not to offend Victorian propriety, Dickens nonetheless brings his attentive reader to the realisation that, as a result of a lopsided education, Louisa reaches a point where her affection for Tom is not merely superlative sisterly affection. When Bounderby comes to inquire about his missing wife, her father stammers that "'there are qualities in Louisa, which—which have been harshly neglected, and—and a little perverted.'" The words are truer than Mr. Gradgrind suspects.

Daniel P. Deneau, "The Brother-Sister Relationship in *Hard Times,*" *The Dickensian,* vol. 60, 1964.

he expects—and certainly because Dickens, too, sees female self-sacrifice as natural. In effect, Dickens puts himself exactly in Tom's position by praising Louisa, Rachael, and Sissy for doing just the sort of things Tom desires. Like Tom, Dickens believes that through unselfish devotion "girls can always get on, somehow." Dickens simultaneously uses the same attitude, in effect, to condemn Tom and praise Louisa.

LOUISA'S INDEPENDENCE

In another telling passage, when Gradgrind catches young Louisa and Tom at the forbidden circus, he blames Tom for instigating the venture, assuming that the boy, though younger, naturally leads. But Gradgrind is mistaken. Louisa haughtily insists she led Tom. Indeed, "Louisa looked at her father with more boldness," and the children's "air of jaded sullenness" was evident "particularly in the girl". Once again Dickens plays both sides of the gender issue. First, he clearly shows that Gradgrind really *is* wrong in assuming that the boy naturally leads. Louisa, Tom tells her afterward, "can always lead me as you like" through her deeply-buried but irrepressible feminine instincts. Dickens wants us to admire Louisa for confidently following her heart beyond Gradgrind's limited teachings and for bringing Tom along after her. At the same time, however, Dickens *condemns* Louisa's unladylike and disobedient independence. Her unfeminine disloyalty to her father must be ascribed to her unfortunate education. So Dickens asks us simultaneously to approve Louisa's independence from her father's system, while blaming that same system for it. Similarly, we must respect Louisa's intellectual capacities even as we blame Gradgrind's system for forcing her to develop them instead of the natural womanly skills involved in making men comfortable. Further, Louisa's haughty reply to her father is itself a loyal defense of her younger brother, whelp though he is. Yet this very loyalty to Tom requires equal disloyalty to her father, toward whom she holds the same womanly duty. Again, Dickens plays both sides at once: We are to respect Louisa's natural womanly feelings in her loyalty to her brother, while simultaneously blaming Gradgrind's system for her disloyalty to him.

Ultimately, Louisa manages to resolve the conflict between father and brother. She returns to her father—who now needs and deserves her affectionate care. Louisa, increasingly "feminine" in outlook, now separates her father from his system: "'I have never blamed you, and I never shall'". She also remains faithful to Tom—even protecting him from justice. Unlike Bounderby's betrayed mother, Mrs. Pegler (who is correspondingly less admirable), Louisa has no illusions about Tom's guilt; she senses it intuitively from the start. Dickens clearly presents Louisa's loyalty despite Tom's unworthiness as admirably feminine. Ironically, however, this very faithfulness causes her inappropriate relationship with Harthouse—both because Harthouse manipulates her through it, and because it motivates her decision to enter an unsatisfying marriage. More importantly, in order to achieve loyalty to father and brother and attain partial feminine fulfillment, Louisa must actually abandon her husband. Dickens asks us to blame Bounderby, who is made to reject her—though not until after she has already left him. Bounderby's unworthiness somehow excuses Louisa for violating her womanly duty to support her husband. Dickens makes us feel that her mistake was marrying Bounderby in the first place, largely under her father and brother's near-criminal influence. Her loyalty to them, despite the limitations and suffering they impose on her, seems even more admirable because they do not deserve it. Yet her disloyalty to Bounderby is made to appear equally admirable, precisely *because* she must escape the same kinds of insensitive limitations and suffering from him.

PUNISHMENT

Moreover, despite Dickens's clear efforts to excuse Louisa, in the end he punishes her for her unfeminine actions and attributes, but mitigates her suffering because she has a naturally loving feminine heart after all. Part of Louisa's sin against her woman's nature is clearly sexual. She has desired a man who is not her husband. Further, she has married a man she despises, who is old enough to be her father—a near-incestuous fate Esther Summerson narrowly avoids in *Bleak House*, written just before *Hard Times*. In the moral system of Dickens's novels, a woman who has sold herself sexually, for whatever reason, is forever denied the comfort and fulfillment of husband and family. Typical of Dickens's good-hearted but fallen women, Louisa must live a life dedicated to serving her father, separated forever from her beloved brother. Though her fate is less harsh than those of

Nancy, Little Em'ly, or, more to the point, Edith Dombey, Dickens describes what is denied Louisa in such desirable terms that it is difficult not to see her state as a punishment:

> Herself again a wife—a mother—lovingly watchful of her children, ever careful that they should have a childhood of the mind no less than a childhood of the body, as knowing it to be even a more beautiful thing, and a possession, any hoarded scrap of which, is a blessing and happiness to the wisest? Did Louisa see this? Such a thing was never to be.

Dickens attempts to mitigate Louisa's suffering by assuring us that other people's children will love her, but the elements of punishment are unmistakable.

Other characters reflect and complicate Dickens's treatment of Louisa. Indeed, nearly every important character functions as part of a large pattern of abandonment. Some desert loved ones for admirable, unselfish purposes. Sissy Jupe's father runs away from her, but, as the eternally loyal Sissy asserts, "'he left me for my good—he never would have left me for his own'". Stephen rejects his fellow workers, but in doing so maintains a higher loyalty to Rachael. Stephen must also leave Rachael, "thinking unselfishly . . . that at least his being obliged to go away was good for her". Other characters abandon duty to others for selfish reasons. Tom largely ignores his sister as soon as he escapes his father's house—except when he needs her to sacrifice something for him. Stephen's fellow Hands reject his honest refusal to join their union. Bounderby fires Stephen and later Mrs. Sparsit for egocentric reasons. Bitzer denies all loyalty toward Gradgrind. Even Mrs. Sparsit's late husband abandoned her shortly after their marriage.

Several cases of abandonment warrant special consideration in relation to Louisa leaving Bounderby. First, Dickens clearly condemns Stephen's wife for leaving him, something similar to what he approves in Louisa. Here the main difference is that the longsuffering Stephen deserves better while Bounderby does not. Dickens also emphasizes distinctions between the two women. Louisa marries Bounderby as an unselfish sacrifice for Tom and manages to evade at least the consummation of her dubious relationship with Harthouse. Stephen's wife is "foul" in her "moral infamy" and confronts Stephen with the threat that she will "'sell thee off agen . . . a score of times'". Consequently, we blame Stephen's wife in ways we do not blame Louisa, and we also recognize

Stephen's need for divorce—though Louisa's desire for separation hardly fits into the same class.

Dickens also emphasizes Bounderby's disloyalty to Louisa—
and to anyone else. His marriage, like his relationships with
Mrs. Sparsit, his mother, and even Gradgrind, is intended to
enhance his self-image and social position as self-made
man. Despite what he tells Stephen about "a sanctity in this
relation of life" that "must be kept up", when Stephen describes his patience toward his wayward wife, Bounderby
thinks, "The more fool you"—foreshadowing the policy he
later adopts toward Louisa. In discussing Louisa's flight with
Gradgrind, Bounderby complains that he has not been "'as
dutifully and submissively treated by your daughter, as
Josiah Bounderby of Coketown ought to be treated by his
wife'". Indeed, Bounderby remarks that he does not wish to
quarrel about Louisa, because "'to tell you the truth, I don't
think it would be worthy of my reputation to quarrel on such
a subject'". Bounderby's rejection of Louisa is unquestionably the best thing that could happen to her. She cannot go
back to him; womanly loyalty to her husband is now impossible. But because Dickens makes Bounderby reject *her* (an
act aggravated by his treatment of his mother), Louisa's desertion is presented as one more count against *him,* and actually becomes a point in her favor, despite violating a central tenet of the Dickensian female code.

Finally, Dickens's treatment of disempowered workers like
Stephen and Rachael parallels his contradictory attitude toward disempowered women. As Dickens condemns Tom's
selfish wishes regarding Louisa while simultaneously ap-
proving Louisa's desire to gratify them, so Dickens criticizes
the mill owners' view of their workers as mere Hands, but
asks us to admire those willing to act as little else. Like the
owners, Dickens essentially treats workers in *Hard Times* as
Hands. When Louisa visits Stephen's home, Dickens remarks
that "for the first time in her life, Louisa had come into one of
the dwellings of the Coketown Hands; for the first time in her
life, she was face to face with anything like individually in
connexion with them". Dickens himself never manages this
in the novel. He even identifies them primarily as "men and
brothers", despite the many female workers. As with Louisa,
Dickens's "good" workers inhabit both sides of crucial divisions, as when Stephen addresses Bounderby: "He spoke
with the rugged earnestness of his place and character—

deepened perhaps by a proud consciousness that he was faithful to his class under all their mistrust; but he fully remembered where he was, and did not even raise his voice".

INJUSTICE

Moreover, Dickens expects both Stephen and Louisa to endure injustice and limited opportunities for growth and self-fulfillment by taking whatever happiness (or solace) they can in self-sacrifice for others who are unworthy of their efforts, and who are clearly incapable of setting the agendas in question fairly. Dickens appears to suggest that workers, like wives, daughters, mothers, and sisters, should merely put faith in their oppressors, represented in *Hard Times* by Bounderby—hardly a rational way to improve their situation. In his ending portraits, Dickens admiringly describes Rachael as "a woman working, ever working, but content to do it, and preferring to do it as her natural lot, until she should be too old to labour any more", at which time presumably she should do the proper thing and die—not that she would have other options. Do your duty, Dickens urges. Take joy or solace there. Meanwhile, I will work to make the owners more sympathetic. This is precisely what he recommends to women. That, too, is why Louisa's bolting from Bounderby seems so uncharacteristic.

In unconsciously playing both sides of irreconcilable contradictions, especially regarding gender issues, Dickens undermines many of his own thematic assertions. Yet he does so in ways harmonious with his time, sex, and class (and therefore largely invisible to his contemporary readers) through conceptual languages he could not escape any more than we can escape our own linguistic and interpretive limitations. As much as any other Dickens novel, *Hard Times* reveals the kinds of cover-ups empowered mid-Victorians needed to hide essential contradictions inherent in pat answers to "the woman question."

Surveillance and Discipline in *Hard Times*

Cynthia Northcutt Malone

Cynthia Northcutt Malone contends that behind *Hard Times'* juxtaposition of individuality and uniformity lurks Dickens's effort to conform individuals to middle-class values. To this end, Dickens deploys a system of disciplinary surveillance—Gradgrind's abstracting gaze or Sissy's silent watchfulness, for example. These watching eyes, according to Malone, are mechanisms of social control, enforcing normalcy, docility, and obedience. The following critical essay originally appeared in *Studies in the Novel.*

"I shall have the satisfaction of causing you to be strictly educated;" Thomas Gradgrind tells Sissy Jupe in *Hard Times*, "and you will be a living proof to all who come into communication with you, of the advantages of the training you will receive. You will be reclaimed and formed." The novel ironically subverts this complacent picture of an invincible Gradgrindian system, of course, for it is Sissy who functions as the principle of reclamation and reforms the former. Through this juxtaposition of Sissy Jupe and Thomas Gradgrind, the novel sets Heart against Head, loving compassion for the particular human heart against soul-deadening uniformity, uniformity that it represents as the product of mid-Victorian social movements and reform efforts. Where Gradgrind's many reform projects would erase difference and enforce uniformity, absorbing the individual life into collective rule, his resistant pupil keeps her eye fixed on the individual life.

The rhetoric of opposition in *Hard Times* is misleading, however, for it masks the complicated dynamics at work in Dickens' representation of social reform—dynamics so complicated that it is difficult to divine any clear social agenda

Reprinted from "The Fixed Eye and the Rolling Eye: Surveillance and Discipline in *Hard Times*," by Cynthia Northcutt Malone, *Studies in the Novel*, Spring 1989. Reprinted with permission. Endnotes in the original have been omitted in this reprint.

in the novel. Recent readings offered by Butwin and Coles illustrate the problem; as a comparison of these readings demonstrates, the argument of *Hard Times* depends, in large measure, on how the reader chooses to frame the novel. I want to argue that the rhetorical oppositions of the novel—individualism versus uniformity, heart versus head—are strategically deployed in the service of the novel's own thoroughly middle-class reform effort. As I will show, *Hard Times* denounces the heavyhanded programs of Utilitarian reformers to build in their place a more sophisticated system of social control. A.P. Donajgrodski has argued that Utilitarians and their opponents often shared "near-identical presuppositions and social values," and *Hard Times* is a case in point. Behind the novel's insistence on difference, on the opposition between the Fact men and Fancy's child, the reform efforts turn out to have a common aim: discipline of the individual to conform to Victorian middle-class social values. Furthermore, as I will demonstrate, *Hard Times* borrows crucial tactics from the very movements and systems it so vigorously denounces. The most important of these tactics is surveillance, the basis of the Utilitarian felicific calculus.

Hard Times is preoccupied with watching; it is filled with observing, surveillant eyes. From the M'Choakumchild school in the opening chapter to the fire-gazing conclusion, *Hard Times* represents a system of disciplinary scrutiny, a hierarchical system of multiple hazes that enforce docility and obedience. The circus serves as a figure in small for the pervasive, multiple-layered system of surveillance at work in the novel as a whole, for the representation of the circus makes that system highly visible. Circus and Society seem to function as opposing terms, but here again, the rhetoric of opposition masks a deeper connection. The circus mirrors society. In the circus, where bodies are most obviously made into spectacle, the disciplinary function of observation is most clearly registered.

SLEARY'S GAZE

As the manager of the circus, Mr. Sleary is eminently constructed to maintain the discipline of the company. Sleary's gaze is always multiple; with one fixed eye and one rolling eye, he is a figure of plural vision—a figure without peripheral vision. The scene of Sleary's farewell speech to Sissy illustrates this point. Concluding his remarks, "he regarded her attentively with his fixed eye" and "surveyed his company with his loose one." Sleary can watch both the stage and the wings, both the spectacle and the spectators. He seems to see all, and when his searching gaze finds a flaw in the spectacle, when the performing body fails to perform correctly, Sleary punishes. "I don't pretend to be of the angel breed mythelf," he tells Sissy, "and I don't thay but what, when you mith't your tip, you'd find me cut up rough, and thwear an oath or two at you." But the disciplinary function of observation is not restricted to Sleary; the other performers and even the spectators participate in the observation of the body, and they also punish, through humiliation and ridicule. Sissy Jupe knows only too well the observing gaze and the observers' punishment, for her father, Signor Jupe, several times "missed his tip" and "was loose in his ponging." Sissy says that the spectators "very often wouldn't laugh," and the other performers "played tricks upon him"; and Jupe vanishes from the company in shame.

The disappearance of Signor Jupe serves as a warning to disobedient bodies, as a lesson held up before the eyes of all the other bodies in the novel. The metaphorical figure that marks his absence, the bottle of nine oils, functions as a visible spectacle of the undisciplined body's fate. By registering Jupe's disappearance in a textual figure at the very outset of the plot, the novel represents and participates in disciplinary surveillance. Throughout the plot, the novel will watch closely and record in textual figures the deaths and disappearances of undisciplined bodies, so that the novel itself becomes a spectacle with a disciplinary function. Like the circus, the novel stands on the side of Fancy, in apparent opposition to dry, dull Fact. Like the circus, the novel serves as improving recreation, offering to watching eyes a moral lesson that would warm the heart of a middle-class reformer; with Cooke Taylor, *Hard Times* implicitly affirms "the great but neglected truth, that moral education, in spite of all the labours of direct instructors, is really acquired in hours of recreation." And like the spectators of the circus, the spectators of the novel are never simply onlookers. *Hard Times* seeks to include its middle-class readers in its reform effort, to incorporate them into the system of intersecting gazes that enforces moral precepts.

I want to organize my discussion of this system around the figure of synecdoche in *Hard Times*, this novel of Head and Hand and Heart, showing that synecdoche serves to name the multiple functions of a larger disciplinary body. The figure of synecdoche articulates this body—and here, of course, I mean to call up the image of Venus in *Our Mutual Friend*. I want to invoke Venus as my muse because I particularly want to explore the ways surveillance functions in this novel to enforce the sexual discipline of the body. Dickens seems to have put aside the marriage plot so central to Victorian fiction in order to take on Industrialism, Utilitarianism, and Education. Yet, while the novel focuses explicitly on a wide range of social problems, its plots remain deeply concerned with bourgeois marriage. *Hard Times* ranges just far enough from the usual Dickensian marriage plot to register the operation and effects of a system that induces conformity to bourgeois codes of sexual behavior.

HEAD

In the novel's articulation of the body, Thomas Gradgrind is, of course, the figured Head. From their elevated position in the system of surveillance, the eyes of Gradgrind train their gaze on all the inhabitants of Coketown, from the smallest child in the M'Choakumchild school to the largest "grown-up baby" in the town. Under the surveillant eyes of Gradgrind and the Hard Fact Fellows, the individual differences within the Coketown masses are absorbed into norms that are recorded, tabulated, and inscribed into Blue Bucks. After extensive observation, these social investigators construct abstract types from the mass of detail. Like James Phillips Kay projecting a single individual, "the artizan," as the fictive representative of the laboring masses in Manchester, the Hard Fact Fellows project an abstracted "Hand," the supposed norm of the Coketown laborer. These norms exert their discipline in turn on the individual Coketown residents, who must construct themselves according to these rules.

The homogenizing, normalizing function of surveillance is perhaps most visible in the novel's representation of education in Coketown. Scrutiny begins in childhood, in "a plain, bare, monotonous vault of a schoolroom." M'Choakumchild's school erases names and assigns each child a number; and this system of education seems to homogenize the student body, to stuff every head—or fill every vessel—with a uniform collection of Facts. Here Bentham's plan for the chrestomathic school is finally realized; these schools like "factories, panopticon style, turning out finished products under the eyes of monitors," were never built, but Dickens fictively erects a Chrestomathia in Coketown. Examinations evaluate the children's grasp of political economy, and the individual child who cannot or will not perform at the level judged "normal" is punished and ridiculed. Sissy Jupe, her father's child, is humiliated and shamed by these examinations. "You don't know," a tearful Sissy tells Louisa, "what a stupid girl I am. All through school hours I make mistakes. Mr. and Mrs. M'Choakumchild call me up, over and over again, regularly to make mistakes. I can't help them. They seem to come natural to me." Political economy, with its emphasis on statistics, was the center of the educational curriculum by the 1850s, and Sissy proves hopeless at these "stutterings":

> "I find (Mr. M'Choakumchild said) that in a given time a hundred thousand persons went to sea on long voyages, and only five hundred of them were drowned or burnt to death. What is the percentage? And I said, Miss;" here Sissy fairly sobbed as confessing with extreme contrition to her greatest error; "I said it was nothing."

> "Nothing, Sissy?"

> "Nothing, Miss—to the relations and friends of the people who were killed. I shall never learn," said Sissy.

The novel sets her in opposition to the disciplinary technologies of statistics and examinations, but Sissy clearly grasps the principles, if not the practice, of these technologies. As the M'Choakumchild examinations register Sissy's inaptitude as a Head, she perfects her complementary function as a Heart. She despairs of statistical observation, but—as we will see—she proves a close observer of the individual human heart.

For the Gradgrind children, the eyes of the Paternal Head are ever watchful; they are under constant surveillance. Gallagher has commented on the differences between family and society in *Hard Times*. I want to suggest that the family operates not as the opposite of society, not as a private space, a retreat from observation, but as a crucial extension or elaboration of the disciplinary gaze. In accord with Bentham's prescription that "the head of a family must be constantly aiding the inexperience of those submitted to his care," Gradgrind enacts the role of the "active" and "vigilant" parent; to his children, he is the "domestic governor" who "can watch over their social intercourse and their studies."

The controlling effect of paternal vigilance is underscored when Louisa and Tom enter the novel imitating their father's surveillance, peeping at the vulgar population through holes in the fence. That peeping comes to an abrupt end when the father comes upon them and puts on his spectacles:

> Phenomenon almost incredible though distinctly seen, what did he then behold but his own metallurgical Louisa peeping with all her might through a hole in a deal board, and his own mathematical Thomas abasing himself on the ground to catch but a hoof of the graceful equestrian Tyrolean flower-act!

There are kinds and kinds of watching, it seems: a disciplinary surveillance and an illicit peeping. Observation is allowable only if the observer functions as a part of the surveillant body. In the family, as in the circus, each observer is part of the disciplinary system, subject to the hierarchy of gazes; each observer is also observed. This moment of peeping calls attention to the hierarchical system surmounted by the Paternal Head.

The necessity for a surveillant system becomes clear as the novel unfolds. This father's gaze is limited; fixed on the rule, Gradgrind's eyes fail to see the essential function of individual differences. Even in the particular case of his daughter's marriage to Josiah Bounderby, Gradgrind applies the Blue Book rules. Discovering that there is a difference in age in "a large proportion" of marriages in the nation, and that the male is generally the older of the partners in these cases, Gradgrind is pleased to find that the thirty-year age difference between Louisa and Bounderby presents no difficulty. He concludes, "The disparity I have mentioned, therefore, almost ceases to be disparity, and (virtually) all but disappears." And when Louisa hesitantly observes that life—her individual life—is brief, Gradgrind responds: "I need not point out to you, Louisa, that it is governed by the laws which govern lives in the aggregate."

The representation of Gradgrind clearly demonstrates the inadequacy of the Head's abstracting gaze. The statistical school, caught up in its calculus of the many, fails to recognize the individual:

> As if an astronomical observatory should be made without any windows, and the astronomer within should arrange the starry universe solely by pen, ink, and paper, so Mr. Gradgrind, in *his* Observatory (and there are many like it), had no need to cast an eye upon the teeming myriads of human be-

ings around him, but could settle all their destinies on a slate, and wipe out all their tears with one dirty little bit of sponge.

The metaphor recalls Bentham's aspiration to become "the Newton of the Moral World"; as Newton explained in precise mathematical terms the movements of the heavenly bodies, so Bentham would explain through the felicific calculus the actions of human beings. To see "the teeming myriads of human beings" through mathematical abstractions, in *Hard Times,* is to see no one at all.

Dickens chews up and spits out the statistical school of Gradgrind, but he is nevertheless its pupil; his strategies of characterization in this novel also depend on observation and abstraction. The abstractions in the novel may be exaggerated, but they depend on a notion of typicality: Gradgrind as the type of Utilitarian, Bounderby as the type of industrial capitalist, Slackbridge as the type of union agitator. I want to suggest that *Hard Times* shows the Head to be not so much wrong as insufficient. The novel uses the tactics of the Head, but it recognizes the need for other tactics, additional strategies of observation.

By failing to recognize individual difference, Gradgrind assigns Louisa to a marriage that threatens sexual discipline. At the announcement of the engagement, two pairs of eyes begin a close observation of Louisa's every move. Both Sissy and Mrs. Sparsit perceive immediately the inappropriateness of the marriage; and both anticipate the probable result, adultery—a result that Harthouse's arrival seems to ensure. So Sissy watches Louisa "in wonder, in pity, in sorrow, in doubt, in a multitude of emotions," while Mrs. Sparsit rubs her mittens in glee, watching Louisa begin the long, long descent of the staircase toward the dark pit at the bottom.

These four eyes are not the only surveillant eyes trained on Louisa, however. The narrator sees what even those close watchers do not, and the narrative record of observation reveals just how dangerously undisciplined Louisa Bounderby is. Daniel Deneau has discussed the "sexual overtones" in the night scene between Louisa and Tom at the Bounderby house. Louisa Bounderby listens to the sounds of the night:

Then she arose, put on a loose robe, and went out of her room in the dark, and up the staircase to her brother's room. His door being shut, she softly opened it and spoke to him, approaching his bed with a noiseless step.

She kneeled down beside it, passed her arm over his neck,

and drew his face to hers. She knew that he only feigned to be asleep, but she said nothing to him.

The greatest threat to sexual discipline is not Harthouse. Tom, we learn, has robbed his sister's husband, and not— Tom himself says—all at once. The novel must banish this bad body. In our last glimpse of Tom, he is lying on his deathbed uttering Louisa's name; we can be sure he will *not* recover and return.

HAND

Stephen Blackpool's dismal marriage parallels Louisa's, and Stephen, too, is headed for a dark pit. The notoriously diffi-cult union plot is ostensibly the central narrative interest in the Stephen Blackpool chapters, but I would like to focus on the plot of marriage and desire. When the Hand seeks re-lease from his wife, Bounderby blusters about the noble in-stitutions of the country. The perfect parody of A. Ure's ideal mill-owner, who would "organize his moral machinery on equally sound principles with his mechanical" and "observe, in reference to his operatives, the divine injunction of loving his neighbours as himself," Bounderby offers no sympathy to the desperate Stephen; turning a blind eye toward his own marital misery, he rules out murder, desertion, bigamy, and adultery and reminds Stephen of his vows: "You didn't take your wife for fast and for loose; but for better for worse. If she has turned out worse—why, all we have got to say is, she might have turned out better."

Two vows structure the plot of Stephen's life: the marriage vow and the problematic vow he makes to Rachael, the vow against joining the union that Dickens' revision of the novel makes incomprehensible. But the logic of the disciplinary system in this plot is clear enough. After his first interview with Bounderby, after Stephen's desire to divorce his wife and to marry Rachael has been made explicit, Stephen watches his wife pour out a cup of poison:

> her eyes stopped at the table with the bottles on it.

> Straightway she turned her back to his corner, with the defi-ance of last night, and moving very cautiously and softly, stretched out her greedy hand. She drew a mug into the bed, and sat for a while considering which of the two bottles she should choose. Finally she laid her insensate grasp upon the bottle that had swift and certain death in it, and, before his eyes, pulled out the cork with her teeth.

Like Louisa and Tom peeping through the fence, Stephen watches in order to escape discipline, not as an extension of disciplinary surveillance. But no sudden, self-willed death is allowed to release this woman from her slow and agonizing decline, or to free Stephen for a second marriage.

It is another Hand that acts in this crisis; it is Rachael, not Stephen, who intervenes. And Rachael's image serves as a disciplinary agent even in her absence. When morning comes, Stephen kneels before Rachael and confesses his temptation, and he concludes: "I nevermore will see or think o' anything that angers me, but thou, so much better than me, shall be by th' side on't."

The crisis is averted, but the subversive impulses of this body have been exposed. Indeed, the near-suicide is all but indistinguishable from near-murder; Stephen cannot say afterward "what I might ha' done to myself, or her, or both!" While it is literally the union plot, and not the plot of desire, that leads to the repudiation of Stephen, it is no surprise that the novel sends him the way of Signer Jupe and Tom Gradgrind. Through the Hands and their Head, Bounderby, the novel drives out this body who has allowed desire to overpower discipline.

Stephen must be taught docility and obedience through a program of unremitting surveillance. A star, the apex of the novel's system of gazes, watches unblinkingly the body incarcerated in the dark pit: "'It ha' shined upon me,' he said reverently, 'in my pain and trouble down below. It ha' shined into my mind.'" The star is linked explicitly to God on the following page when Stephen muses, "I thowt it were the star as guided to Our Saviour's home." The plot ends with Stephen going to "his Redeemer's rest," with his body borne on a stretcher to its resting place, another dark pit permanently monitored by the All-Seeing Eye of the Father.

HEART

Under the watchful gaze of the night sky, Stephen leaves the novel with his hand clasped in Rachael's. But the surveillant body of *Hard Times* has not only its Paternal Head and its Hands; it has also a Heart. When Louisa narrowly misses falling into the pit, Gradgrind acknowledges that the Head requires the complementary function of the Heart, the function embodied in Sissy Jupe; he notes that "what the Head had left undone and could not do, the Heart may have been doing silently" through "mere love and gratitude."

Like Bentham's Chevalier Paulet, Gradgrind takes in the fatherless child to educate her, employ her in domestic service, and incorporate her into a system of monitoring gazes. Her inaptitude for political economy acknowledged and accepted, Sissy is given the latitude to find and develop her own particular function. She perfects her function as the Heart of the disciplinary system, and her silent watchfulness reinforces the Head's surveillance.

Through the language of loving concern for each human heart, Sissy teaches the importance of observing carefully the aptitudes of each particular body; and her relationship with Louisa demonstrates the usefulness of this strategy. Sissy begins her observation of the individual body, Louisa, when Gradgrind announces Louisa's engagement. Apparently anticipating the collapse of discipline, Sissy turns her gaze toward Louisa; but Louisa averts her eyes: "Louisa had known it, and seen it, without looking at her. From that moment she was impassive, proud and cold—help Sissy at a distance—changed to her altogether." Louisa escapes that gaze for the period of her unhappy marriage and her descent of the staircase, but she chafes under Sissy's eyes once more when she returns to her father's house in search of moral guidance: "A dull anger that she should be seen in her distress, and that the involuntary look she had so resented should come to this fulfilment, smouldered within her like an unwholesome fire." Resentment of Sissy's gaze has continued this long while, internalized and smoldering in Louisa's breast.

Like Stephen, Louisa must learn docility under disciplinary surveillance. At first she keeps her face hidden, refusing to meet Sissy's eyes, but the "soft touch" of a "sympathetic hand" breaks down her obstinate resistance and calls forth penitent confession. Like Stephen before Rachael, Louisa kneels before Sissy: "Forgive me, pity me, help me! Have compassion on my great need, and let me lay this head of mine upon a loving heart!" And Sissy does "help," for she sends away the two threatening bodies, Harthouse and the whelp.

Sissy's role as the reclaimer and rehabilitator of Louisa deserves close attention. By representing this watchdog of bourgeois morality as a child of the lower classes, *Hard Times* constructs a socially useful myth. Through Sissy Jupe, the novel seems to argue, with F.M.L. Thompson, that the working classes did not need instruction in respectable behavior; indeed, *Hard Times* goes further, representing Rachael and Sissy as the moral giants of the novel. This strategy masks the novel's interest in propagating a program of middle-class reform. If the true reformers are the untutored—or untutorable—lower classes, then the novel does not support a code rooted in class interest, but a natural code of values, a set of principles inscribed on the Heart.

The opposition of Fancy and Fact in *Hard Times* turns out to be another useful fiction. "People mutht be amuthed, Thquire, thomehow," Sleary tells a disapproving Gradgrind; "they can't be alwayth a working, nor yet they can't be alwayth a learning. Make the betht of uth; not the wurtht." An explanation of how the Fact fellows might make the best of Sleary's circus is suggested by Donajgrodski, who argues that "'secondary institutions' apparently hostile to established social order . . . may paradoxically be mechanisms of social control." Fancy complements Utilitarian programs of Fact by easing their intolerable rigidity. The leggy spectacle of Sleary's Horse-Riding may offer little in the way of Useful Knowledge, but it may serve as a safety valve.

Louisa becomes the pupil of Fancy; and once she has "grown learned in childish lore," she, too, becomes an educator. The morally renovated Louisa escapes the punishment meted out to Tom and to Stephen, but no second marriage, no children are allowed the sinner come home: "Such a thing was never to be." Instead, Louisa's plot, like Stephen's, ends with the erring figure thoroughly disciplined, firmly under a monitoring gaze.

The closing lines focus on the continuing effort of reform. Reform has risen out of the lower orders to renovate the middle-class Louisa, and Louisa, in turn, takes the program of recreational reform to "her humbler fellow-creatures." After showing us this improving spectacle, the novel exhorts us to participate in reform. Its final gesture is to turn its gaze to the middle-class readers, cozily gathered at the domestic hearth:

> Dear reader! It rests with you and me, whether, in our two fields of action, similar things shall be or not. Let them be! We shall sit with lighter bosoms on the hearth, to see the ashes of our fires turn grey and cold.

The Problems of a Weekly Serial

John Butt and Kathleen Tillotson

Hard Times was originally published as a weekly serial in *Household Words*. Dickens, accustomed to writing in the longer monthly serial unit, found the necessary shortness of a weekly installment extremely restricting, even writing to a friend, "The difficulty of the space is CRUSHING." In the following critical excerpt, John Butt and Kathleen Tillotson trace Dickens's number plans and trial titles as the author adapted to the space requirements dictated by the weekly format. Butt and Tillotson have written extensively on Victorian literature. Tillotson's books include *Novels of the Eighteen Forties* and *Mid-Victorian Studies.*

Household Words had been running for some eighteen months when *Bleak House* was completed at the end of August 1853. While Dickens was engaged with his book he had no time to write anything for his magazine more substantial than articles; but once the book was out of the way, he could listen to the persuasions of Forster, Bradbury and Evans, and Wills. 'There is such a fixed idea on the part of my printers and copartners in *Household Words,* that a story of me, continued from week to week, would make some unheard of effect with it that I am going to write one'; so he told Miss Coutts on 23 January 1854. The decision had been taken some time earlier, however. On 20 January he sent Forster a list of fourteen titles for 'the *Household Words* story', begging him to look at them 'between this and two o'clock or so, when I will call. It is my usual day, you observe, on which I have jotted them down—Friday! It seems to me that there are three very good ones among them. I should like to know whether you hit upon the same.' Though he had not yet set

Excerpted from *Dickens at Work,* by John Butt and Kathleen Tillotson (London: Methuen, 1957). Reprinted by permission of Routledge.

himself to write, it would seem that he had already discussed the theme of the novel with Forster; for if he had not, he could scarcely have expected Forster to choose between titles for a single story so strictly committing as these: *According to Cocker, Prove it, Stubborn Things, Mr Gradgrind's Facts, The Grindstone, Hard Times, Two and Two are Four, Something Tangible, Our Hard-headed Friend, Rust and Dust, Simple Arithmetic, A Matter of Calculation, A Mere Question of Figures, The Gradgrind Philosophy.*

These rejected titles and those in the manuscript—*Fact, Hard-headed Gradgrind, Hard Heads and Soft Hearts, Heads and Tales, Black and White*—remain of interest, since they seem to indicate the limits within which the book would move. The irony implicit in *Something Tangible, A Matter of Calculation,* and *A Mere Question of Figures* suggests that the novel will open up areas of experience beyond the reach of Mr Gradgrind's philosophy, and the importance of feelings, disregarded by the political economists, is represented in *Hard Heads and Soft Hearts,* while *Heads and Tales* seems to forecast the opposition of fact and fancy so prominent in the scenes at Sleary's Circus troupe. These titles show that the story would appropriately appear in the columns of *Household Words,* whose policy Dickens had defined in an initial address (30 March 1850):

> . . . No mere utilitarian spirit, no iron binding of the mind to grim realities, will give a harsh tone to our *Household Words.* In the bosoms of the young and old, of the well-to-do and of the poor, we would tenderly cherish that light of Fancy which is inherent in the human breast; which, according to its nurture, burns with an inspiring flame, or sinks into a sullen glare but which (or woe betide that day!) can never be extinguished.

The same day on which he consulted Forster about the title, Dickens sat down to plan the book. On a sheet of paper preserved in the manuscript he wrote first the date and then a memorandum on quantity, which reads as follows:

> One sheet (16 pages of Bleak House) will make 10 pages and a quarter of Household Words. Fifteen pages of my writing, will make a sheet of Bleak House.

> A page and a half of my writing, will make a page of Household Words.

> The Quantity of the story to be published weekly, being about five pages of Household Words, will require about seven pages and a half of my writing.

and at the head of the first number plan he has, subsequently, written:

> Write and calculate the story in the old monthly N⁰⁵.

These calculations conceal the real difficulty. They amount
to saying that one monthly number is the equivalent of four
weeklies; but they do not emphasize that the weekly number
is now the unit, and that within its brief limits characters
must be presented, background sketched, and atmosphere
created. A monthly number of thirty-two pages had been a
convenient unit for two or three episodes; one or two
episodes had now to be related in the equivalent of eight
pages. It is no wonder that Dickens found himself hampered.
In February he wrote to Forster:

> The difficulty of the space is CRUSHING. Nobody can have an
> idea of it who has not had an experience of patient fiction-
> writing with some elbow-room always, and open places in
> perspective. In this form, with any kind of regard to the cur
> rent number, there is absolutely no such thing.

The sense of this restriction never left him: 'I am in a dreary
state,' he told Wills on 18 April, 'planning and planning the
story of *Hard Times* (out of materials for I don't know how
long a story)' and in the end he was forced to enlarge his
weekly stints to ten pages of his manuscript.

ECONOMY AND POWER

But though the difficulties of the weekly number exasper-
ated him, and though there is reason to suppose that some
material was forcibly excluded, there is no doubt that Dickens was able to adapt his manner to the new conditions, and
it might be argued that the discipline was good for him. The
necessary shortness of the chapters is matched by an economy in detail, noticeable throughout the novel and especially obvious if the opening chapters of *Hard Times* are
compared with the opening chapters of *Bleak House*. It is appropriate, no doubt, that the symbolical fog of *Bleak House*
should be more leisurely presented than the symbolical fact
of *Hard Times;* but it is difficult to believe that in any
monthly novel Dickens would have been content with those
mere eight but sufficient words which set the scene, 'a plain,
bare, monotonous vault of a schoolroom'. The initial description of Mr Gradgrind's square appearance is conveyed
in a traditional manner, but it is considerably shorter than
the initial descriptions of Sir Leicester Dedlock and Mr Tulk-

inghorn in *Bleak House,* chapter ii; and more remarkable still, both in economy and in power, is the symbolically contrasting appearance of Sissy Jupe and Bitzer as the sunlight plays upon them:

> whereas the girl was so dark-eyed and dark-haired, that she seemed to receive a deeper and more lustrous color from the sun, when it shone upon her, the boy was so light-eyed and light-haired that the self-same rays appeared to draw out of him what little color he ever possessed. His cold eyes would hardly have been eyes, but for the short ends of lashes which, by bringing them into immediate contrast with something paler than themselves, expressed their form. His short-cropped hair might have been a mere continuation of the sandy freckles on his forehead and face. His skin was so unwholesomely deficient in the natural tinge, that he looked as though, if he were cut, he would bleed white.

It is not merely that Bitzer's body has been deprived by Coketown smoke of the life-giving sun, or that his mind has been repressed by a lifeless education, but that he is emptier and shallower than Sissy; there is no depth to him. The monthly novels are not without comparable moments. The juxtaposition of Miss Flite and the young wards at the end of *Bleak House,* chapter iii, is equally well contrived, she suitably enough at the *bottom* of the steep, broad flight of stairs, they looking down upon her, and her words are equally powerful to suggest more than they say,

> 'Youth. And hope. And beauty. And Chancery. And Conversation Kenge! Ha! Pray accept my blessing!'

This, however, is only a small part of a much larger episode. It lacks the rounded completeness of the scene in *Hard Times.*

MONTHLY UNITS

But though Dickens recognized how his manner required adapting to weekly presentation, he was also determined to 'write and calculate the story in the old monthly N^{os}'. This is shown not only by the memorandum but by the whole appearance of the manuscript. In it the novel is divided into five monthly parts, each separately foliated as his custom was when writing a monthly serial, and each represented by a separate number plan. The first of these makes clear that after deciding what shall happen during the month he arranged this material in chapters before distributing the chapters into weekly issues. He evidently felt the need to see these chapters grouped into units larger than a weekly number, even though the monthly unit could not force itself upon the reader's attention and might not even be apparent to him. These larger monthly units would serve as stages by which to measure the progress made and the distance still to be covered. Thus the opening words of chapter viii, the last of the first monthly 'part'—'Let us strike the key-note again, before pursuing the tune'—seem to indicate that the exposition is completed; and the ending of the second 'part' with Louisa Gradgrind's marriage to Bounderby, the third with Stephen Blackpool leaving Coketown, and the fourth with the breakdown of Louisa's marriage, all mark important stages completed in the development of the story.

Though the reader may appreciate the completion of the stage without observing that a monthly 'part' is completed also, his attention is called to still larger movements in the story by the division of the novel into 'books'. The device had frequently been used since its adoption from the epic by Fielding in *Joseph Andrews*. But Dickens had not hitherto employed it. Perhaps he had taken notice of Thackeray's refinement in *Esmond* (1852) of not merely numbering his books, as the custom was, but of naming them. The second number plan of *Hard Times* shows him considering this device ('republish in 3 books? / 1. Sowing / 2. Reaping / 3. Garnering'). By then it was perhaps too late to adopt it in serial publication: we do not know whether the first weekly issue, without an indication of book number, was already in print when the second monthly 'part' was under consideration. But the notion was kept in mind, and when the novel was reissued in volume form it was divided into books with the titles already determined, the divisions coinciding with what had been the end of the second and fourth monthly 'parts'.

Of earlier novels, only *Dombey and Son* lends itself to a similar division, with well-marked stages reached at the end of Number V (the death of Paul), Number X (Mr Dombey's second marriage), and Number XV (the flight of Florence). But from *Hard Times* onwards each novel, except for *Edwin Drood*, is divided into books even in the serial issues. This is further evidence of the attention which Dickens was now paying to construction. He was quite justified in telling Carlyle that *Hard Times* was 'constructed . . . patiently, with a view to its publication altogether in a compact cheap form'.

Dickens's first purpose was to establish the dominion of Fact and of its high priest, Mr Gradgrind. The draft titles show that Mr Gradgrind was to be the representative of a theory. It is therefore appropriate that he should first appear in his own school impressing his theories upon the rising generation, who will show the effect of his teaching as the story develops.

Although Dickens had settled upon the name, opinions, and perhaps the nature of his principal character before beginning to write, he was still undetermined about his supporters. Mr Gradgrind was to have two children—the first number plan specifies 'Louisa Gradgrind' and 'Young Thomas'—who would doubtless exist to disappoint him in different ways; but whether his wife was still alive was not yet decided. Dickens was evidently tempted to produce another repellent widower with a sister in attendance, as Miss Murdstone had attended upon Mr Murdstone, and Mrs Chick upon Mr Dombey. The number plan shows his purpose settling: 'Mrs. Gradgrind—or Miss? Wife or Sister? Wife.' Having fixed upon that, he turned to consider the remainder of the household: 'Any little Gradgrinds?

Say 3.   Adam Smith ⎫
             Malthus   ⎬ no parts to play'
             Jane   ⎭

Jane Gradgrind is later to play a small, yet not unimportant, part; and Mrs Gradgrind is to become one more of Dickens's ineffectual mothers, closer in type to Mrs Matthew Pocket in the future than to Mrs Nickleby in the past. Her entry is carefully timed—postponed from chapter iii ('Mrs. Gradgrind—badly done transparency, with not enough light behind it. No not yet') to chapter iv ('Now, Mrs. Gradgrind'). No member of his household could have had less effect upon Mr Gradgrind or upon his children, and that was perhaps the reason that she displaced the sister in Dickens's choice: she serves to emphasize more powerfully than any sister that Mr Gradgrind alone influenced the course of his children's career.

Gradgrind is to be recognized not only in his house and family, but also by the company he keeps. He is seen in school with a representative of the Department of Practical Art, who in his determination to remove flowers from the design of carpets and foreign birds and butterflies from the design of crockery, is as anxious as Gradgrind to submit the imagination to the chains of fact and real circumstance. But the representative of the Department of Practical Art has served a limited purpose by the end of chapter ii, and no more is seen of him.

Much more prominent among Gradgrind's friends is Josiah Bounderby, for whose appearance the reader's expectations are raised at the end of the first weekly number (chapter iii). 'What would Mr. Bounderby say?' cried Mr Gradgrind on finding his elder children peeping through a hole in the circus tent. But Dickens himself had not pronounced the name with equal confidence when meditating his number: "What will Mr. Bound say?" is the version on the number plan (and in the manuscript of chapter iii), subsequently altered to 'Bounder' and finally to 'Bounderby'. Dickens may already have known his man; certainly the very next entry on the number plan shows that he knew what parts he was to play ('Mr. Bounderby, the Bully of humility. Dawn of Bounderby and Louisa'), and in their partnership Gradgrind supplies the ethos of heartless calculation in which Bounderby can oppress the Coketown operatives; but the momentary hesitation over his name shows that Bounderby was not so prominent in Dickens's scheme as Gradgrind.

A final entry on the first number plan points to Gradgrind's third associate: 'The man who, being utterly sensual and careless, comes to very much the same thing in the end as the Gradgrind school? Not yet.' This was James Harthouse, who is not introduced until the third month. He is a young man of good family who had found army and diplomatic life a bore, and had now been persuaded by an elder brother in Parliament to 'go in' for statistics, make a place for himself amongst the 'hard Fact fellows', and canvass one of the industrial seats. Finding Coketown as much of a bore as the army and the diplomatic service, he whiles away his time there by attempting to seduce Louisa Bounderby. If Dickens had already foreseen this role, it is surprising that he should have contemplated introducing Harthouse in the first month, since he could not perform his function in the plot until Bounderby and Louisa were married. A possible explanation is that Dickens, with his mind on the fable, needed Harthouse as a supporter to Gradgrind; but recognizing that Harthouse could best be employed as a seducer of Louisa, he permitted the requirements of the fable to give place temporarily to the requirements of the plot.

Bounderby also has his supporter. Just as Captain Cuttle is incomplete without Mrs MacStinger and Captain Bunsby, and Mr Toots without the Game Chicken, so Bounderby is incomplete without Mrs Sparsit. The distance he has reached from the humblest origins, born in a ditch and abandoned by his mother, is most readily measured by his now employing as a housekeeper this lady of seemingly the highest family connexions. But Mrs Sparsit's aristocratic connexions are of doubtful authenticity, and so are Bounderby's origins. The reader is left to guess this and merely to suspect that the eminently respectable countrywoman, Mrs Pegler, is betraying a suspiciously maternal interest in a most unlovable mill-owner. Dickens is already preparing the ground for the scene of Bounderby's exposure, or rather of his deflation, for at his first appearance he is seen to have

> a great puffed head and forehead, swelling veins in his temples, and such a strained skin to his face that it seemed to hold his eyes open, and lift his eyebrows up. A man with a pervading appearance on him of being inflated like a balloon, and ready to start.

But though all but the most unsophisticated reader can see that a rich retribution is in store for Bounderby, this assumption of humility on his part and of gentility on Mrs Sparsit's serves a more immediate purpose. Here at the very centre of the dominion of Fact are people indulging in Fancy, a peculiarly repulsive Fancy maybe, but Fancy still. Here, in the punning of one of the rejected titles, is a man proud of his head but flourishing his tale. This apposition of Fact and Fancy is forcibly presented throughout the first three weekly parts. The young Gradgrinds have been brought up on Fact, but when we first meet them they are contriving to satisfy their starved Fancy by peeping through a hole in a circus tent. Coketown too is 'Fact, fact, fact, everywhere in the material aspect of the town; fact, fact, fact, everywhere in the immaterial'; but in an obscure corner of Coketown, Fancy is ensconced in the shape of a circus. The district is so obscure that Mr Gradgrind and Mr Bounderby, like two evil characters in *The Pilgrim's Progress,* do not know where to find it and are forced to enlist the help of the clown's daughter. The circus people are lodged at an inn named, in a suitable frolic of Fancy, the Pegasus's Arms, and are expert in all sorts of fanciful behaviour, in dancing upon rolling casks, standing upon bottles, catching knives and balls, twirling hand-basins, and dancing upon the slack wire and the tight-rope. But for all that they are the salt of the earth:

> there was a remarkable gentleness and childishness about these people, a special inaptitude for any kind of sharp prac-

tice, and an untiring readiness to help and pity one another, deserving often of as much respect, and always of as much generous construction, as the every-day virtues of any class of people in the world.

And their leader, Mr Sleary, has a philosophy adapted to the world of Fancy just as Mr Gradgrind's is adapted to the world of Fact:

> 'People must be amuthed, Thquire, thomehow,' continued Sleary, rendered more pursy than ever, by so much talking; 'they can't be alwayth a working, nor yet they can't be alwayth a learning. Make the betht of uth; not the wurtht. I've got my living out of the horthe-riding all my life, I know; but I conthider that I lay down the philothophy of the thubject when I thay to you, Thquire, make the betht of uth: not the wurtht!'

This is the milieu from which Sissy comes to be an inmate of the Gradgrind household, there to be educated in Mr Gradgrind's system. It is some measure of the man's inherent goodness that he receives her as an inmate. He is redeemable, and the course of the novel shows that he will be redeemed by Sissy. He fails to educate her head, but she succeeds in educating his heart.

Dickens's Use of Nature

Paul Schacht

Paul Schacht asserts that Dickens cared deeply about the laws of nature—universal principles that pertain to all people, times, and places. In the following essay, Schacht examines how Dickens used natural laws—physical laws and the notion of natural liberty, for example—to reinforce thematic material. For instance, Dickens warns that "all closely imprisoned forces rend and destroy," suggesting that Gradgrindery is wrong not only on moral grounds but also because it violates the laws of nature. Schacht is an associate professor of English at the State University of New York at Geneseo.

At the thematic center of *Hard Times* stands a law of nature: "All closely imprisoned forces rend and destroy." Though in its immediate context this statement merely refers to the "dull anger" Louisa Gradgrind feels, but does not express, towards Sissy Jupe, it is also the essential warning of the novel. If vital human forces like imagination and emotion are denied their natural "play" for too long, they will find some explosive release from containment, as they do in the dissipation and gambling of Thomas Gradgrind, Jr., the murderous thoughts of Stephen Blackpool, the adulterous yearnings of Louisa, and the unionism of the Coketown hands: "when the night comes, Fire bursts out." One might compare this warning with John Stuart Mill's example of the person who, in blatantly disregarding a law of nature, only succeeds in demonstrating its inexorability: "a person who goes into a powder magazine either not knowing, or carelessly omitting to think of, the explosive force of gunpowder, is likely to do some act which will cause him to be blown to atoms in obedience to the very law which he has disregarded." Dickens's society has placed itself in precisely this position.

Hard Times thus makes the case that Gradgrindery is

Excerpted from "Dickens and the Uses of Nature," by Paul Schacht, *Victorian Studies*, vol. 34, no. 1 (Autumn 1990). Reprinted by permission of Indiana University Press.

wrong not only on moral but on rational, "scientific" grounds; it violates rather than conforms to the laws of nature, or at best conforms with dangerous selectivity. To underscore the point, the outraged narrator of *Hard Times* occasionally adopts, with self-conscious irony, the rationalistic tone of Gradgrind himself, as if like Marx he wished to claim that he has "proceeded from the premises of political economy" and "accepted its language." The success of this rhetorical posture may be judged by comparing the following passages from *Hard Times* and *The Wealth of Nations* (Adam Smith):

> Surely, none of us in our sober senses and acquainted with figures, are to be told at this time of day, that . . . exactly in the ratio as [the Coketown hands] worked long and monotonously, the craving grew within them for some physical relief—some relaxation, encouraging good humour and good spirits, and giving them a vent . . . which craving must and would be satisfied aright, or must and would inevitably go wrong, until the laws of the Creation were repealed? (*Hard Times*)

> Great labour, either of mind or body, continued for several days together, is in most men naturally followed by a great desire of relaxation, which, if not restrained by force or by some strong necessity, is almost irresistible. It is the call of nature, which requires to be relieved by some indulgence, sometimes of ease only, but sometimes too of dissipation and diversion. If it is not complied with, the consequences are often dangerous, and sometimes fatal. (Smith)

The close similarity of these passages—all the more remarkable given the unlikelihood of direct influence—suggests how faithfully Dickens has echoed the rhetoric of "natural" economic theory; amidst the many reverberations here, the Gradgrindian formulation "exactly in the ratio" is merely the loudest. The similarity extends, of course, not only to words, logical structure, and fundamental assumptions but to the central idea expressed; and this may strike the reader as odd. If Dickens and Smith agree about the laborer's "natural" need for "relief" and "relaxation," on what exactly do they differ? Has Dickens misunderstood Smith's idea of natural liberty? Has he made the mistake of lumping Smith together with the "real" culprits—the Victorian factory-owners who misguidedly followed only half of Smith's advice, insisting on their "natural liberty" from state interference while ignoring their responsibility to heed the "call of nature" that demanded periodic respite for their workers? Does not his confusion bear out [Humphry] House's and

[Raymond] Williams's point that Dickens's quarrel is only with the "consequences," the "effects" of Smith's theory rather than its "formal substance"? On the contrary: Dickens's and Smith's agreement on this matter of natural law only strengthens Dickens's criticism of Smith's theory *as* theory. For Dickens, the problem of natural liberty as an *idea* is that it creates the illusion of conformity among the laws of nature, suggesting implicitly if not explicitly that to follow one particular law, the law of self-interest, is to "follow nature" altogether. Thus, as *Hard Times* repeatedly points out, the notion of natural liberty tempts one to view the rational pursuit of self-interest as the sum-total of a person's obligation to society, and it involves little incentive and no positive duty to acknowledge any "call of nature" other than that which originates within. Smith's acknowledgement of another call, inconsistent and perhaps directly at odds with the call of self-interest, belies the illusion of nature's conformity, however; and Dickens's rhetorical strategy deliberately explodes it. Here again Mill's "Nature" serves as a useful gloss on Dickens's reasoning: "By every choice which we make either of ends or of means," Mill writes, "we place ourselves to a greater or less extent under one set of laws of nature instead of another." And again he supplies a clarifying illustration: "When, for example, a person is crossing a river by a narrow bridge to which there is no parapet, he will do well to regulate his proceedings by the laws of equilibrium in moving bodies, instead of conforming only to the law of gravitation, and falling into the river." The Gradgrinds and Bounderbys, Dickens in effect argues, walk their own narrow bridge in the mistaken belief, fostered by Smith's doctrine, that no choice of laws need be made.

LAWS OF THE CREATION

As important as the physical law that "all closely imprisoned forces rend and destroy" is another of the "laws of the Creation," the biological law that a man must reap what he sows. The titles for the three books of *Hard Times*—Sowing, Reaping, Garnering—clearly pit Gradgrindery against the values of Christianity, but they just as pointedly turn Gradgrind's scientific language against him. After all, it is Gradgrind who first introduces the metaphor of cultivation when he announces as a matter of scientific "principle" that you "can only form the minds of reasoning animals" by planting facts and rooting out everything else. Here as elsewhere Gradgrind's reasoning proves scientifically as well as morally dubious. He begins from the false assumption about human nature indicated by his definition of his students as "reasoning animals"; he ends by producing a daughter in whose heart the "golden waters were not there. They were flowing for the fertilization of the land where grapes are gathered from thorns, and figs from thistles." Dickens's metaphor neatly conflates scientific and Biblical language to indicate the double failure of Gradgrind's thinking.

ENVIRONMENTAL LAWS

Readers who saw *Hard Times* in its original, serial form could have compared Dickens's point about grapes and figs not only with Matthew 7:16 but also with a science piece which appeared in *Household Words* along with chapters 13 and 14 of the novel. In "Nature's Changes of Dress," the medical journalist E.A. Hart (1835–98) discussed at length the determining power of heat, soil, and other environmental factors in producing the varieties of plant life. In effect the essay provides scientific sanction for Dickens's environmental treatment of character in the novel. "The laws which regulate the distribution of plants over the surface of the earth," we are told, "are peremptory and severe"—they cannot be controverted. In language that seems to point the moral of Gradgrind's dangerously mistaken experiment in human culture, Hart informs us that

> in every latitude we find plants to which that special territory is assigned as their domain, beyond which their passport will not carry them. . . . The Gulf-stream may carry the tropic seed to the coasts of Norway,—the bird or insect may bear the vegetable germ from Indian woods to plant it in a northern soil; but offended Nature avenges the transgression of her changeless laws. The seed never germinates, but is blighted by the asperities of a new and more rigorous clime.

Offended Nature avenges Gradgrind's transgression of her "changeless laws" with the blighted lives of his own children. Two of Hart's other contributions to *Household Words* similarly enhanced the scientific credibility of *Hard Times*. The number immediately preceding the first installment of Dickens's novel carried a Hart piece entitled "Plant Architecture," in which the author himself explicitly abstracted a political lesson from his observations of nature. If we examine the "internal economy" of the plant, Hart informed Dickens's readers, we find that the individual cells composing it "seem to hold a double relation—aptly typifying our own position: since like us they have both an individual existence, (in respect to which they are only concerned in performing their own duties and exercising their own special functions,) and a social position which calls upon them to aid in operations that aim at the general good." The second part of this double relation is precisely what Gradgrind ignores in teaching that "the whole social system is question of self-interest" and what Hart, like Dickens, attempted to emulate in advocating sanitary and other social reforms. The other Hart article—the lead for the first number of volume 9—looks forward to Dickens's satire on the Department of Practical Art six weeks later: "Displaying in their form and essence an union of the sweetest utilitarianism with the most ideal beauty, the flowers preside over the birth of the plants under conditions giving rise to fancies that have fed the imagination of generations of poets. . . ."

DICKENS'S GENIUS

Although Hard Times *has a checkered critical history, most readers agree that the passages describing Coketown represent Dickens at his finest.*

It was a town of red brick, or of brick that would have been red if the smoke and ashes had allowed it; but as matters stood, it was a town of unnatural red and black like the painted face of a savage. It was a town of machinery and tall chimneys, out of which interminable serpents of smoke trailed themselves for ever and ever, and never got uncoiled. It had a black canal in it, and a river that ran purple with ill-smelling dye, and vast piles of buildings full of windows where there was a rattling and a trembling all day long, and where the piston of the steam-engine worked monotonously up and down like the head of an elephant in a state of melancholy madness. It contained several large streets all very like one another, and many small streets still more like one another, inhabited by people equally like one another, who all went in and out at the same hours, with the same sound upon the same pavements, to do the same work, and to whom every day was the same as yesterday and tomorrow, and every year the counterpart of the last and the next.

Charles Dickens, *Hard Times.*

No doubt largely through Rousseau's influence, the analogy between plant development and character development was a staple of progressive educational theory by the time Dickens drew it in *Hard Times*. Most notably, it informed Friedrich Fröbel's (1782–1852) term for his influential experiment, the kindergarten, in which Dickens took an interest and on which Henry Morley would report for *Household Words* of 21 July 1855. Dickens himself had already worked the metaphor extensively in *Dombey and Son* to characterize the educational shortcomings of Mrs. Pipchin's establishment (where cactus and creeping vegetables throve in soil that "was more than usually chalky, flinty, and sterile") and Dr. Blimber's Academy (that "great hothouse" where "all the boys blew before their time" and "Nature was of no consequence at all.") But in one often-quoted passage of *Dombey and Son* the analogy is employed more broadly to challenge the scientific good sense of unqualified "natural" liberty. This is the passage where Dickens argues the value of inquiring "what Nature is, and how men work to change her." He takes issue with the "magistrate or judge" who admonishes "the unnatural outcasts of society; unnatural in brutal habits, unnatural in want of decency, unnatural in losing and confounding all distinctions between good and evil; unnatural in ignorance, in vice, in recklessness, in contumacy, in mind, in looks, in everything." In doing so, of course, he takes issue with the moralistic assumption that the poor owe their abject position to their own weakness of character. Thomas Chalmers had argued that "character is the parent of comfort, not vice versa"; and thus his Gradgrindian solution to the pauper problem was that we must "plant in their bosoms a principle of independence—give a high tune of delicacy to their characters." But here Dickens holds to the opposite, environmentalist assumption: follow "the good clergyman or doctor"—the man of religion or the man of science—into the dens of the poor, he recommends, and having breathed the polluted air, "vainly attempt to think of any simple plant, or flower, or wholesome weed, that, set in this foetid bed, could have its natural growth, or put its little leaves off to the sun as GOD designed it."

"UNNATURAL HUMANITY"

Invoking current medical wisdom about the pathogenic nature of "noxious particles" and "vitiated air," Dickens argues that where we "generate disease" we also "breed, by the same certain process," youth without innocence or modesty, middle-age without maturity, and old age that is "a scandal on the form we bear." Dickens then throws the magistrate's words back at him: "Unnatural humanity! When we shall gather grapes from thorns, and figs from thistles; when fields of grain shall spring up from the offal in the bye-ways of our wicked cities, and roses bloom in the fat churchyards that they cherish; then we may look for natural humanity, and find it growing from such seed." This time the appropriate counterpart to Matthew 7:16 is to be found in the language of those severely scientific gentlemen, the members of the Statistical Society of London, who in March, 1848 reported on the "State of the Inhabitants and their Dwellings in Church Lane, St. Giles's," concluding that "with many of the young, brought up in such hot-beds of mental pestilence, the hopeless, but benevolent attempt is making to implant, by means of general education the seeds of religion, virtue, truth, order, industry, and cleanliness; but which seeds to fructify advantageously, need, it is to be feared, a soil far less rank than can be found in these wretched abodes." Since Dickens's "unnatural humanity" passage had appeared in December, 1847, he could not have written it with this report in mind; but as with the passage from Smith, influence is not the question here. The point is that Dickens seems to have calculated—and the wording of the report shows just how correctly—that in his Biblical/biological metaphors he had found a language whose appropriateness, if not moral force, the hard-headed devotees of "fact" could not deny.

Theme, Form, and the Naming of Names in *Hard Times*

Philip V. Allingham

The following essay examines nomenclature in *Hard Times*. In his study, Philip V. Allingham decodes characters' names to reveal the complex web of allusion and association intended by Dickens. According to Allingham, Dickens is often subtle in choosing names that not only reveal and conceal character identity but also bestow meaning and highlight thematic material. Allingham teaches at Lakehead University in Ontario, Canada.

F.R. Leavis's rationale for excluding the works of Dickens from *The Great Tradition* (1948) was that such a story as *Hard Times* must be read as a moral fable rather than a genuine novel. Leavis cites the name Dickens has chosen for Mr Gradgrind's 'utilitarian abode, Stone Lodge', as an example of Dickens's investing everything in the book with a clearly apparent 'representative significance'. Leavis interprets the schoolroom scene which opens the story as a stylized piece of Jonsonian comedy, and Bounderby as 'consistently a Jonsonian character in the sense that he is incapable of change'. With such names as 'Sleary', Leavis implies that Dickens's nomenclature in *Hard Times For These Times* is also perfectly consistent with the practices of Jonson and Bunyan.

As David Craig has pointed out, however, not all the names in the novel are laden with the obvious symbolic associations of the Comedy of Humours; for instance, 'the Gradgrind children whom Dickens wants to establish fully as individuals, i.e. Louisa and Tom, are not given parody names'.

Further, in 'A Landscape with Figures', J.M. Benn suggests that some characters in this novel are neither allegories nor metaphors, and that Gradgrind in particular 'plays a double

Reprinted from "Theme, Form, and the Naming of Names in *Hard Times for These Times*," by Philip V. Allingham, *The Dickensian*, Spring 1991, by permission of the author. Endnotes in the original have been omitted in this reprint.

role, the human father and the allegorical Utilitarian'. If Benn is correct, then *Hard Times* is not solely the fable F.R. Leavis argues it to be, but also an exploration of life-like character and circumstances in a genuine dystopia.

The key to the story's theme would then seem to lie in the characters' names. If the meanings of the characters are simply the meanings of their names, as in Jonsonian comedy, then the story is a fable. If, however, the names hide as much as they reveal and are more often subtle than obvious in their symbolic associations, *Hard Times* must be accepted as a novel in the modern sense.

The origins of the names of the twenty-three characters tend to be biblical, topical, historical, and colloquial. In the *Dickensian* for 1935 Frank G. Roe established that almost all the names (with the exception of 'Jupe' and 'Bitzer') have not come from life. Since Dickens has concocted most of the names, they bear close examination, for as in his previous works they are his initial means of revealing both his appraisals of and the natures of the characters. [As Harry Stone has noted:] 'For Dickens, names were truly magical; they concealed and revealed identity'.

THOMAS GRADGRIND

Behind Dickens's caricature of a retired hardware merchant turned educator lie the very real figures of John Stuart Mill, Jeremy Bentham, and David Ricardo, whose Utilitarian views on philosophy and political economy were odious in the extreme to such liberals as Lemon and Dickens. Although [, as Raymond Williams has pointed out,] 'Dickens has Mill's *Political Economy* (1849) very much in mind in his general indictment of the ideas which built and maintained Coketown,' in the second chapter he is emphatic that Gradgrind is *not* a John but a Thomas. The contemporary Thomas at whom Dickens had tilted with great effect in the persons of both Scrooge the miser in *A Christmas Carol* (1943) and Filer the statistician in *The Chimes* (1844) was Thomas Robert Malthus (1766–1834), whose *Essay on the Principle of Population* (1798) had proposed that disease and famine were necessary and useful checks on population. Gradgrind's being a disciple of Malthus is made manifest by the names he has selected for his two youngest children: 'Adam Smith' (after the eighteenth-century promulgator of the doctrine of *laissez-faire*, which spawned England's factories) and 'Malthus' (after the originator of the callous expression 'redundant (in *A Christmas Carol,* 'surplus') population'. [According to T.W. Hill:]

> Dickens, an author, bestowed upon his children the names of authors he admired. . . . It seems natural, therefore, that he should cause Gradgrind, the believer in FACTS, to name his children, one from Adam Smith the founder of Political Economy presented in an impersonal way as based on facts, and the other from Thomas Malthus, whose Essay on the Principle of Population is based on statistics and facts without any reference to human emotions.

Gradgrind's Christian name also implies a biblical allusion to Thomas 'The Apostle who doubted (*John* xx, 25); hence the phrase, a doubting Thomas, applied to a sceptic' [in *Brewer's Dictionary of Phrase and Fable*]. St Thomas had not been a bad man; indeed, he is reported to have done considerable missionary work later in India. However, he was prepared to take nothing on faith. Although 'Gradgrind' has since become a class-name for the cruel Victorian factory-owner, Dickens from the outset suggests that his Gradgrind is no more beyond redemption than is that inveterate miser Scrooge. [As Myron Magnet notes,] 'Misguided though he is, he believes the Coketown pupils are being taught with the success he sincerely wishes'. His education scheme, after all, he intended to produce a better world, a world with 'no nonsense', but also with a minimum of starvation and unemployment.

The name 'Gradgrind' is associated with the drudgery of the factory-system in Dickens's working notes, which indicate that he was toying with such variations for the novel's title as 'The Grindstone,' 'The universal grindstone', 'Two and Two are Four' 'Prove it!' (Stone) on Friday, January 20th, 1854. Behind the gritty cacophony of the double alliterative 'Gradgrind' we hear the roaring of the assembly-line machinery that mutilated the factory girl who was the subject of Henry Morley's editorial 'Ground in the Mill' in *Household Words* on April 22, 1854. As a verb 'grind' means 'oppress, harass with exactions', as well, of course, as 'crush'. The Coketown educational reformer, 'interposing between his pupils and reality a blanket of words, abstract notions, mathematical tables and formulae, crushes the world of actual experience by laying upon it too heavy an explanatory superstructure' (Magnet). Gradgrind's oppressed pupils enter his pedagogic factory imaginative Sissy Jupes (perhaps with a pun on 'dupes'), but leave it calculating, anaemic Bitzers.

The 'Grad' in 'Gradgrind' is probably an abbreviation of 'gradually', perhaps reminiscent of Von Logau's remark about the slowness but inevitability of the devine retribution that both Gradgrindery in life and its leading practitioner in the novel invite:

> Though the mills of God grind slowly, yet they grind exceedingly small;
>
> Though with patience He stands waiting, with exactness grinds He all (*Sinngedichte*, III, ii, 24).

In *Allegory in Dickens* (1977) Jane Vogel sees the name 'Gradgrind' as part of a pattern of stoning, noting that like schoolmaster Headstone and step-father Murdstone, 'Mr Gradgrind . . . *grad*ually *grinds* childish fancy, curiosity about wonders seen and unseen . . . on the remorseless grindstone of fact, rule, law'. For Vogel, the stones of Stone Lodge and Gradgrind are the tablets of the Mosaic law, the strict adherence to which kills such spirits as Stephen Blackpool's.

SISSY JUPE

The Coketown system's attempted 'grinding' down or depersonalization of Sissy begins with Gradgrind's initially addressing her as 'Girl number twenty', suggesting the impersonal, almost military organization of the Manchester Lancasterian School. To give Gradgrind his due, he does endeavour to learn the new student's name. However, as a repressor of sentiment, he hastens to supplant 'Sissy' with the formal 'Cecilia'. As the course of the book reveals, she is indeed no coward (a connotation that would not have occurred to Dickens's readers, since the slang term 'sissy' originated at the close of the nineteenth century), for it is she who dismisses Harthouse. But is this stroller's child a fitting representative of St Cecilia, the second- or third-century virgin Christian martyr now regarded as the patron saint of music?

She is an interloper in the rigid, ordered, disciplined, and soulless streets of Coketown, a representative of the shabby but imaginative world of the horseriders, who, with their circus slang, are [, writes Geoffrey Johnston Sadock,] 'an unmistakable allegorical counterpart of the pragmatic, mechanical, and imprisoned masses of Coketown'.

Although she has grown up in the society of horses, Sissy [,writes Frank Edmund Smith,] 'is unable to understand facts freed from their relation to people'; consequently, she is overwhelmed by Gradgrind's challenge to define in a precise, dispassionate way the smooth, graceful, flesh-and-blood creatures with whom her father earns his livelihood. In that she represents that knowledge which defies articulation but must rather be intuited, Sissy is a fitting agent for the patron saint of music and femininity.

Her petname in Dickens's time even lacked the additional sense of 'sister', since that use the *OED* records as having originated after the novel's publication, in America. However, the femininity which her 'irradiated' hair, and her blushing and curtseying suggest her surname tends to reinforce. While in the north of England and in Scotland a jupe was [according to the *Oxford English Dictionary*, V, 633] 'A loose jacket, kirtle, or tunic worn by men', a usage recorded by Dickens's friend Carlyle in his *French Revolution* (I, II, ii) in 1837, in the south of England the word, a French borrowing, would have betokened a woman's skirt.

In this dreary industrial town Sissy is the first positive person whom the reader meets. In that she is the victim of the classroom ogre, his 'dupe' in question period, Sissy immediately arouses the reader's sympathy. However, in that he has been so thoroughly taken in by the bureaucratic, Department of Practical Art point-of-view in the matter of wallpaper and carpet patterns it is Gradgrind who is the real dupe. His system is nonsense to Sissy's common sense, which does not preclude fancy. She is not fool enough to believe that one could [, writes Steven Connor,] 'hurt a picture of a flower'.

Sissy's aestheticism Dickens clearly reveals by contrasting her responses to the wallpaper and carpet questions to those of her fellow pupils. Her healthiness, modesty, dark-haired beauty are contrasted by the unwholesomeness of her schoolroom and schoolyard antagonist, the aged child Bitzer, who later opposes Sissy's attempt to rescue Tom.

BITZER

> Balanced against her normalcy, Bitzer . . . lives . . . in the coldness of unadulterated fact. He never gets excited; he has no interests or desires that involve feeling. . . . Sterile, neutral, zombielike, Bitzer watches, calculates, bides his time, becomes a perfect factual success (Smith).

As much a denial of the imagination and rites of childhood as Bounderby, Bitzer is the novel's villain in embryo. In the initial schoolroom scene, his overrationalization of matters yields exactly what his master requires: a cold, factual analysis of a horse, devoid of any sense of the animal's vitality. Bitzer's name suggests that, although he can provide a series of discrete pieces of data on any given subject, he is but a trivia machine that can offer neither a coherent literal nor a moving figurative perception. Like young Victor Frankenstein, Bitzer can collect and even assemble the building blocks of matter, but the product is as soulless and lifeless as the bricks that compose the lookalike buildings of Coketown itself.

It is quite possible, as David Sloane has suggested, that Dickens was satirising a particular person in the character of Bitzer. Just as Slackbridge in the novel is probably an elaboration of the caricature Gruffshaw in 'On Strike', who in turn is based on an actual union leader named 'Mortimer Grimshaw' (according to K.J. Fielding in 'The Battle for Preston' in 1954), so Bitzer may well be based [, as suggested by David E. Stone,] on George Parker Bidder, or the 'Caculating Boy', as he was known. The connection may explain Bitzer's affinity for numbers. However, the association with 'Bittern' (lye), 'bitters', 'bit' (including the mechanical device for controlling a horse, and a slang term for money), and especially 'bitter' should not be disregarded.

As a verb, 'bit' means 'to curb, restrain' *(OED, I, 882)* and it is the development of the nobler aspects of human nature that Gradgrindery has curbed in Bitzer. In his utter practicality amounting to heartlessness he represents a concept that Dickens had explored in the last of the Christmas Books, *The Haunted Man* (1848). Like the street urchin in that novella, Bitzer is impervious to the beneficent effect of memory, for his brain records mere data, not human experience. Accordingly, when Gradgrind pleads as the youth's former schoolmaster for his son's release, Bitzer returns with interest the 'fundamental principle' Gradgrind taught him, one of the essential tenets of Utilitarianism, namely that all human transactions are inherently 'politico-economical'.

An interesting (though possibly irrelevant) side-note is that in the north of England 'bitts' were instruments involved in blasting mines [according to James Orchard Halliwell's *A Dictionary of Archaic and Provincial Words*]. The association adds force to Dickens's image of the earlier Gradgrind as a 'cannon loaded to the muzzle with facts', for

Bitzer is Gradgrind's blasting mechanism for blowing the other pupils 'clean out of the regions of childhood at one discharge'. It is poetic justice that Bitzer should function as Gradgrind's own petard, hoisting his former master with his own inflexible doctrine.

The opening scene's other character, a freshly-graduated teacher (anonymous until the close of the chapter) has an equally telling (albeit more Jonsonian) appellation: M'Choakumchild. [George Bernard] Shaw found this device so obvious that he dismissed it as 'almost an insult to the serious reader'.

MR AND MRS M'CHOAKUMCHILD

Typical of the fact-wielding assassins of 'the robber Fancy' that the new training colleges had begun dispatching in 1853, M'Choakumchild and wife are rather shadowy figures. A gradgrinding schoolmaster thoroughly imbued with 'fact, fact, fact,' he has lost the vital connection between formal learning and direct experience. The 'feeble stragglers' from the labouring, anguished world outside the classroom, those like Sissy Jupe who have come to receive 'a sound, practical education' are to be processed, 'regulated and governed' in every way—to become like Bitzer, a prototype of the Hitler Youth who would sooner betray his own parent rather than his doctrine, a grim foreshadowing of the Orwellian nightmare a full century before its unveiling.

The 'M' 'in the master's name, like his obsession with 'the elements of Political Economy', may be an allusion not merely to the dour, thrifty Scot of tradition, but to one Scot in particular—Adam Smith. Appropriately, the effect of the name is suggestive of choking, suffocating, and stifling. The master's name may also imply both an artichoke (a thorny vegetable) and a stiff, unbending clerical collar—and even 'chock' (as in 'chock-full').

The name, curiously spelled with an 'oa', may even echo the 'choakee', an Anglo-Indian colloquialism for prison or lock-up, adopted in England shortly before the novel's publication. After all, if 'The jail might have been the infirmary, the infirmary might have been the jail', why may not the schoolhouse partake of the character, form, and function of these other institutions? Such a connection is neither obvious, nor an affront to the serious reader.

JOSIAH BOUNDERBY

> He is . . . the embodiment of the aggressive money-making
> and power-seeking ideal which was a driving force of the In-
> dustrial Revolution. That he is also a braggart, a liar and in
> general personally repellent is of course a comment on Dick-
> ens's method. . . . The very name (and Dickens uses his
> names with conscious and obvious effect), incorporating
> *bounder* incorporates this typical feeling (Williams).

However, Partridge shows that expression as originating
at Cambridge in 1883. Williams' connecting the modern use
of the term with mid-Victorian associations is an example of
the specious reasoning that excluded *Hard Times* from the
Great Tradition. As a Bully of Humility, however, Bounderby
is a juggernaut, a possible connection being the 'bounder' of
the 1850's—a four-wheeled cab.

Although he does indeed represent the evils that ideologi-
cally underpin the Coketown system, Bounderby's name does
not, then, automatically suggest the sort of allegorical and static nature that Williams derives from it. As Benn notes,

> His first metaphor is metal; . . . as he is a north-country
> banker, brass. He also represents the bullying bluster of the
> master-class; his second, more strongly developed metaphor,
> is wind.

Rather than on his name, Benn focuses, quite correctly, on
Bounderby's nature and on Dickens's methods for readily
communicating it. His dominant qualities—his energy, constant activity, and racy volubility—are consistent with 'bounding', leaping, springing, and pouncing. In Dickens's day the
secondary association of the name would have been either
'One who sets or marks out bounds or limits,' or 'A limit, a
boundary; a landmark' (*OED*, I, 1023). In fact, he is both. He
is a negative force, limiting and confining. Principally, he is
antithetical to youth, denying Louisa of hers while attempting
to cover up any vestiges of his own, actual childhood with fabricated anecdotes from a carefully-fostered Horatio Alger
myth. In counselling Gradgrind against retaining Sissy Jupe
in the school and in pensioning his own mother off at thirty
pounds *per annum* (echoing Judas's betrayal of Christ), like
Ebenezer Scrooge of Scrooge and Marley, the City, Josiah
Bounderby of Coketown has set a bound or limit to his own
humanity. In Hebrew 'Ebenezer' signifies a marker-stone, just
as in English 'Bounderby' did. Then, too, Bounderby is quite
literally a Coketown landmark more distinctive than any edi-

fice: he is, as he always proclaims as if reading the subscription on the pedestal of his own monument, Josiah Bounderby of Coketown.

The suffix in his name associates Bounderby with the north of England as surely as the brass metaphor, reminiscent of such place names as Grimsby and Whitby, and of such descriptive personal appellations as *'idelsby* (= idler, Mr Idleness), *lewdsby, . . . rudesby, sneaksby, . . .* Cf. also such appellations as . . . *Slyboots.* Some have suggested identity with *boy'* (*OED*, I, 1023). The process of paranomasia with the suffix 'by' seems to be chiefly pejorative, so that a reasonable translation of 'Bounderby' might be (uttered in contempt or derision) 'Mr Marker', or 'Mr Energetic'.

The character's Christian name is as telling in its associations as his surname. The most famous modern historical personages to bear the name are the great eighteenth-century industrialist Josiah Wedgwood (1730 95) and his successor (1769–1843). The senior Josiah was elected to the Royal Society for his scientific ingenuity, was a leading member of the circle of industrialists known as the Lunar Society of Birmingham.

Victorian readers could hardly have missed Dickens's allusion to the powerful Wedgewood family. Nor would they have failed to detect the irony of the biblical allusion to the zealous, iconoclastic King Josiah of *Second Kings.* Having seen Israel falling into the immoral worship of such foreign deities as Baal, Josiah had stood for the Mosaic Law. His energy, however, was directed towards the restoration of righteousness, not the foundation of a soulless and degrading system in which men are reduced to 'Hands'. Since the biblical Josiah succeeded his father Amon at the age of eight, he presumably enjoyed little of a natural childhood, a point which accords with Bounderby's fictionalized youth. The comic antithesis of the Book of Deuteronomy, discovered in his reparation of the Temple, would be the works of the Utilitarian prophets Malthus, Smith, Ricardo, and Bentham.

That Bounderby is neither an innovative Wedgewood nor a virtuous Josiah underscores his imposture, for this appellation he deliberately chose to retain, even though he has spurned the identity of a 'pegler'—implying one who 'pegs along', that is, makes his way 'with vigour or haste' *(OED,* VII, 618), as his mother does when she meets Stephen. To suit a rags-to-riches rise he has chosen a name that connotes 'bounding' over obstacles in preference to one that suggests the 'persistent hammering away' at them. [As Richard E. Lougy notes,] such a leap of his new surname asserts, from gutter-urchin to prosperous capitalist, 'affirms rather than denies the existing order. . . . Bounderby's fictionalized past arises out of an adult mind wholly attuned to the values of an industrialized society. . . .' The name he has renounced suggests the 'slow and steady wins the race' attitude of the pre-industrial era. Although Lougy contends that 'Mrs Pegler, . . . in keeping with the romance motif, comes across as a hybrid between an unwitting Fury and a more conventional English witch', her name is anything but romantic. In that Bounderby has recreated himself in name and birth, he prefigures such twentieth-century re-creators as J. Vissarionovich Dzugashvili (Stalin), and numerous actors and actresses who have found their real names unsuitable for the artificial world of stage and screen.

In this respect, there is a curious link between the world of fancy, Sleary's circus, and the world of fact, the Coketown of Gradgrind and Bounderby, that Dickens's characterizing the machinery of the place as 'melancholy mad elephants' implies from the first. That the name 'Kidderminster' is so admirably suited to a member of a 'graceful equestrian Tyrolean flower-act' leads one to suspect that 'Kidderminster' is a pseudonym designed to evoke a Teutonic association. Since it may be translated as either 'Child city' or 'Child-cathedral', it is doubly fitting for the aged youth who is symbolic of the irresponsible, imaginative, tawdry world of the horse-riders. Ostensibly, Bounderby has rejected the romantic nonsense that Sleary's folk personify; in fact, he embraces both aspects of the circus world in his idealized Christian and surnames, and in his abnegation of the true character of both his mother and his childhood. Like Bitzer, Bounderby is a figure of nullity and sterility; both [, according to Richard Fabrizio,] 'effectively eliminate motherhood, matricides by intent', and have no natural issue.

MRS SPARSIT (*NÉE* SCADGERS)

While Janet Karsten Larson writes: she relies upon aristocratic credentials as leverage in social power games, she also uses the high society name to manipulate her perception of herself. Ironically, it is much less to the Scadgerses, who are blueblood relations, than to the Powlers, with whom she is related only by marriage, that Mrs Sparsit looks for a source of self-esteem.

Mrs Sparsit's acquiescing in Harthouse's misnaming her 'Mrs Powler', a repetition of her failure to correct Bitzer's addressing her as 'my lady' (II, i, 88) just a few minutes earlier, shows not so much 'that she has privately renamed herself' (Larson) as that she, like Bounderby, has rejected her real identity in favour of one grander, more powerful (and 'Powler' surely encloses 'power').

In 'Scadgers', her maiden name, lies less power. She and Lady Scadgers, her great aunt who arranged her marriage to the profligate but well-connected Sparsit, had a falling out just after her husband's death as an insolvent debtor in Calais, 'a popular Continental retreat for English people escaping from their creditors: a whole story is suggested of arranged marriages and pretended gentility', [according to Angus Easson]. Indeed, Mrs Sparsit has lived a pretender, first that she is a Powler by blood, secondly that she is on good terms with her titled relative, and thirdly that she is to be Mrs Bounderby.

Lougy associates her with 'Robert Graves' "capricious and all-powerful Threefold Goddess, . . . mother, bride, and layer out".' She displays an almost supernatural power for spying, and prying, and 'prowling about the house'. A true Scadger, she parlays her original position as Bounderby's house-keeper into a sinecure at the bank through manipulating the Bully of Humility with his own guilt (in marrying Louisa instead of her) and pride (in having her, an impoverished aristocrat, run 'attendance on his car').

Shortly after the book's publication, the term 'scadger' according to Partridge came to mean 'A mean fellow, a contemptible beggar of loans'. However, the term 'cadger', upon which Dickens has constructed the name, had suggested 'sponger' from early in the nineteenth century. The origin of the same 'Scadgers' may therefore suggest the cause of the falling out between Lady Scadgers and her niece, each of whom may have attempted to borrow from the other after the death of Mr Sparsit. While the 'sparse' in her name may apply to her means, it may also link her sowing of dissent between the Bounderbys to the pattern of sowing that pervades Book One, for as a verb 'sparse' means 'To disperse; to scatter' (Halliwell).

However, the root of Mrs Sparsit's name, 'spar', seems to reveal her character best; in general use it has four meanings in the middle of the nineteenth century. To begin with, it signified the shutting up, in, or out of a person. While she seeks to exclude Louisa from her home and position, and supplant her, Mrs Sparsit is content to wait and watch as Louisa descends the staircase to ignominy. Shut up within Mr Bounderby's house at the beginning, she is the goddess of the sacred precinct whom all visitors must acknowledge and worship. Later, like the dragon of myth, Mrs Sparsit sits enclosed in her room above a treasure, attended by a single suppliant and awaiting the arrival of the handsome youth (James Harthouse, a name suggesting 'hunter'), who instead of trying to steal her hoard will help her to recover it. When victory finally seems within her grasp, Louisa eludes her at the railway station, leaving Mrs Sparsit in the rain, a picture of misery, rancour, and frustration. Her witch-like powers have been cancelled by the water, showing her in her true colours: 'a stagnant verdure' of moss.

Her intended victim having pulled herself free from Mrs Sparsit's carefully laid web, the drenched and vexed widow reminds the reader of a washed-out spider. Her priding herself on the accuracy of her perceptions and predictions, her constant calculations, 'her manner of sitting, . . . her extraordinary facility of locomotion . . . [and her ability to] shoot with consummate velocity from the roof to hall' all support her spider-like character. Sitting in the window of whatever room she happens to visit, Mrs Sparsit in her patient knitting and gleeful anticipation of vengeance foreshadows a far bloodier-minded antagonist, Madame Defarge, presiding genius of the guillotine in *A Tale of Two Cities*. Like the Frenchwoman, Mrs Sparsit sits, unhurried and grimly methodical, yet ever ready to spar verbally with any and all comers, a Sibyl envisioning the descent into the underworld of the object of her antipathy. Fabrizio labels her 'a gross caricature of Penelope, always pictured with distaff . . .'. The wife of the absent hero utilized her web to confound marriage proposals and keep her numerous suitors at bay; Mrs Sparsit employs hers to eliminate a marriage rival.

Had she been so fortunate as to land Bounderby in her net, Mrs Sparsit would have extended Dickens's 'fistic phraseology' by coming up to scratch with her spouse at every opportunity, arguing, debating, and bandying words with the Noodle of her eye face to face, rather than at one remove, with the Noodle's portrait. Confining, enclosing, and shutting up being in her very nature, Mrs Sparsit contains her own true feelings with aplomb until the very last, when Bounderby delivers her dismissal with a conscious-salving cheque.

STEPHEN BLACKPOOL AND SLACKBRIDGE

> Blackpool is neither a reflection of some real working man . . . , nor a one-dimensional allegory, the figure of Good in some medieval morality play. Blackpool is a complex proto-type, a factory worker perplexed by ambient abundance and intelligence that results in depletion and injustice (Fabrizio).

The working notes indicate that Dickens contemplated the names 'John' and 'George Prodge' (the latter for its associations of 'Man and Earth' and 'Hodge' or rural labourer) before settling on 'Stephen Blackpool' (Stone). While Frank G. Roe in the *Dickensian* for 1935 hypothesizes that Dickens chose 'Blackpool' for its regional character, suggesting as it does an actual city in Lancashire, Fabrizio postulates that the name is deliberately intended to connote his muddled psychological state in that 'Muddle and his name are forms of the same idea, a denial of clarity—the muddying or blackening of a pool of water'. For Fabrizio, then, what Coketown does to this good man's spirit is analogous to its operation on the town's surrounding countryside, converting its potentially healing waters into a spumous track made black and thick with the dye of industrial waste. In the end, appropriately, the blighted wasteland's Old Hell Shaft swallows Tom Gradgrind's scapegoat.

J. Miriam Benn contends that 'Stephen Blackpool's name defines his allegorical role: he is a Lancashire saint and martyr'. Geoffrey Sadock maintains that Dickens has modelled the humble weaver trapped by a bad marriage and a heartless system on the first Christian martyr, Saint Stephen. Although the more usual modern spelling is 'Steven', a form established in England in the middle ages, the form 'Stephen' alludes to the Hellenized Jew 'Stephanos' (in Greek signifying 'garland' or 'crown'), whose feast is celebrated immediately after Christ's own, on December 26th. Nine popes and one English king (proverbially a good fellow—'a worthy peer' as the song from Shakespeare's *Othello* styles him; but politically inept) have borne the name with the Greek spelling.

One of seven church officials, Stephen, a Jew of Greek culture, in trying to convert his fellow Hellenists aroused the antipathy of the more conservative and became a marked man in Jerusalem. His sentiment that even the Temple could be destroyed without the loss of the true faith the elders and scribes regarded as blasphemous. Although he defended himself in the Sanhedrin with eloquence and conviction, Stephen was stoned to death for blasphemy (*Acts* vii, 58).

Sadock utilizes Dickens's adaptation of the life of the saint to refute Leavis's contention that the novelist failed to communicate a sense of the part played by religion in the emotional and intellectual life of nineteenth-century England.

> The peculiarly Eucharistic meal Stephen partakes of on the night before his death and the image of the inviolate virgin by whom he is mourned complete the heavy Christian references. . . .

For Jane Vogel, the antitype to Christ-Stephen is

> *Slackbridge*, symbolically a *slack bridge*, a spiritual No Thoroughfare, sign of treacherous footing over the void. No Two Cities, Christ-celebrating sunrise is seen from the vantage point of a Slackbridge. Following him, men follow a false saviour and reject the Stephen-revealed, true way.

The connection between the Dickensian Stephen and his biblical counterpart is reinforced by the character of the language in which Slackbridge denounces him. At the first meeting of the United Aggregate Tribunal, Slackbridge stigmatizes him as being as great a traitor to his class as 'he who sold his birthright for a mess of pottage' (Esau in *Genesis* xxv, 34) and 'Judas Iscariot'. At the second 'Consult'—after Bounderby's bills have proclaimed Stephen a bank-robber—Slackbridge characterizes him as having betrayed the honour of the proletariat to the employer-class, who see already little reason why the labourers should not crawl on their bellies all their lives, 'like the serpent in the garden'. Thus primed, when Slackbridge demands the ostracism of the 'viper', despite a few negative voices, 'the general assemblage subscribed to the gospel acording to Slackbridge', Dickens's adaptation of Milton's Satan.

While Stephen's acting as a good Samaritan to Mrs Pegler is necessary to the mechanism of the plot, his main function is to act as a representative of the oppressed class from which Louisa Bounderby's husband has growth rich and upon whose backs the weight of her father's doctrine of fact unalloyed by sentiment falls so grievously. Her encounter with Stephen, promoted by instincts we have hitherto not seen in operation, marks the turning point in our sympathies towards Louisa. She is so overcome that, forgetting the gulf between them, she momentarily reaches out, as if his mere touch would restore her moral vision. Stephen expresses his thanks wordlessly, but with 'a *grace* [italics mine] . . . that Lord Chesterfield could not have taught his son in a century'.

MRS BLACKPOOL

With no identity other than as a dependant of her husband, the 'evil spirit' of Stephen's existence is the proletarian counterpart of Mrs Gradgrind. Although Warrington Winters locates Mrs Blackpool's genesis in the 'bottomless abyss' of Dickens's 'desperate animosity' towards his mentally-unbalanced wife, noting that 'Both the Dickenses and the Blackpools had been married exactly eighteen years', she may well have taken life from Bertha Rochester (*née* Mason) in Charlotte Bronte's *Jane Eyre* (1847). Both husbands are 'bound hand and foot, to a dead woman, and tormented by a demon in her shape'.

Mrs Blackpool represents in Dickens's notes the 'Law of Divorce' question. There she is indicated only once, and then merely as Stephen's 'bad wife' (Stone). Unlike Bronte, Dickens does not permit his entrapped husband an easy escape. With a great house and servants, Rochester is able to isolate and restrain his lunatic spouse; with but one friend and little property, Stephen is powerless to prevent his wife's continually despoiling what little he has.

Her condition is never satisfactorily explained. She is brutal and animalistic because the story requires that she be so, and because that is the nature of the system upon which Coketown has been erected. Her addictions to alcohol and opium are as logical a consequence of the system's godless degradation of human nature as the smoke-filled skies, polluted river and man-killing pits are of its assault on nature itself. Excluded from the comfort of eighteen Christian denominations and any wholesome recreation save the Sunday walk, what else can 'A.B.' do but resort to 'law haunts' and lower vices? The Coketown process is so depersonalizing and dehumanizing that it robs Mrs Blackpool of both her Christian name and her soul: she is a mere animal seeking release from pain. For Dickens, already chafing under a marriage rendered unhappy through incompatibility of temperament (though still four years away from a definite separation and the affair with Ellen Ternan), Mrs Blackpool may even represent Kate Dickens.

RACHAEL

Although Winters proposes Georgina Hogarth, who had virtual management of the Dickens *ménage* at the time he wrote the novel, as the source for Rachael, the biblical character of the same name bears examining.

The daughter of the wily Laban, and eventually the favourite wife of the Hebrew patriarch Jacob, by whom when not in her 'first bloom' (I, x, 50) she conceived Joseph and Benjamin, Rachael had to wait fourteen years to marry the man who loved her. Jacob served seven years for her hand, only to be deceived and given the older sister, Leah, instead (Laban then compelled the frustrated youth to serve yet another seven years for Rachael's hand; *Genesis*, xxix-xxxv). Vogel contends that Dickens's 'Rachael symbolizes the joy of man's desiring the unattainable, or won only at soul-wearing cost, under the old covenant' of antiquated marriage laws.

When Herod ordered the Massacre of Innocents, the wailing of anguished mothers was the fulfillment of Jeremiah's prophecy that with the coming of the Messiah there would be heard the voice of 'Rachael weeping for her children, and refusing all consolation, because they were no more' (*Mathew*, 11, 18). In *Hard Times* the weeping would be for Stephen, the children Rachael and he never had, and the sister that the industrial system destroyed, the novel's only factory child. Significantly, Rachael often addresses Stephen as 'lad', as if he were still the youth who courted her friend, or even a surrogate child. And yet, she is more than an externalization of one side of Stephen's dilemma, for she is permitted rage, vexation, and grief in her own right. She is among the tale's least verbal characters, and yet her communications, verbal and nonverbal, and full of deepest meanings. Although she and Stephen, for example, have never spoken of their marrying, that notion thoroughly informs their relationship. Her Lancashire accent, like Stephen's, suggests her akwardness in speech and yet makes her insistently real. Patiently and quietly she suffers like Stephen, but is capable of independent thought and action, as when she seizes the initiative by going to Bounderby. She even defies social convention by walking hand-in-hand with her friend's husband.

As a character representing a principle, Rachael is much allied to Sissy Jupe; indeed, the two symbolically join forces in seeking to exonerate Stephen when accused, and to find him when lost. If Sissy stands for the wisdom of the heart,

Rachael represents the Christian spirit in action, even to her rival (in stark contrast to Mrs Sparsit's antipathy towards Louisa). Rachael is only a partially explored character because she must also serve the moral truth of the fable, as is suggested by her single name. Although she represents many of Sissy's values, she possesses neither nickname, indicative of 'family and social order' (Fabrizio), nor surname, indicative of identity in the community.

As T.W. Hill has noted, Dickens propounds but does not expound social problems in *Hard Times*. His interest lies in telling a story that happens to utilize such elements as Utilitarianism, trade unionism, and schools. Since the story is not told at two distinct levels, as is Orwell's *Animal Farm*, and since a number of characters on this unusually uncluttered canvas develop an inner life all their own, *Hard Times* is neither Lougy's 'romance' nor Leavies's 'dramatic poem'.

Coketown is both a recognizable place in a familiar landscape and a hypothetical construct, a nightmare world of melancholy-mad, elephantine machines that is to the nineteenth century what the chief city of Airstrip One in the third most populous province of Oceania in 1984 is to the twentieth, a 'soap-bubble, without its beauty'. The names of Coketown's inhabitants partake of this dual nature; such names as Sleary and Bitzer are humourously descriptive and easily apprehended, while others such as Sparsit and Bounderby require decoding to yield a complex nexus of associative and allusive meanings, and others such as Louisa are not intended to convey any allusion or association at all. While some characters are never released from the single dimension their names imply, others such as Gradgrind do escape to be seen in the round. Benn is dissatisfied with Dickens's transforming Gradgrind's from an allegorical into a multidimensional nature, but Dickens has prepared the reader for this change from the very opening. The story is one of imaginative fulfillment and the movement from factual analysis towards intuitive perception. The final note, spiritual harmony, requires the vanquishing not of Gradgrind the character, but Gradgrind the principle. Thus, Bitzer operates as a surrogate for his ex-master in being cozened by Sleary and his 'learned dog'.

This scene illustrates that the satisfaction of reading *Hard Times* lies not in the decoding of an allegorical scheme but in rationalizing the work's fabulous and realistic elements.

The Paradox of the Clown

Joseph Butwin

In *Hard Times*, the circus offers a favorable, regenerative alternative to Coketown's soul-deadening utilitarian philosophy. In the following essay, Joseph Butwin examines what he perceives as a paradox: The clown represents human kindness and cooperation on the one hand, yet it also serves as an emblem of morbidity and shame. These incongruous images of the clown are apparent, for example, when the debased Tom—hardly a congenial figure—appears as a blackface clown and also through Signor Jupe's many downfalls, which include abandoning his own daughter. Butwin is an associate professor of English at the University of Washington.

In the novels of Charles Dickens there are few more complete images of familial esprit de corps, social cooperation, and good humor than Sleary's Horse-Riding in *Hard Times*. Critics generally agree that Dickens saw in Sleary's brief apologia the common denominator of his own comic art: "People mutht be amuthed, Thquire, thomehow." In addition to amusement, the circus offers an admirable, if somewhat unrealistic, alternative to the cutthroat competition that characterizes industrial Coketown. Acrobatics allows people to be flexible, agile, and eccentric even while they are bound by the form and cooperation represented, say, by the human pyramid.

> The father of one of the families was in the habit of balancing the father of another of the families on the top of a great pole; the father of a third family often made a pyramid of both those fathers, with Master Kidderminster for the apex, and himself for the base; all the fathers could dance upon rolling casks, stand upon bottles, catch knives and balls, twirl hand-basins, ride upon anything, jump over everything, and stick at nothing. All the mothers could (and did) dance, upon the

Excerpted from "The Paradox of the Clown in Dickens," by Joseph Butwin, *Dickens Studies Annual*, vol. 5 (1974). Reprinted by permission of AMS Press. Endnotes in the original have been omitted from this reprint.

slack wire and the tight-rope, and perform rapid acts on bare-backed steeds.

And yet Dickens chooses to mar this image of a saving remnant by eventually placing at its center the most disgusting of creatures, Tom Gradgrind done up as a blackface clown.

> In a preposterous coat, like a beadle's, with cuffs and flaps exaggerated to an unspeakable extent; in an immense waist-coat, knee-breeches, buckled shoes, and a mad cocked hat; with nothing fitting him, and everything of coarse material, moth-eaten and full of holes; with seams in his black face, where fear and heat had started through the greasy composition daubed all over it; anything so grimly, detestably, ridiculously' shameful as the whelp in his comic livery, Mr. Gradgrind never could by any other means have believed in, weighable and measurable fact though it was. And one of his model children had come to this!

The clownish costume becomes a brickbat used to punish "the whelp." If people must be amused, who is responsible for this amusement?—a grim, detestable, shameful creature done up in rags. Another clown, Signor Jupe, drinks heavily, beats his dog, abandons his daughter, and weeps after every unsuccessful attempt to make people laugh. Given the choice, his daughter, Sissy, leaves the circus and makes her way in a more conventional if corrupt outer world. Why does the seemingly congenial image go sour? . . .

THE SHAME OF THE CLOWN

In *Hard Times* Dickens traces the shame of the clown. It begins in the Stone Lodge, that fortress of middle-class opinion belonging to Mr. Thomas Gradgrind of Coketown. There we hear the daughter of the clown identifying her family for the daughter of the house:

> "[Mother] was;" Sissy made the terrible communication nervously; "she was a dancer. . . ."
>
> "Father's a;" Sissy whispered the awful word, "a clown. . . ."
>
> "Merrylegs;" she whispered the awful fact; "is his performing dog."

Of course Dickens does not consider the facts "awful." He simply acknowledges but does not endorse the prejudices that account for Sissy's shame.

And yet in the course of the novel Sissy is abandoned by a father who wallows in shame and sorrow, and she is not allowed to remain with the saving remnant of circus folk. Tom's appearance as a blackface clown is made to demonstrate disgrace. The whole approach to the circus cannot be summarized by Sleary's defense nor by Gradgrind's disdain. It lies with Charles Dickens, somewhere between the two.

Our first exposure to Sleary's establishment is on Gradgrind's walk through the middle ground between Coketown and his Stone Lodge. The terrain "was neither town nor country yet was either spoiled." The circus on the outskirts of town is a variation of the French *fête foraine*, the demipastoral, demirespectable diversion shunted to the suburbs. The result is a debased pastoral, tainted like the very suburbs by the waste of the town. This would be the landscape of Picasso's sad saltimbanques wandering through the same wasteland sixty years later. Beyond the town and beyond the law the clowns carry on their extraordinary version of pastoral. Just as their turf is not quite city and not quite country, the performers themselves are barely human and barely animal, or in the case of Sleary himself, "never sober and never drunk." E.W.B. Childers with his legs too short and his back too broad is "a remarkable sort of Centaur, compounded of the stable and the playhouse." Kidderminster is a cupid with a rough voice. And altogether their language bears uncertain relation to standard English. "Nine oils, Merrylegs, missing tips, garters, banners, and ponging"—Bounderby's list could go on.

Although it is with Gradgrind that we first encounter Sleary's Horse-Riding, the fact that he is unresponsive to "the sound of music" leaves the task of introduction to Dickens himself. Gradgrind "took no heed" of what follows, and what follows sounds very much like the gently satirical portraits of theatrical life that can be found in the early *Sketches* of Astley's and Greenwich Fair. The music that Gradgrind unconsciously censors is described as "a clashing and banging band . . . in full bray," and if we accept the narrative voice, Gradgrind's insensitivity is an act of reasonable self-defense. The circus tent itself is a curious mingling of Gothic architecture and modern advertisement which suggests a whimsical version of Ruskin's critique of the age: "A flag, floating from the summit of the temple" bears the name of Sleary's Horse-Riding and claims the "suffrages" of the people. "Sleary himself, a stout modern statue with a money-box at its elbow, in an ecclesiastical niche of early Gothic architecture, took the money." The repetition of "money . . . money" turns the God of this particular church into Mammon for a new saint whose attribute is his coffer, an anticipation of Ruskin's Britannia of the Market Place.

The strictly commercial aspect of the establishment continues in the descriptive voice that is borrowed from the circus barker and the playbill: "Miss Josephine Sleary, as some very long and very narrow strips of printed bill announced, was then inaugurating the entertainments with her graceful equestrian Tyrolean flower-act. Among other pleasing but always strictly moral wonders which must be seen to be believed, Signor Jupe was that afternoon to 'elucidate the diverting accomplishments of his highly trained performing dog Merrylegs.'" As in the description of the clowns out front at Greenwich Fair, the stilted Latinized language is just the kind of misleading puffery that reveals its opposite, low comedy. The same Jupe flings fountains of iron into the air—"a feat never before attempted in this or any other country," performs in a "hippo-comedietta," and punctuates the performance "with his chaste Shakspearean quips and retorts." The circus is a mixed bag of absurdity wrapped in the inevitably false dignity of modern publicity. The foreign diversions ("Tyrolean," "signor") offer the enticement of exoticism with the promise of respectable restraint ("strictly moral" and "chaste"). That mingling of the exotic, the Gothic, and the moral could be seen on any contemporary patent medicine bottle as well.

A CRITIQUE OF SOCIETY

Read in the vein of the *Sketches*, the passage satirizes the commercial side of circuses, advertisers, and the society that is willing to receive them. But in the context of the early pages of *Hard Times* the circus serves as another kind of critique of society, that is, of the society already represented within the novel by Gradgrind in the schoolroom. Next to that stifling prison, the noise, variety, inconsistency, and comedy of the Horse-Riding is a valuable refreshment. A moment later, when Gradgrind drags his children away, we are left with the sense that they are missing what would be the better half of their education. "I would sooner catch them reading poetry," their father complains. And the novel is among other things the story of how poetry or the circus might have been made to serve and correct the "starved imagination." Anyone who cannot imagine a man in the moon or a great bear in the stars will also reject the unlikely promises of the Tyrolean flower-act. Thus in this context, to receive (if not exactly believe) the claims of the circus is a mark not of corrigible folly (as it might be in the *Sketches*) but is itself a correction of the greater folly of hyperrational factualism. In this case the circus—also "poetry"—is a vital, even natural, alternative to the school and the Stone Lodge to which the "metallurgical Louisa" and little Tom are taken home "like a machine."

The clown himself, in spite of a life infused with the spirit of the circus, is sad. Signor Jupe has a private life. It is described to us, and, as we would expect, it is the contrary of his advertised public life. Only his daughter knows. Even the other members of the troupe "never knew how he felt" and would make him the butt of their jokes backstage. "He was far timider than they thought," Sissy explains to Louisa. Like Mayhew's street clown, Jupe can only wish his daughter out of the circus. And as self-esteem declines, his wishes for Sissy rise. It was "because he felt himself to be a poor, weak, ignorant, helpless man . . . that he wanted me so much to know a great deal, and be different from him."

He drinks and he weeps. Only when Sissy reads to him from what at the Stone Lodge would be forbidden books is he distracted from his sorrows, "wondering whether the sultan would let the lady go on with the story, or would have her head cut off before it was finished." Scheherezade's art, like his own, is a matter of life and death, and life depends on approval of the audience. "But they wouldn't laugh sometimes, and then father cried." His audience laughs less and less, and he comes home drunk, beats the dog and falls to the floor, weeping. On the day that he left Sissy behind he came home in tears from another dismal performance. "At last poor father said that he had given no satisfaction again, and never did give any satisfaction now, and that he was a shame and disgrace, and I should have done better without him all along." Shame, disgrace, and tears seem to be the lot of the clown.

THE CLOWN'S GUISE

The novel runs its course between the first and last appearances of Sleary's Horse-Riding. When the circus returns, shame and disgrace have devolved upon Thomas Gradgrind and his son. It is then that we see them as sad clowns wearing the mark of their fall. The misguided "whelp" has embezzled money from Bounderby's bank and is being helped to escape through Sleary's good offices. Gradgrind Sr. comes with Louisa and Sissy to meet Tom at the Horse-Riding where he has been incorporated into the act in the disguise of a blackface clown. The children thus return to the circus from which they once had been dragged. When the show is over, "Mr. Gradgrind sat down forlorn, on the Clown's performing chair in the middle of the ring." On one of the benches beyond the otherwise empty ring his son appears, "ridiculously shameful . . . in his comic livery." Seeing both in the guise of clowns, we are reminded of the father's misguidance and the son's sloth. Gradgrind's model family has failed, and when we look at the whelp as a clown we see that a certain kind of art—or artifice—has also failed. The disgrace of some clowns becomes the shame of all, and in *Hard Times* these exemplars of an art that appears to be comic and socially regenerative are made to suffer, and, what is worse, made to appear worthy of their punishment.

MR. SLEARY'S LISP

Sena Jeta Naslund describes how the reader—to understand what Sleary says—must pronounce the sentences as if he or she were Sleary.

"Thith ith a bad piethe of bithnith, thith ith."

"I conthider that I lay down the philothophy of the thubject when I thay to you, Thquire, make the betht of uth; not the wurtht!"

Thus spake Mr. Sleary, "who was troubled with asthma, and whose breath came far too thick and heavy for the letters." In addition to having a speech impediment, Mr. Sleary also has "one fixed eye and one loose eye." Yet Mr. Sleary, who is also stout and flabby and has a head muddled by his fondness for "Therry" or "a glath of bitterth," is surely the most whole character of a novel strikingly concerned with the question of how we achieve wholeness and interconnectedness in ourselves and in society. . . .

Mr. Sleary's centrality to the vision of the novel consists not only of what he is and what he does but also in the fact that to understand what Mr. Sleary says or means at all, the reader must play Sleary's role. *Sotto voce,* the reader mouths his way through Sleary's sentences. Part of the meaning of *Hard Times* is that the imagination makes it possible to identify with other people and the parts that they play and thus to sympathize with them. Dickens insures that Sleary's words will not be rec-

For one thing, they are not funny. Both Dickens and Henry Mayhew [author of *London Labour and the London Poor*] allude to an audience that laughs, but neither is willing to leave his reader with an impression that what the clown does actually deserves laughter. In the sketch of Astley's we are given this little dialogue between the clown and the ringmaster at a pause in Miss Woolford's riding act. The clown begins—

> "I say, sir!" —"Well, sir?" (it's always conducted in the politest manner). —"Did you ever happen to hear I was in the army, sir?" —"No, sir." —"Oh, yes, sir—I can go through my exercise, sir." —"Indeed, sir!" —"Shall I do I it now, sir?" —"If you please, sir; come, sir—make haste" (a cut with the long whip, and "Ha' done now—I don't like it," from the clown). Here the clown throws himself on the ground, and goes through a variety of gymnastic convulsions, doubling himself up, and untying himself again, and making himself look very like a man

ognized merely visually by the reader: the reader *cannot* recognize "thith" as an English word. However, when he pronounces it to himself, like a child learning to read, "thith" resolves itself into "this." The reader has had to speak like Sleary, to be Sleary for the moment, in order to grasp the meaning.

This special technique of engaging the reader's active participation in Sleary's role is pecularily appropriate for the medium of print. In the quite excellent recent production of *Hard Times* for television, Mr. Sleary was not given a lisp. An audience hearing a character in a play lisp is not in the same position as a reader who must himself re-create the lisp in order to understand what he's reading. Dickens's creation of Sleary is one of his strokes of genius that cannot be equivalently represented in film.

"Tho that both thides may be equally theen" it should be admitted that a reader could memorize a formula starting with "th = s" and visually replace the *th*'s, but it seems to take one less far from the story to sound out the sentence and to let its meaning take shape as one participates in the utterance. I think that this is the kind of reading that Dickens counts on from his public, and it makes the manner of apprehending Sleary's total meaning congruent with his message. We cannot be literal in looking at his words; we must be imaginative.

Sena Jeter Naslund, "Mr. Sleary's Lisp: A Note on *Hard Times*," *Dickens Studies Newsletter*, June 1981.

in the most hopeless extreme of human agony, to the vocifer-
ous delight of the gallery, until he is interrupted by a second
cut from the long whip.

Dickens goes on to recite "similar witticisms" and to record
"the delight of every member of the audience," but we are
left with a sense that the act itself is vacuous and that the
laughter, following convulsions and whippings, is somewhat sinister. Mayhew's judgment of the street clown's comedy is untouched with irony: "He told me several of his jests;
they were all of the most venerable kind, as for instance:
—'A horse has ten legs: he has two forelegs and two hind
ones. Two fores are eight, and two others are ten.' The other
jokes were equally puerile."

At the end of *Hard Times,* before Sissy and Louisa recognize the whelp hidden in the act at Sleary's, they are de-
tained if not diverted by a clown show. The personages of
the Astley's act—ringmaster, bareback rider, and clown—
rehearse a similarly inane joke which serves to draw out the
tension of the larger scene.

Mr. Sleary had only made one cut at the Clown with his long
whip-lash, and the Clown had only said, "If you do it again,
I'll throw the horse at you!" when Sissy was recognised both
by father and daughter. But they got through the Act with
great self-possession; and Mr. Sleary, saving for the first in-
stant, conveyed no more expression into his locomotive eye
than into his fixed one. The performance seemed a little long
to Sissy and Louisa, particularly when it stopped to afford the
Clown an opportunity of telling Mr. Sleary (who said, "Indeed, sir!" to all his observations in the calmest way, and with
his eye on the house) about two legs sitting on three legs
looking at one leg, when in came four legs, and laid hold of
one leg, and up got two legs, caught hold of three legs, and
threw 'em at four legs, who ran away with one leg. For, although an ingenious Allegory relating to a butcher, a three-
legged stool, a dog, and a leg of mutton, this narrative con-
sumed time; and they were in great suspense.

Sorrowful off stage and inane on. How then do we take the
apology of the "philosophical" Sleary that punctuates the
novel at beginning and end? "Don't be croth with uth poor
vagabondth. People mutht be amuthed. They can't be alwayth
a learning, nor yet they can't be alwayth a working, they an't
made for it. You *mutht* have uth, Thquire. Do the withe thing
and the kind thing too, and make the betht of uth; not the
wurtht!" If this defense of comic art is based on what we know
of clowns in *Hard Times* and elsewhere in Dickens, it is fairly
desperate. "You *mutht* have uth," becomes a kind of warning:

make the best of us. In Gradgrind's world this would mean—
we are useless paupers but we do serve to amuse people; we
neither advance work nor instruction; we are, in fact, a bur-
den but one that *must* be borne. Or a necessary evil appealing
to the baser and duller side of man, a side that cannot be ignored, like original sin. Or a corrective element, a dose of
which is necessary to make the working world work.

DICKENS'S DOUBTS

Dickens is speaking to himself. His sense of the clownish element includes his own doubts. (By saying "clownish" instead of "comic" I acknowledge the negative charge, the side
of the clown that does not amuse and is not amused.) Dickens would seem to throw a bit of himself into the admoni-
tory reproof of the ringmaster. For amusement's sake he can
turn the tawdry clown into comedy through his playful treatment of the subject. Otherwise the clown is a vehicle for his
sense of the shallowness of mere amusement. People must
be amused but only after "working" and "learning," and
even then a glance backstage reveals something much more
grim. In *Hard Times* the clown wrests a concession from
Gradgrind and from Dickens himself.

But only a concession. Sissy could not remain in Sleary's
menagerie any more than Nicholas Nickleby could remain
with the Crummles troupe in Portsmouth. Both are bidden
to another world. The circus in *Hard Times* is an alien place,
not quite urban, not quite English, and its inhabitants are not
quite human. It may be instructive and exemplary, but it is
impossible. Even when their father leaves, Sissy still could
choose this world. Sleary offers her one kind of family
where the bonds are all the stronger for its acrobatic and
professional precariousness; Gradgrind offers her another.
Sleary offers apprenticeship to the circus art; Gradgrind offers "a sound practical education" which Sissy knows to
have been her father's interest. Gradgrind's condition is that
she break all ties with the circus, that, as he says later, she
even *forget* her past connection. "From this time you begin
your history. . . . You will be reclaimed and formed." The
rigidity of this separation is mistaken and, luckily, also impossible. Sissy cannot be wholly reformed to match his own
lost children. But when she is removed from the circus
world, she is in a sense reclaimed for the other world which
is, after all, Gradgrind's world.

CHAPTER 2

Dickens and the Industrial World

READINGS ON

HARD TIMES

Dickens's Critique of Materialism

Edgar Johnson

Edgar Johnson sees *Hard Times* as "an analysis and a condemnation of the ethos of industrialism"—a culmination of social criticism that extends from *Dombey and Son* to *Bleak House.* The author tells why he finds *Hard Times* a piercing morality drama in both thought and technique, and why the novel has been unpopular with many readers. Johnson has written and edited a number of books, including *Charles Dickens: His Tragedy and Triumph,* from which the following critical essay is excerpted. Johnson's other publications include *The Heart of Charles Dickens: His Letters to Angela Burdett Coutts* and *A Treasury of Satire.*

Hard Times brings to a culmination an orderly development of social analysis that extends in Dickens's work form *Dombey and Son* through *Bleak House.* That development has its roots, indeed, far earlier, and is to be found, although fragmentarily, in the social attitudes underlying *Oliver Twist* and the prison scenes of *Pickwick Papers.* With *Dombey and Son,* however, Dickens achieved his first clear picture of the workings of a monetary society; and even while he was still writing that story he underlined his hostility to Mr. Dombey's world through Scrooge and the fantasy of *A Christmas Carol.* Although *David Copperfield* is mainly an exploration of personal emotion, the social comment is an organic part of its pattern. It lurks in the legal morasses of Doctors' Commons and runs through the conscienceless exploitation of child labor in the bottling warehouse; its emphasis on money is as clear in the ostentatious display of Mr. Spenlow as in the mean rapacity of Uriah Heep; its spiritual essence is painted in Steerforth's cynical middle-class indifference to the hu-

Excerpted from *Charles Dickens: His Tragedy and Triumph,* by Edgar Johnson. Copyright © 1952, 1977, 1980 by Edgar Johnson. Reprinted by permission of Georges Borchardt, Inc., for the author.

manity of the poor and the callousness of his seduction of Little Em'ly.

Bleak House carries on that analysis to a detailed examination the rotten workings of the social system in almost every major institution and activity of society. Except for one: the operations of that colossus of mechanized industry that had swollen its dominion until it had almost all of modern society subjected to its power. That power Dickens saw as an inhuman, life-denying tyranny. *Bleak House* reveals the monstrous tentacles of acquisitive power in general, crushing human fulfillment in its foggy coils. *Hard Times* deals with industrial power, but is not so much a picture of its ramifications as a presentation of its underlying principles. It is an analysis and a condemnation of the ethos of industrialism.

These facts partly explain why *Hard Times* has been unpopular with many readers and has been disliked by most critics. People could laugh unrestrainedly at Dick Swiveller and Pecksniff and Micawber, who can only amuse, not hurt us, but no such irresponsible mirth is possible with Bounderby and Gradgrind, who have the world appallingly under their control. In Dickens's earlier novels it had been easy to think of him as a warm-hearted, unphilosophic humanitarian indignant at individual cruelties. Even in *Bleak House* the reader might not realize the total meaning of the indictment, and could comfort himself by imagining that Dickens was merely prejudiced against some groups in society—lawyers, moneylenders, members of the aristocracy, politicians. But there is a desperate endeavor among commentators to ignore or belittle the dark masterpieces of Dickens's maturity because they will not let us close our eyes on the clamorous problems that threaten us with disaster. The harsh truth of Mr. Merdle and the Circumlocution Office in *Little Dorrit* is dismissed as "twaddle," and *Our Mutual Friend*'s astringent satire on Podsnap and the Veneerings as mere clowning in a dusty desert of a book. Except for a few critics such as F.R. Leavis, who do not care for Dickens's earlier work, only radicals and revolutionaries like Ruskin and Bernard Shaw have praised *Hard Times*.

INDICTING INDUSTRIALISM

For in *Hard Times* there is no mistaking Dickens's violent hostility to industrial capitalism and its entire scheme of life. Here he is proclaiming a doctrine not of individual but of social sin, unveiling what he now sees as the real state of modern society. "This," Shaw says, "is Karl Marx, Carlyle, Ruskin, Morris, Carpenter, rising up against civilization itself as a disease, and declaring that it is not our disorder but our order that is horrible; that it is not our criminals but our magnates that are robbing and murdering us; and that it is not merely Tom-ail-Alone's that must be demolished and abolished, pulled down, rooted up, and made for ever impossible so that nothing shall remain of it but History's record of its infancy, but our entire social system." "Here you will find," Shaw continues, "no more villains and heroes, but only oppressors and victims, oppressing and suffering in spite of themselves, driven by a huge machinery which grinds to pieces the people it should nourish and ennoble, and having for its directors the basest and most foolish of us instead of the noblest and most farsighted." And thus, he summarizes, the indignation with which Dickens began "has spread and deepened into a passionate revolt against the whole industrial order of the modern world."

The change that reaches its climax in *Hard Times*, however, is not only in revolutionary thought, it is in method as well. And this disturbs still another group of Dickens's readers, grown used to a profusion of comic episode and a tremendous crowded canvas thronged with characters almost as numerous as life itself, all painted in vivid contrasting scenes of light and dark with a brilliant external realism. This is the method of *Dombey* and of *Bleak House*, those complicated and elaborate literary structures like some enormous medieval building whose bays and wings and niches are filled with subordinate figures and with bright genre groups of all kinds clustering in a hundred patterns ranging from grotesque fancy to portraits from nature.

Had Dickens been following this method in *Hard Times*, he would have had scenes among the clerks in Bounderby's bank like those in Mr. Dombey's countinghouse and scenes among the hands in Bounderby's factories like those of pasting on the labels in Murdstone and Grinby's warehouse. He would have had scenes of a cotton spinner getting tangled in the threads of his loom as comic as the marchioness smiting herself on the chin with her corkscrew, and extended scenes of clamorous industrial activity as vivid as the brief glimpses of glaring furnace mouths in Little Nell's nocturnal wanderings through the Black Country. He would have had scenes of the home lives of the factory laborers as warm as those of the Toodle family, and as grim as those of the brickmakers in *Bleak House.* All this would have been no less easy for Dickens's creative vitality, perhaps even easier, than the technique he did follow. Dictated partly, no doubt, by the need of compressing his story into a short novel of brief weekly installments, that technique was even more determined by Dickens's resolution to make it a formidable and concentrated blow against the iniquity of a heartless materialism.

COKETOWN

In consequence, *Hard Times* is a morality drama, stark, formalized, allegorical, dominated by the mood of piercing through to the underlying *meaning* of the industrial scene rather than describing it in minute detail. Therefore Coketown, which might be Hanley, Preston, Birmingham, or Leeds, or, for that matter, Fall River or Pittsburgh, is drawn once for all in a few powerful strokes: "It was a town of red brick, or of brick that would have been red if the smoke and ashes had allowed it; but as matters stood it was a town of unnatural red and black like the painted face of a savage. It was a town of machinery and tall chimneys, out of which interminable serpents of smoke trailed themselves for ever and ever, and never got uncoiled. It had a black canal in it, and a river that ran purple with ill-smelling dye, and vast piles of buildings full of windows where there was a rattling and a trembling all day long, and where the piston of the steam-engine worked monotonously up and down like the head of an elephant in a state of melancholy madness. It contained several large streets all very like one another, and many small streets still more like one another, inhabited by people equally like one another, who all went in and out at the same hours, with the same sound upon the same pavements, to do the same work, and to whom every day was the same as yesterday and tomorrow, and every year the counterpart of the last and the next."

"The streets were hot and dusty on the summer day, and the sun was so bright that it even shone through the heavy vapour drooping over Coketown, and could not be looked at steadily. Stokers emerged from low underground doorways into factory yards, and sat on steps, and posts, and palings, wiping their swarthy visages, and contemplating coals. The whole town seemed to be frying in oil. There was a stifling

smell of hot oil everywhere. The steam-engines shone with
it, the dresses of the Hands were soiled with it, the mills
throughout their many stories oozed and trickled with it.
The atmosphere of those Fairy palaces was like the breath of
the simoom: and their inhabitants, wasting with the heat,
toiled languidly in the desert. But no temperature made the
melancholy mad elephants more mad or more sane. Their
wearisome heads went up and down at the same rate, in hot
weather and cold, wet weather and dry, fair weather and
foul. The measured motion of their shadows on the walls,
was the substitute Coketown had to show for the shadows of
rustling woods; while, for the summer hum of insects, it
could offer, all the year round, from the dawn of Monday to
the night of Saturday, the whir of shafts and wheels."

"Seen from a distance, in such weather, Coketown lay
shrouded in a haze of its own, which appeared impervious
to the sun's rays. You could only know the town was there,
because you knew there could have been no such sulky
blotch upon the prospect without a town. A blur of soot and
smoke, now confusedly tending this way, now that way, now
aspiring to the vault of Heaven, now murkily creeping along
the earth, as the wind rose and fell, or changed its quarter: a
dense formless jumble, with sheets of cross light in it, that
showed nothing but masses of darkness:—Coketown in the
distance was suggestive of itself, though not a brick of it
could be seen."

Every packed detail of this entire setting is surcharged
with significant emotional and intellectual comment, and
every character among the small unified group, symbolic
and stylized, who act out their drama in the gritty industrial
world, serves to deepen and intensify the meaning. Josiah
Bounderby, banker and manufacturer, is its blatant greed
and callous inhumanity in action. Thomas Gradgrind, retired wholesale hardware dealer, man of facts and figures, is
the embodiment of utilitarian economic theory and its endeavor to dry up life into statistical averages. Young Thomas
Gradgrind, devoted first and only to his own advantage, is
the mean product of the paternal theories—"that not unprecedented triumph of calculation which is usually at work
on number one." The daughter Louisa is their predestined
tragic victim going to her doom, in her face "a light with
nothing to rest upon, a fire with nothing to burn." The consummate achievement of Mr. Gradgrind's system is repre-

sented by Bitzer, one of the pupils graduated from the day school founded by Gradgrind: for Bitzer everything is a matter of bargain and sale, accessible to no appeal except that of self-interest.

In contrast to these, Sissy Jupe, the strolling juggler's child, spending her childhood among the acrobats and equestrians of Sleary's Horse-riding, symbolizes everything in human nature that transcends the soul-crushing hideousness and mere instrumentalism of Coketown: she is vitality, generosity, uncalculating goodness. It is significant that she has been born and nourished among a people whose activities are not dominated by pure utility, but have at least some association with those of art, self-fulfilling, self-justified, and containing their ends within themselves. The contrast between her "dark-eyed and dark-haired" warmth, glowing with an inward sun-filled luster, and Bitzer's cold eyes and colorless hair and etiolated pallor, renders in pure sensation, as F.R. Leavis points out, the opposition between "the life that is lived freely and richly from the deep instinctive and emotional springs" and "the thin-blooded, quasi-mechanical product of Gradgrindery."

SPEECH

Nor does Dickens concern himself in *Hard Times* with any of the small tricks of verisimilitude in speech. The characters express themselves in a stylized idiom that is as far removed from everyday diction as it is true to the inward essence of their natures. Louisa speaks in a solemn poetry filled from the beginning with vibrant forewarnings of her destiny, and Sissy, the stroller's child, confronts Harthouse, the smart, sarcastic worldling, with the stern justice of an angelic messenger. Bounderby's housekeeper, Mrs. Sparsit, with her Roman nose and Coriolanian eyebrows, has a grotesque and mournful dignity of utterance fitting to a world of mad melodrama. And in the wild exuberance of his humor, Dickens allows Mr. Bounderby to talk with the extravagant absurdity of a figure in an insane harlequinade. When Mrs. Sparsit, rendered inarticulate by an inflamed throat and pathetic with sneezes, is trying in vain to tell Mr. Gradgrind that Louisa has deserted Bounderby for Harthouse, the aggrieved husband seizes and shakes her. "If you can't get it out, ma'am," he exclaims, "leave *me* to get it out. This is not a time for a lady, however highly connected, to be totally inaudible, and seemingly swallowing marbles."

In all Dickens's previous novels there had been scenes in which the characters burst into a theatrical diction of an ornate dignity or talked a gabble fantastically ridiculous. Nicholas and Ralph Nickleby assail each other in words of purple rhetoric and Edith Dombey addresses both her husband and Mr. Carker in the accents of a tragedy queen, but the successes Dickens achieves in such passages are won in the teeth of their language. And with Mrs. Nickleby, Sampson Brass, Pecksniff, Sairey Gamp, Captain Cuttle, Mr. Toots, and Jack Bunsby he had risen to heights of triumphant nonsense. "But now," as Shaw remarks, "it is no longer a question of passages;"—or even of an occasional character— "here he begins at last to exercise quite recklessly his power of presenting a character to you in the most fantastic and outrageous terms, putting into its mouth from one end of the book to the other hardly a word which could conceivably be uttered by any sane human being, and yet leaving you with an unmistakable and exactly truthful portrait of a character that you recognize at once as not only real but typical."

In the same way, the overtones of symbolism and allegory had always moved through Dickens's earlier novels, in solution, as it were, and only at times rendered in definite statement. They are implicit in the social myth of Little Nell's mad grandfather and his mania for the "shining yellow boys" seen against the stock-market-gambling fever of the 1840's. They glimmer in the Christmas pantomime transformation-scenes that end *Martin Chuzzlewit,* with old Martin as the beneficent Prospero bringing the pageant to a close. They are symmetrically balanced in the ice and frozen cupids of Mr. Dombey's dinner table and the warmth of the Little Midshipman where Florence and Captain Cuttle are the wandering princess and the good monster of a fairy tale. They emerge again in the image of Uriah Heep as an ugly and rebellious genie and Betsey Trotwood as the fairy godmother. They underlie that entire symbolic bestiary of wolves, tigers, cats, captive birds, flies, and spiders that moves among the fog and falling tenements and self-consuming rottenness of *Bleak House.* But in these novels, except for the last, the symbolism always lurked below the surface or played over it in a fanciful and exuberant embroidery of metaphor. Even in *Bleak House* symbolism had never taken charge, nor determined and limited every detail in the structure.

GRADGRINDISM

Hard Times opens, significantly, in a schoolroom. Here the children are to be indoctrinated in the tenets of practicality, encouraged to think of nothing except in terms of use, crammed full of information like so many "little vessels . . . ready to have imperial gallons of facts poured into them until they were full to the brim." "Now, what I want," Mr. Gradgring tells the schoolmaster, "is, Facts. Teach these boys and girls nothing but Facts. Facts alone are wanted in life. Plant nothing else and root out everything else. You can only form the minds of reasoning animals upon Facts: nothing else will every be of service to them. This is the principle on which I bring up my own children, and this is the principle on which I bring up these children. Stick to Facts, sir!"

In the Gradgrind world there are to be no imagination, no fancy, no emotion, only fact and the utilitarian calculus. When Sissy Jupe—"Girl number twenty," Mr. Gradgrind calls her, obliterating human identity itself in the blank anonymity of a number—defends her taste for a flowery-patterned carpet by saying, "I am very fond of flowers . . . and I would fancy—" the government inspector of schools pounces upon her triumphantly: "Ay, ay, ay! But you mustn't fancy. That's it! You are never to fancy"; and "You are not, Cecilia Jupe," Mr. Gradgrind repeats sepulchrally, "to do anything of that kind." "Fact, fact, fact!" says the government official. "Fact, fact, fact!" echoes Thomas Gradgrind.

For Sissy's loving humanity, though, this bleak factuality is quite impossible. "'Here are the stutterings,'" she misquotes her schoolteacher—"Statistics," corrects Louisa—of a town of a million inhabitants of whom only twenty-five starved to death in the course of a year. What does she think of that proportion? "I thought it must be just as hard on those who were starved whether the others were a million, or a million million." So "low down" is Sissy in "the elements of Political Economy" after eight weeks of study, that she has to be "set right by a prattler three feet high, for returning to the question, 'What is the first principle of this science?' the absurd answer, 'To do unto others as I would that they should do unto me.'"

Mr. Gradgrind's stand at school is the stand he takes among his own children at home. "No little Gradgrind had ever seen a face in the moon; it was up in the moon before it could speak distinctly. No little Gradgrind had ever learnt the silly jingle, Twinkle, twinkle, little star; how I wonder what you are! No little Gradgrind had ever known wonder on the subject, each little Gradgrind having at five years old dissected the Great Bear like a Professor Owen, and driven Charles's Wain like a locomotive engine-driver. No little Gradgrind had ever associated a cow in a field with that famous cow with the crumpled horn . . . or with that yet more famous cow who swallowed Tom Thumb: it had never heard of these celebrities, and had only been introduced to a cow as a graminivorous ruminating quadruped with several stomachs."

But the facts in which Gradgrindery is interested are only the cut-and-dried facts of intellectual definition, not the facts of living and breathing reality. It wants to learn nothing about the behavior of horses and how they are trained, which Sissy Jupe knows from Sleary's Horse-riding: "You musn't tell us about the ring, here." Instead, it trots out Bitzer's "definition of a horse": "Quadruped. Graminivorous. Forty teeth, namely twenty-four grinders, four eye-teeth, and twelve incisive. . . . Hoofs hard, but requiring to be shod with iron. Age known by marks in mouth."—"Now girl number twenty" says Mr. Gradgrind, "you know what a horse is."

The factual education approved by Mr. Gradgrind is identical in spirit with that which was inflicted upon John Stuart Mill and which left him in his young manhood despairingly convinced that his emotional and imaginative nature had been starved to death. Mr. M'Choakumchild, the schoolmaster, has been "turned out," with "some one hundred and forty other schoolmasters . . . in the same factory, on the same principles, like so many pianoforte legs. . . . Orthography, etymology, syntax, and prosody, biography, astronomy, geography, and general cosmography, the sciences of compound proportion, algebra, land-surveying and levelling, vocal music, and drawing from models, were all at the ends of his ten chilled fingers. He had worked his stony way into Her Majesty's most Honourable Privy Council's Schedule B, and had taken the bloom off the higher branches of mathematics and physical science, French, German, Latin, and Greek. He knew all about all the Water Sheds of all the world (whatever they are), and all the histories of all the peoples, and all the names of all the rivers and mountains, and all the productions, manners, and customs of all the countries, and all their boundaries and bearings on the two and thirty points of the compass. . . .

"He went to work in this preparatory lesson, not unlike Morgiana in the Forty Thieves: looking into all the vessels ranged before him, one after another, to see what they contained. Say, good M'Choakumchild. When from thy boiling store, thou shalt fill each jar brim fun by-and-by, dost thou think thou wilt always kill outright the robber Fancy lurking within—or sometimes only maim him and destroy him!"

HARD-FACTS PHILOSOPHY

The principles that dominate Mr. Gradgrind's school are the principles that dominate Coketown and its industry. His hard-facts philosophy is only the aggressive formulation of the inhumane spirit of Victorian materialism. In Gradgrind, though repellent, it is honest and disinterested. In Bounderby, its embodiment in the business world, with his bragging self-interest, it is nothing but greed for power and material success, Victorian "rugged individualism" in its vulgarest and ugliest form. And Bounderby is nothing but the practice of that business ethos, for which "the relations between master and man were all fact, and everything was fact between the lying-in hospital and the cemetery, and what you couldn't state in figures, or show to be purchasable in the cheapest market and saleable in the dearest, was not, and never should be, world without end, Amen."

The wonderful wit and insight with which Dickens withers laissez-faire capitalism is not to be lost sight of "because he chooses to speak," as Ruskin says, "in a circle of stage fire." Carlyle never voiced a more burning denunciation of the dismal science of classical economic theory or the heartlessness of "cash-nexus" as the only link between man and man. The hundred years that have passed since *Hard Times* was written have done hardly more to date the cant with which businessmen defend industrial exploitation than they have to brighten the drab and brutal thing. Laboring men who protested wanted "to be set up in a coach and six and to be fed on turtle soup and venison, with a gold spoon"; the laboring class "were a bad lot altogether, gentlemen," "restless," "never knew what they wanted," "lived upon the best, and bought fresh butter; and insisted upon Mocha coffee, and rejected all but prime parts of meat, and yet were eternally dissatisfied and unmanageable." As for the Labor unions: "the united masters" should not "allow of any such class combinations."

One more cluster of these sardonic clichés recalls the capitalists of our own day who were going to dispose of their
businesses and go to Canada if Franklin Delano Roosevelt
were re-elected. The Coketown industrialists, Dickens observes dryly, were always crying that they were ruined:
"They were ruined, when they were required to send labouring children to school; they were ruined when inspectors
were appointed to look into their works; they were ruined,
when such inspectors considered it doubtful whether they
were justified in chopping people up with their machinery;
they were utterly undone when it was hinted that perhaps
they need not always make quite so much smoke. . . . Whenever a Coketowner felt he was ill-used—that is to say, whenever be was not left entirely alone, and it was proposed to
hold him accountable for the consequences of any of his
acts—he was sure to come out with the awful menace that
he would 'sooner pitch his property into the Atlantic.' This
had terrified the Home Secretary within an inch of his life,
on several occasions.

"However, the Coketowners were so patriotic after all,
that they never had pitched their property into the Atlantic
yet, but, on the contrary, had been kind enough to take
mighty good care of it."

SLACKBRIDGE

The only weaknesses in Dickens's handling of the industrial
scene are his caricature of the union organizer Slackbridge
and his portrayal of that noble but dismal representative of
the laboring classes, Stephen Blackpool. Slackbridge, with
his windy and whining rhetoric ("Oh my friends and fellow-
countrymen, the slaves of an iron-handed and a grinding
despotism! Oh my friends and fellow-sufferers, and fellow-
workmen, and fellow-men!") is a figment of imagination.
"He was not so honest," Dickens says, as the workers he ad-
dressed, "he was not so manly, he was not so good-
humoured; he substituted cunning for their simplicity, and
passion for their safe solid sense. An ill-made, high-
shouldered man, with lowering brows, and his features
crushed into an habitually sour expression, he contrasted
most unfavourably, even in his mongrel dress, with the great
body of his hearers in their plain working clothes."

Such a description is a piece of sheer ignorance, not because union leaders cannot be windbags and humbugs as

other politicians can, but because labor organizers are not like Slackbridge and do not talk like him, and did not do so in Dickens's day any more than in ours. Dickens knew human nature too well not to know that fundamentally laboring men were like all men, and he knew domestic servants and artisans working for small tradesmen, but of the class manners and behavior of industrial laborers he had made no more than a superficial observation in some half-dozen trips through the Midlands. He had attended only one union meeting in his life, during the Preston strike in January, 1854. "It is much as if a tramp," Shaw comments with witty but not untruthful exaggeration, "were to write a description of millionaires smoking large cigars in church, with their wives in low-necked dresses and diamonds."

There is a possibility, to be sure, that the brief chapter in which Slackbridge appears was designed to reassure a middle-class audience that might otherwise grow restive and worried over the radical sound of the book. Dickens's own personal support of the labor movement, however, is unequivocally clear. He had already stated in *Household Words* his belief that laborers had the same right to organize that their employers had, and shortly after the conclusion of *Hard Times* he was to appeal to working men to force reforms from the Government. *Hard Times* itself burns with indignant sympathy for the injustice under which the workers suffered and is violent in its repudiation of Bounderby's career and Gradgrind's philosophy.

Hardly less typical of the laboring class than Slackbridge is the independent workman Stephen Blackpool, who is ostracized by his fellow workers for not joining the union and blacklisted by Mr. Bounderby for having the courage to defend their cause. Stephen's isolated stand cuts him off from the support of his own class and the patronage of the factory owners. For all this, it is in Stephen's mouth that Dickens puts a dark summation of the life of the industrial workers: "Look round town—so rich as 'tis—and see the numbers o' people as has been broughten into bein heer, for to weave, an to card, an to piece out a livin', aw the same one way, somehows, twixt their cradles and their graves. Look how we live, and wheer we live, an in what numbers, an by what chances, and wi' what sameness; and look how the mill is awlus a goin, and how they never works us no nigher to ony dis'ant object—'ceptin awlus Death."

And to Stephen, too, Dickens gives a denunciation of laissez faire and the hostile division it creates in society: "Let thousands upon thousands alone, aw leading the like lives and aw faw'en into the like muddle, and they will be as one, and yo will be as anoother, wi' a black impassable world betwixt yo, just as long or short a time as sitch-like misery can last. . . . Most o' aw, rating 'em as so much Power, and reg'latin 'em as if they was figures in a soom, or machines: wi'out loves and likens, wi'out memories and inclinations, wi'out souls to weary and souls to hope—when aw goes quiet, draggin' on wi' 'em as if they'd nowt o' th' kind, and when aw goes onquiet, reproachin 'em for their want o' sitch human feelins in their dealins wi' you—this will never do't, sir, till God's work is onmade."

DICKENS'S WARNING

When Stephen's crushed body is brought up from Old Hell Shaft into which he had stumbled, his dying words are as if the crushed people themselves were speaking from the pit into which the modern world had fallen: "I ha into the pit . . . as wi'in the knowledge o' old fok now livin, hundreds and hundreds o' men's lives—fathers, sons, brothers, dear to thousands an thousands, an keeping 'em fro' want and hunger. I ha' fell into a pit that ha' been wi' th' Fire-damp crueller than battle. I ha' read on't in the public petition, as onny one may read, fro' the men that works in the pits, in which they ha' pray'n and pray'n the lawmakers for Christ's sake not to let their work be murder to 'em, but to spare 'em for th' wives and children that they loves as well as gentlefok loves theirs. When it were in work, it killed wi'out need; when 'tis let alone, it kills wi'out need. See how we die an no need, one way an another—in a muddle—every day!"

And, in the end, as if from the depths of Old Hell Shaft Dickens sounds once more a prophetic warning to the "Utilitarian economists, skeletons of schoolmasters, Commissioners of Fact, genteel and used-up infidels, gabblers of many little dog's eared creeds," lest "in the day of [their] triumph, when romance is utterly driven out" of the souls of the poor, "and they and a bare existence stand face to face, Reality will take a wolfish turn and make an end of you."

Dickens's Portrait of the Modern World

George Bernard Shaw

In this widely read essay that originally appeared as an introduction to *Hard Times*, British author and dramatist George Bernard Shaw declares that "Dickens's occasional indignation has spread and deepened into a passionate revolt against the whole industrial order of the modern world." Unlike Dickens's earlier books, which target individual criminality, *Hard Times* seemingly indicts the entire social, political, and industrial life of England. Shaw asserts that *Hard Times*, in short, was written to make the reader feel threatened and uncomfortable. Despite the novel's bleak socioeconomic critique, Shaw goes on, Dickens "casts off, and casts off forever, all restraint on his wild sense of humor."

John Ruskin once declared *Hard Times* Dickens's best novel. It is worth while asking why Ruskin thought this, because he would have been the first to admit that the habit of placing works of art in competition with one another, and wrangling as to which is the best, is the habit of the sportsman, not of the enlightened judge of art. Let us take it that what Ruskin meant was that *Hard Times* was one of his special favorites among Dickens's books. Was this the caprice of fancy? or is there any rational explanation of the preference? I think there is.

Hard Times is the first fruit of that very interesting occurrence which our religious sects call, sometimes conversion, sometimes being saved, sometimes attaining to conviction of sin. Now the great conversions of the XIX century were not convictions of individual, but of social sin. The first half of the XIX century considered itself the greatest of all the centuries. The second discovered that it was the wickedest of all the cen-

Reprinted from George Bernard Shaw's introduction to the 1912 Waverly (London) edition of *Hard Times*.

turies. The first half despised and pitied the Middle Ages as
barbarous, cruel, superstitious, ignorant. The second half saw
no hope for mankind except in the recovery of the faith, the
art, the humanity of the Middle Ages. In Macaulay's *History of
England*, the world is so happy, so progressive, so firmly set
in the right path, that the author cannot mention even the National Debt without proclaiming that the deeper the country
goes into debt, the more it prospers. In Morris's *News from
Nowhere* there is nothing left of all the institutions that
Macaulay glorified except an old building, so ugly that it is
used only as a manure market, that was once the British
House of Parliament. *Hard Times* was written in 1854, just at
the turn of the half century; and in it we see Dickens with his
eyes newly open and his conscience newly stricken by the dis-
covery of the real state of England. In the book that went immediately before, *Bleak House,* he was still denouncing evils
and ridiculing absurdities that were mere symptoms of the
anarchy that followed the industrial revolution of the XVIII
and XIX centuries, and the conquest of political power by
Commercialism in 1832. In *Bleak House* Dickens knows nothing of the industrial revolution: he imagines that what is
wrong is that when a dispute arises over the division of the
plunder of the nation, the Court of Chancery, instead of settling the dispute cheaply and promptly, beggars the dis-
putants and pockets both their shares. His description of our
party system, with its Coodle, Doodle, Foodle, etc., has never
been surpassed for accuracy and for penetration of superficial
pretence. But he had not dug down to the bed rock of the imposture. His portrait of the ironmaster who visits Sir Leicester
Dedlock, and who is so solidly superior to him, might have
been drawn by Macaulay: there is not a touch of Bounderby
in it. His horrible and not untruthful portraits of the brickmakers whose abject and battered wives call them 'master',
and his picture of the now vanished slum between Drury
Lane and Catherine Street which he calls Tom All Alone's,
suggest (save in the one case of the outcast Jo, who is, like
Oliver Twist, a child, and therefore outside the old self-help
panacea of Dickens's time) nothing but individual delinquen-
cies, local plague-spots, negligent authorities.

THE HORROR OF COKETOWN

In *Hard Times* you will find all this changed. Coketown,
which you can see to-day for yourself in all its grime in the

Potteries (the real name of it is Hanley in Staffordshire on the London and North Western Railway), is not, like Tom All Alone's, a patch of slum in a fine city, easily cleared away, as Tom's actually was about fifty years after Dickens called attention to it. Coketown is the whole place; and its rich manufacturers are proud of its dirt, and declare that they like to see the sun blacked out with smoke, because it means that the furnaces are busy and money is being made; whilst its poor factory hands have never known any other sort of town, and are as content with it as a rat is with a hole. Mr Rouncewell, the pillar of society who snubs Sir Leicester with such dignity, has become Mr Bounderby, the selfmade humbug. The Chancery suitors who are driving themselves mad by hanging about the Courts in the hope of getting a judgment in their favor instead of trying to earn an honest living, are replaced by factory operatives who toil miserably and incessantly only to see the streams of gold they set flowing slip through their fingers into the pockets of men who revile and oppress them.

Clearly this is not the Dickens who burlesqued the old song of the Fine Old English Gentleman, and saw in the evils he attacked only the sins and wickednesses and follies of a great civilization. This is Karl Marx, Carlyle, Ruskin, Morris, Carpenter, rising up against civilization itself as against a disease, and declaring that it is not our disorder but our order that is horrible; that it is not our criminals but our magnates that are robbing and murdering us; and that it is not merely Tom All Alone's that must be demolished and abolished, pulled down, rooted up, and made for ever impossible so that nothing shall remain of it but History's record of its infamy, but our entire social system. For that was how men felt, and how some of them spoke, in the early days of the Great Conversion which produced, first, such books as the *Latter Day Pamphlets* of Carlyle, Dickens's *Hard Times*, and the tracts and sociological novels of the Christian Socialists, and later on the Socialist movement which has now spread all over the world, and which has succeeded in convincing even those who most abhor the name of Socialism that the condition of the civilized world is deplorable, and that the remedy is far beyond the means of individual righteousness. In short, whereas formerly men said to the victim of society who ventured to complain, 'Go and reform yourself before you pretend to reform Society', it now has to admit that until Society is reformed, no man can reform himself except in the most insignificantly small ways. He may cease picking your pocket of half crowns; but he cannot cease taking a quarter of a million a year from the community for nothing at one end of the scale, or living under conditions in which health, decency, and gentleness are impossible at the other, if he happens to be born to such a lot.

DICKENS'S GREATEST BOOK

John Ruskin, a contemporary of Dickens, asserts that Hard Times *is the author's greatest book, citing apparent Dickensian wit, insight, and purpose.*

The essential value and truth of Dickens's writings have been unwisely lost sight of by many thoughtful persons, merely because he presents his truth with some colour of caricature. Unwisely, because Dickens's caricature, though often gross, is never mistaken. Allowing for his manner of telling them, the things he tells us are always true. I wish that he could think it right to limit his brilliant exaggeration to works written only for public amusement; and when he takes up a subject of high national importance, such as that which he handled in *Hard Times,* that he would use severer and more accurate analysis. The usefulness of that work (to my mind, in several respects the greatest he has written) is with many persons seriously diminished because Mr Bounderby is a dramatic monster, instead of a characteristic example of a wordly master; and Stephen Blackpool a dramatic perfection, instead of a characteristic example of an honest workman. But let us not lose the use of Dickens's wit and insight, because he chooses to speak in a circle of stage fire. He is entirely right in his main drift and purpose in every book he has written; and all of them, but especially *Hard Times,* should be studied with close and earnest care by persons interested in social questions. They will find much that is partial, and, because partial, apparently unjust; but if they examine all the evidence on the other side, which Dickens seems to overlook, it will appear, after all their trouble, that his view was the finally right one, grossly and sharply told.

John Ruskin, *Cornhill Magazine,* August 1860.

You must therefore resign yourself, if you are reading Dickens's books in the order in which they were written, to bid adieu now to the lighthearted and only occasionally in-

dignant Dickens of the earlier books, and get such entertainment as you can from him now that the occasional indignation has spread and deepened into a passionate revolt
against the whole industrial order of the modern world.
Here you will find no more villains and heroes, but only oppressors and victims, oppressing and suffering in spite of
themselves, driven by a huge machinery which grinds to
pieces the people it should nourish and ennoble, and having
for its directors the basest and most foolish of us instead of
the noblest and most farsighted.

Many readers find the change disappointing. Others find
Dickens worth reading almost for the first time. The increase in strength and intensity is enormous: the power that
indicts a nation so terribly is much more impressive than
that which ridicules individuals. But it cannot be said that
there is an increase of simple pleasure for the reader,
though the books are not therefore less attractive. One cannot say that it is pleasanter to look at a battle than at a merry-
go-round; but there can be no question which draws the
larger crowd.

To describe the change in the readers' feelings more precisely, one may say that it is impossible to enjoy Gradgrind
or Bounderby as one enjoys Pecksniff or the Artful Dodger or
Mrs Gamp or Micawber or Dick Swiveller, because these
earlier characters have nothing to do with us except to
amuse us. We neither hate nor fear them. We do not expect
ever to meet them, and should not be in the least afraid of
them if we did. England is not full of Micawbers and Swiv-
ellers. They are not our fathers, our schoolmasters, our employers, our tyrants. We do not read novels to escape from
them and forget them: quite the contrary. But England is full
of Bounderbys and Podsnaps and Gradgrinds; and we are all
to a quite appalling extent in their power. We either hate and
fear them or else we are them, and resent being held up to
odium by a novelist. We have only to turn to the article on
Dickens in the current edition of the *Encyclopedia Britan-
nica* to find how desperately our able critics still exalt all
Dickens's early stories about individuals whilst ignoring or
belittling such masterpieces as *Hard Times, Little Dorrit,
Our Mutual Friend*, and even *Bleak House* (because of Sir
Leicester Dedlock), for their mercilessly faithful and pene-
trating exposures of English social, industrial, and political
life; to see how hard Dickens hits the conscience of the gov-

erning class; and how loth we still are to confess, not that we are so wicked (for of that we are rather proud), but so ridiculous, so futile, so incapable of making our country really prosperous. *The Old Curiosity Shop* was written to amuse you, entertain you, touch you; and it succeeded. *Hard Times* was written to make you uncomfortable; and it will make you uncomfortable (and serve you right) though it will perhaps interest you more, and certainly leave a deeper scar on you, than any two of its forerunners.

DICKENS'S HUMOR

At the same time you need not fear to find Dickens losing his good humor and sense of fun and becoming serious in Mr Gradgrind's way. On the contrary, Dickens in this book casts off, and casts off for ever, all restraint on his wild sense of humor. He had always been inclined to break loose: there are passages in the speeches of Mrs Nickleby and Pecksniff which are impossible as well as funny. But now it is no longer a question of passages: here he begins at last to exercise quite recklessly his power of presenting a character to you in the most fantastic and outrageous terms, putting into its mouth from one end of the book to the other hardly one word which could conceivably be uttered by any sane human being, and yet leaving you with an unmistakable and exactly truthful portrait of a character that you recognize at once as not only real but typical. Nobody ever talked, or ever will talk, as Silas Wegg talks to Boffin and Mr Venus, or as Mr Venus reports Pleasant Riderhood to have talked, or as Rogue Riderhood talks, or as John Chivery talks. They utter rhapsodies of nonsense conceived in an ecstasy of mirth. And this begins in *Hard Times.* Jack Bunsby in *Dombey and Son* is absurd: the oracles he delivers are very nearly impossible, and yet not quite impossible. But Mrs Sparsit in this book, though Rembrandt could not have drawn a certain type of real woman more precisely to the life, is grotesque from beginning to end in her way of expressing herself. Her nature, her tricks of manner, her way of taking Mr Bounderby's marriage, her instinct for hunting down Louisa and Mrs Pegler, are drawn with an unerring hand; and she says nothing that is out of character. But no clown gone suddenly mad in a very mad harlequinade could express all these truths in more extravagantly ridiculous speeches. Dickens's business in life has become too serious for troubling over the small change of verisimilitude, and denying himself and his readers the indulgence of his humor in inessentials. He even calls the schoolmaster M'Choakumchild, which is almost an insult to the serious reader. And it was so afterwards to the end of his life. There are moments when he imperils the whole effect of his character drawing by some overpoweringly comic sally. For instance, happening in *Hard Times* to describe Mr Bounderby as drumming on his hat as if it were a tambourine, which is quite correct and natural, he presently says that 'Mr Bounderby put his tambourine on his head, like an oriental dancer'. Which similitude is so unexpectedly and excruciatingly funny that it is almost impossible to feel duly angry with the odious Bounderby afterwards.

This disregard of naturalness in speech is extraordinarily entertaining in the comic method; but it must be admitted that it is not only not entertaining, but sometimes hardly bearable when it does not make us laugh. There are two persons in *Hard Times,* Louisa Gradgrind and Sissy Jupe, who are serious throughout. Louisa is a figure of poetic tragedy; and there is no question of naturalness in her case: she speaks from beginning to end as an inspired prophetess, conscious of her own doom and finally bearing to her father the judgment of Providence on his blind conceit. If you once consent to overlook her marriage, which is none the less an act of prostitution because she does it to obtain advantages for her brother and not for herself, there is nothing in the solemn poetry of her deadly speech that jars. But Sissy is nothing if not natural, and though Sissy is as true to nature in her character as Mrs Sparsit, she 'speaks like a book' in the most intolerable sense of the words. In her interview with Mr James Harthouse, her unconscious courage and simplicity, and his hopeless defeat by them, are quite natural and right; and the contrast between the humble girl of the people and the smart sarcastic man of the world whom she so completely vanquishes is excellently dramatic; but Dickens has allowed himself to be carried away by the scene into a ridiculous substitution of his own most literary and least colloquial style for any language that could conceivably be credited to Sissy.

'Mr Harthouse: the only reparation that remains with you is to leave her immediately and finally. I am quite sure that you can mitigate in no other way the wrong and harm you have done. I am quite sure that it is the only compensation you have left it in your power to make. I do not say that it is much, or that it is enough; but it is something, and it is necessary. Therefore, though without any other authority than I have given you, and even without the knowledge of any other person than yourself and myself, I ask you to depart from this place to-night, under an obligation never to return to it.'

This is the language of a Lord Chief Justice, not of the dunce of an elementary school in the Potteries.

SLACKBRIDGE AND TRADE UNIONS

But this is only a surface failure, just as the extravagances of Mrs Sparsit are only surface extravagances. There is, however, one real failure in the book. Slackbridge, the trade union organizer, is a mere figment of the middle-class imagination. No such man would be listened to by a meeting of English factory hands. Not that such meetings are less susceptible to humbug than meetings of any other class. Not that trade union organizers, worn out by the terribly wearisome and trying work of going from place to place repeating the same commonplaces and trying to 'stoke up' meetings to enthusiasm with them, are less apt than other politicians to end as windbags, and sometimes to depend on stimulants to pull them through their work. Not, in short, that the trade union platform is any less humbug-ridden than the platforms of our more highly placed political parties. But even at their worst trade union organizers are not a bit like Slackbridge. Note, too, that Dickens mentions that there was a chairman at the meeting (as if that were rather surprising), and that this chairman makes no attempt to preserve the usual order of public meeting, but allows speakers to address the assembly and interrupt one another in an entirely disorderly way. All this is pure middle-class ignorance. It is much as if a tramp were to write a description of millionaires smoking large cigars in church, with their wives in low-necked dresses and diamonds. We cannot say that Dickens did not know the working classes, because he knew humanity too well to be ignorant of any class. But this sort of knowledge is as compatible with ignorance of class manners and customs as with ignorance of foreign languages. Dickens knew certain classes of working folk very well: domestic servants, village artisans, and employees of petty tradesmen, for example. But of the segregated factory populations of our purely industrial towns he knew no more than an observant professional man can pick up on a flying visit to Manchester.

It is especially important to notice that Dickens expressly says in this book that the workers were wrong to organize themselves in trade unions, thereby endorsing what was perhaps the only practical mistake of the Gradgrind school that really mattered much. And having thus thoughtlessly adopted, or at least repeated, this error, long since exploded, of the philosophic Radical school from which he started, he turns his back frankly on Democracy, and adopts the idealized Toryism of Carlyle and Ruskin, in which the aristocracy are the masters and superiors of the people, and also the servants of the people and of God. Here is a significant passage.

> 'Now perhaps,' said Mr Bounderby, 'you will let the gentleman know how you would set this muddle (as you are so fond of calling it) to rights.'

> 'I donno, sir. I canna be expecten to't. Tis not me as should be looken to for that, sir. Tis they as is put ower me, and ower aw the rest of us. What do they tak upon themseln, sir, if not to do it?'

And to this Dickens sticks for the rest of his life. In *Our Mutual Friend* he appeals again and again to the governing classes, asking them with every device of reproach, invective, sarcasm, and ridicule of which he is master, what they have to say to this or that evil which it is their professed business to amend or avoid. Nowhere does he appeal to the working classes to take their fate into their own hands and try the democratic plan.

Another phrase used by Stephen Blackpool in this remarkable fifth chapter is important. 'Nor yet lettin alone will never do it.' It is Dickens's express repudiation of *laissez-faire.*

There is nothing more in the book that needs any glossary, except, perhaps, the strange figure of the Victorian 'swell', Mr James Harthouse. His pose has gone out of fashion. Here and there you may still see a man—even a youth—with a single eyeglass, an elaborately bored and weary air, and a little stock of cynicisms and indifferentisms contrasting oddly with a moral anxiety about his clothes. All he needs is a pair of Dundreary whiskers, like the officers in Desanges's military pictures, to be a fair imitation of Mr James Harthouse. But he is not in the fashion; he is an eccentric, as Whistler was an eccentric, as Max Beerbohm and the neo-dandies of the *fin de siècle* were eccentrics. It is now the fashion to be energetic, and hustle as American millionaires are supposed (rather erroneously) to hustle. But the soul of the swell is still unchanged. He has changed his name again and again, become a Masher, a Toff, a Johnny and what not; but fundamentally he remains what he always was, an Idler, and therefore a man bound to find some trick of thought and speech that reduces the world to a thing as empty and purposeless as himself. Mr Harthouse reappears, more seriously and kindly taken, as Eugene Wrayburn and Mortimer Lightwood in *Our Mutual Friend.* He reappears as a club in The Finches of the Grove of *Great Expectations.* He will reappear in all his essentials in fact and in fiction until he is at last shamed or coerced into honest industry and becomes not only unintelligible but inconceivable.

Note, finally, that in this book Dickens proclaims that marriages are not made in heaven, and that those which are not confirmed there, should be dissolved.

Dickens's Sociological Argument

Humphry House

Humphry House contends that Dickens's sociological argument that industry impoverishes human life renders *Hard Times* valuable and provocative. In his critique of the novel, House discusses labor and industry in the nineteenth century and how Dickens's misconceptions impacted his writing. Despite his praise for the novel's sociological message, however, House finds *Hard Times* imperfect in design. For example, the character Gradgrind is inadequate because Dickens "did not understand enough of any philosophy even to guy [ridicule] it successfully." Similarly, Blackpool fails because Dickens avoids "the proper tragic solution." House is the author of *The Dickens World*, from which the following essay is excerpted.

Though most readers find *Hard Times* dry and brain-spun, Dickens said of it himself that he had not meant to write a new story for a year, when the idea laid hold of him by the throat in a very violent manner.

What this central idea was there is no means of knowing; but it is plain that *Hard Times* is one of Dickens's most thought-about books. One of the reasons why, in the 1850s, his novels begin to show a greater complication of plot than before, is that he was intending to use them as a vehicle of more concentrated sociological argument. All his journalism shows too that he was *thinking* much more about social problems, whereas earlier he had been content to feel mainly, and to record a thought, when it occurred, in emotional dress. The objection to such a character as Gradgrind is not just that he is a burlesque and an exaggeration—so are Squeers and Pecksniff—but rather that in him the satire is

Excerpted from *The Dickens World*, 2nd ed., by Humphry House (Oxford: Oxford University Press, 1942). Reprinted by permission of Oxford University Press.

directed against a kind of thought: he is in fact the only major Dickens character who is meant to be an 'intellectual':
'His character was not unkind, all things considered; it
might have been a very kind one indeed if he had only made
some round mistake in the arithmetic that balanced it, years
ago.' Dickens was caught with the idea of a man living by a
certain philosophy, as in the past he had often been caught
with the idea of a man living by a master vice such as mis-
erhood or hypocrisy or pride. Such vices he understood, but
he did not understand enough of any philosophy even to be
able to guy it successfully. But he obviously felt during the
'fifties, when Public Health and Administrative Reform were
keeping him so closely to social-political problems, that
there must be some essential flaw in the reasoning of such
a man as Bright. The creation of Gradgrind is an attempt to
track it down. The despondent atmosphere of the whole
book reflects the failure to do so.

This atmosphere is concentrated in Stephen Blackpool. In
him Dickens tried to rescue the idea of personality in an individual industrial worker. Stephen's successive defeats by
the Law, by the Trade Union, and by his employer might
have become the material of genuine tragedy, if Dickens had
been prepared to accept his death from the beginning as inevitable and unanswerable; but he was hankering all the
time after a way to avoid the proper tragic solution, and the
result is nothing but a slow record of inglorious misery and
defeat. Dickens did not want to admit that Stephen's bargaining power—whether against Bounderby, his marriage,
or life itself—was negligible, but wrote as if there might be
an unexpected solution at every turn. There is no difficulty
about Stephen's relation to the Law or about his relation to
Bounderby; the true crux is in the part of the plot that deals
with the Trade Union, and in making it so Dickens was apparently trying to work out, in the actual writing of the book,
the implications of his old ideal of *man to man* benevolence
in the relations between employers and labour in large-scale
industry. Three points were emphasized in the treatment of
the Union—Stephen's inexplicable obstinacy in refusing to
join it; Dickens's hatred of Slackbridge; and the difference of
mood and attitude of the other workers towards Stephen as
men and as Union members under Slackbridge's influence.

For the Union meeting itself he did a thing which was very
rare for him—he deliberately went in search of copy, to Pre-

ston, to watch the effects of a strike of the cotton workers there which had dragged on for weeks. He seems to have gone expecting to find discontent, disorder, and even rioting, and his first impression caused surprise and a sort of sentimental gladness that everything was so quiet and the men generally so well-behaved. When he came to write up the visit for the article *On Strike* in *Household Words* (Feb. 11, 1954) there was overlaid upon this first impression a certain horror at the idleness. He seemed to be asking whether these were perhaps after all the lazy poor, in whose existence he had never believed. The article describes the two meetings of the strikers that he attended, and they are obviously the foundation for the Union meeting in *Hard Times:* it stresses their order and courtesy, the efficiency of the business and the competence of the men's local leaders; it decries the influence of an outside orator who is a prototype of Slackbridge; it makes clear that the men fully believed in the justice of their case, but that, at the same time, they had no hatred or resentment for most of the employers: it does, however, quote one example of a threatening notice against a particular man, together with various other placards and verses: the moral approval seems to be all on the side of the strikers. But the political conclusion is not that the strike is right:

> In any aspect in which it can be viewed, this strike and lock-out is a deplorable calamity. In its waste of time, in its waste of a great people's energy, in its waste of wages, in its waste of wealth that woke to be employed, in its encroachment on the means of many thousands who are laboring from day to day, in the gulf of separation it hourly deepens between those whose interests must be understood to be identical or must be destroyed, it is a great national affliction. But, at this pass, anger is of no use, starving out is of no use—for what will that do, five years hence, but overshadow all the mills in England with the growth a bitter remembrance?—political economy is a mere skeleton unless it has a little human covering and filling out, a little human bloom upon it, and a little human warmth in it.

The only practical suggestion is that the dispute should be submitted immediately to impartial arbitrators agreed upon by both sides. This paragraph is extremely important and interesting, because in it Dickens accepts the fundamental ethical and political proposition of the political economy he generally so much deplores. The interests of employers and employed must be assumed to be identical or must be destroyed. The doctrine of the identity of interests was common to the utilitarians and the economists: on the question of *theory* there is no real difference between Dickens and W.R. Greg: he is not in the least a Socialist.

GRADGRIND

This paragraph also helps to explain why the satire of Mr. Gradgrind is comparatively ineffective; for Dickens is not even intending to attack the whole philosophy which he thought was represented in the Manchester men; he is only attacking the excessive emphasis on statistics; in fact he is repeating Mr. Filer over again, and he seems to have no uneasiness about whether such satire is adequate or important. He is through all these years, however, extremely uneasy in his attempts to find a channel through which the desires and needs of an ordinary decent working man like Blackpool can find expression. Why, when he recognized the capacity of such men for conducting their own business, did he reject the Trade Union solution, and reject it as emphatically as a Manchester man like Greg?

On the whole the 'Combinations' of the 'thirties and 'forties, whether organized locally, by trades, or nationally, had avowed revolutionary aims. The extent to which their members advocated the use of physical force was less important than the fact that they were widely believed to do so; but, physical force aside, they were revolutionary in the sense that they did not accept the doctrine of the natural identity of interests between Capital and Labour, and were in their political activities more or less conscious of a class-struggle; and this consciousness was shared by their opponents. The Chartist failure of '48 meant widespread disillusionment in the possibilities of working-class political action, and the reviving unions of the 'fifties concentrated more on the immediate problem of collective bargaining within particular trades than on the formation of huge amalgamations with political aims. Dickens seems to have realized that this change was happening, but he shared two common popular misconceptions about it; the first was that the leaders of such unions were bound to be demagogic frauds like Gruffshaw and Slackbridge; and the second was that the unions were likely to violate liberty by being exclusive and tyrannical towards workers who refused to join them: both points were heavily underlined in *Hard Times*. The first of these objections was a legacy from the earlier amalgamating, revolutionary period, and was very largely justified. For in the period of Chartism and the large national unions the working-class movement was grotesquely top-heavy and therefore unstable: the middle-class mistrust of 'demagogues' and 'paid agitators', whatever its motives may have been, was justified in the sense that national leadership had not developed out of solidly organized cells of local opinion. Local organization even in the 'fifties was likely, as in the Preston strike, to be an *ad hoc* affair called into being by a particular dispute; and Dickens was faithful in his reporting, in *On Strike,* of the way that outside influence was likely to be overridden: but in *Hard Times* he regarded local opinion as dynamically inferior to Slackbridge's bluster: he meant to imply that Stephen was socially boycotted in spite of a predominating feeling in his favour, and the other workers bamboozled out of their better selves; and he made the distortion seem more serious by giving Stephen no better reason for not joining them than a mysterious promise. The objection to unions on the ground of exclusiveness and tyranny followed inevitably from the general misunderstanding of their nature: Dickens realized that when Stephen had been both boycotted by his fellow-workers and sacked by Bounderby he had no chance of getting another job; but he did not draw from this the conclusion that an individual worker *cannot* be the equal of an employer in bargaining power, and that the ideal bargaining for labour-price talked of by the economists only had any meaning when the bargaining was done by a unanimous combination. His emotional admiration for the conscientious blackleg was not based on any alternative argument. But he did not abandon all hope of finding some means other than the unions by which such men as Stephen might be politically and socially articulate; he was still groping after it later in the year in the address *To Working Men* and the other articles on Public Health we have already discussed.

However, the failure of *Hard Times* in two main strands of its plot and in so many of its major characters does not lessen the force of the mixture of fascination and repulsion that Dickens felt for the industrial scene in which the book was set. The fascination, which appears in the descriptions of the night railway journey out from Coketown to Bounderby's house, of the people surging around mills in the morning, and returning at night to their various homes, has the interest in life and movement, which is plain everywhere in his work, heightened by greater speed and tension. The repulsion is generally more marked, as it is in the Black Country parts of *The Old Curiosity Shop;* the dismal appearance of the competing chapels, the rigidity of the Bounderby bank and the grim business discipline which intrudes on every detail even of domestic life, express once more the Southerner's dismay at what he could not assimilate; but underlying it there is unresting indignation at the impoverishment of human life that such things implied. This indignation is not crude and immature anger, but rather a disturbed mood that colours every perception, contributing a great deal to the unpopularity of *Hard Times.* The book is ultimately unsatisfying and oddly uncomfortable to nearly all its readers; but this very fact is the main thing that has to be considered in assessing its value as a novel; unanswerable disquiet was normal among the very few who were not misled into the easy optimism in which Bagehot typifies the 'fifties; Ruskin's exaggerated praise of *Hard Times* may be understood as a recognition that a work of art, by conveying this at least to others, might make up for many other imperfections; and even those writers whose economics and social criticism were more solid and thoughtful than Dickens's betray in their own ways shifting of opinion and misplacement of emphasis— Mill, Ruskin, and Arnold are examples—which equally, express the practical embarrassment of the time.

CHAPTER 3

Dickens Reconsidered

Hard Times: An Analytic Note

F.R. Leavis

The following essay, written in 1947 by British critic
F.R. Leavis, resulted in a flood of renewed critical interest in *Hard Times*. In contrast to many critics who
find *Hard Times* flawed and less significant than
other works by Dickens, Leavis calls the novel the
"one that has all the strength of [Dickens's] genius,
together with a strength no other of them can show—
that of a completely serious work of art." Leavis's influential essay was included as a final chapter in his
book *The Great Tradition*, a study of English fiction
published in 1948.

Hard Times is not a difficult work; its intention and nature
are pretty obvious. If, then, it is the masterpiece I take it for,
why has it not had general recognition? To judge by the critical record, it has had none at all. If there exists anywhere an
appreciation, or even an acclaiming reference, I have missed
it. In the books and essays on Dickens, so far as I know them,
it is passed over as a very minor thing; too slight and in-
significant to distract us for more than a sentence or two
from the works worth critical attention. Yet, if I am right, of
all Dickens's works it is the one that has all the strength of
his genius, together with a strength no other of them can
show—that of a completely serious work of art.

A MORAL FABLE

The answer to the question asked above seems to me to bear
on the traditional approach to 'the English novel'. For all the
more sophisticated critical currency of the last decade or
two, that approach still prevails, at any rate in the appreciation of the Victorian novelists. The business of the novelist,
you gather, is to 'create a world', and the mark of the master

Excerpted from *The Great Tradition*, by F.R. Leavis, published by Chatto & Windus.
Reprinted with permission from the Executors of the F.R. Leavis Estate and the Ran-
dom House Group, Ltd.

is external abundance—he gives you lots of 'life'. The test of life in his characters (he must above all create 'living' characters) is that they go on living outside the book. Expectations as unexacting as these are not, when they encounter significance, grateful for it, and when it meets them in that insistent form where nothing is very engaging as 'life' unless its relevance is fully taken, miss it altogether. This is the only way in which I can account for the neglect suffered by Henry James's *The Europeans*, which may be classed with *Hard Times* as a moral fable—though one might have supposed that James would enjoy the advantage of being approached with expectations of subtlety and closely calculated relevance. Fashion, however, has not recommended his earlier work, and this (whatever appreciation may be enjoyed by *The Ambassadors*) still suffers from the prevailing expectation of redundant and irrelevant 'life'.

I need say no more by way of defining the moral fable than that in it the intention is peculiarly insistent, so that the representative significance of everything in the fable—character, episode, and so on—is immediately apparent as we read. Intention might seem to be insistent enough in the opening of *Hard Times*, in that scene in Mr. Gradgrind's school. But then, intention is often very insistent in Dickens, without its being taken up in any inclusive significance that informs and organizes a coherent whole; and, for lack of any expectation of an organized whole, it has no doubt been supposed that in *Hard Times* the satiric irony of the first two chapters is merely, in the large and genial Dickensian way, thrown together with melodrama, pathos and humour—and that we are given these ingredients more abundantly and exuberantly elsewhere. Actually, the Dickensian vitality is there, in its varied characteristic modes, which have the more force because they are free of redundance: the creative exuberance is controlled by a profound inspiration.

DICKENS'S COMPREHENSIVE VISION

The inspiration is what is given in the grim clinch of the title, *Hard Times*. Ordinarily Dickens's criticisms of the world he lives in are casual and incidental—a matter of including among the ingredients of a book some indignant treatment of a particular abuse. But in *Hard Times* he is for once possessed by a comprehensive vision, one in which the inhumanities of Victorian civilization are seen as fostered and sanctioned by a hard philosophy, the aggressive formulation of an inhumane spirit. The philosophy is represented by Thomas Gradgrind, Esquire, Member of Parliament for Coketown, who has brought up his children on the lines of the experiment recorded by John Stuart Mill as carried out on himself. What Gradgrind stands for is, though repellent, nevertheless respectable; his Utilitarianism is a theory sincerely held and there is intellectual disinterestedness in its application. But Gradgrind marries his eldest daughter to Josiah Bounderby, 'banker, merchant, manufacturer', about whom there is no disinterestedness whatever, and nothing to be respected. Bounderby is Victorian 'rugged individualism' in its grossest and most intransigent form. Concerned with nothing but self-assertion and power and material success, he has no interest in ideals or ideas—except the idea of being the completely self-made man (since, for all his brag, he is not that in fact). Dickens here makes a just observation about the affinities and practical tendency of Utilitarianism, as, in his presentment of the Gradgrind home and the Gradgrind elementary school, he does about the Utilitarian spirit in Victorian education.

All this is obvious enough. But Dickens's art, while remaining that of the great popular entertainer, has in *Hard Times,* as he renders his full critical vision, a stamina, a flexibility combined with consistency, and a depth that he seems to have had little credit for. Take that opening scene in the school-room:

> "'Girl number twenty,'" said Mr. Gradgrind, squarely pointing with his square forefinger, "I don't know that girl. Who is that girl?"

> "'Sissy Jupe, sir,'" explained number twenty, blushing, standing up, and curtsying.

> "'Sissy is not a name,'" said Mr. Gradgrind. "Don't call yourself Sissy. Call yourself Cecilia."

> "'It's father as call me Sissy, sir,'" returned the young girl in a trembling voice, and with another curtsy.

> "'Then he has no business to do it,'" said Mr. Gradgrind. "Tell him he mustn't. Cecilia Jupe. Let me see. What is your father?"

> "'He belongs to the horse-riding, if you please, sir.'"

> 'Mr. Gradgrind frowned, and waved off the objectionable calling with his hand.

> "'We don't want to know anything about that here. You mustn't

tell us about that here. Your father breaks horses, don't he?"

"'If you please, sir, when they can get any to break, they do break horses in the ring, sir."

"'You mustn't tell us about the ring here. Very well, then. Describe your father as a horse-breaker. He doctors sick horses, I dare say?"

"'Oh, yes, sir!'"

"'Very well, then. He is a veterinary surgeon, a farrier, and horse-breaker. Give me your definition of a horse."

(Sissy Jupe thrown into the greatest alarm by this demand.)

"'Girl number twenty unable to define a horse!" said Mr. Gradgrind, for the, general benefit of all the little pitchers. "Girl number twenty possessed of no facts in reference to one of the commonest animals! Some boy's definition of a horse. Bitzer, yours."

"'Quadruped. Graminivorous. Forty teeth, namely, twenty-four grinders, four eye-teeth, and twelve incisive. Sheds coat in the spring; in marshy countries, sheds hoofs too. Hoofs hard, but requiring to be shod with iron. Age known by marks in mouth." Thus (and much more) Bitzer.'

Lawrence himself, protesting against harmful tendencies in education, never made the point more tellingly. Sissy has been brought up among horses, and among people whose livelihood depends upon understanding horses but 'we don't want to know anything about that here'. Such knowledge isn't real knowledge. Bitzer, the model pupil, on the button's being pressed, promptly vomits up the genuine article, 'Quadruped. Graminivorous', etc.; and 'Now, girl number twenty, you know what a horse is'. The irony, pungent enough locally, is richly developed in the subsequent action. Bitzer's aptness has its evaluative comment in his career. Sissy's incapacity to acquire this kind of 'fact' or formula, her unaptness for education, is manifested to us, on the other band, as part and parcel of her sovereign and indefeasible humanity: it is the virtue that makes it impossible for her to understand, or acquiesce in, an ethos for which she is 'girl number twenty', or to think of any other human being as a unit for arithmetic.

POETRY AND SYMBOLISM

This kind of ironic method might seem to commit the author to very limited kinds of effect. In *Hard Times*, however, it associates quite congruously, such is the flexibility of Dickens's art, with very different methods; it co-operates in a truly dramatic and profoundly poetic whole. Sissy Jupe, who might be taken here for a merely conventional *persona*, has already, as a matter of fact, been established in a potently symbolic rôle: she is part of the poetically-creative operation of Dickens's genius in *Hard Times*. Here is a passage I omitted from the middle of the excerpt quoted above:

> 'The square finger, moving here and there, lighted suddenly on Bitzer, perhaps because he chanced to sit in the same ray of sunlight which, darting in at one of the bare windows of the intensely white-washed room, irradiated Sissy. For the boys and girls sat on the face of an inclined plane in two compact bodies, divided up the centre by a narrow interval; and Sissy, being at the corner of a row on the sunny side, came in for the beginning of a sunbeam, of which Bitzer, being at the corner of a row on the other side, a few rows in advance, caught the end. But, whereas the girl was so dark-eyed and dark-haired that she seemed to receive a deeper and more lustrous colour from the sun when it shone upon her, the boy was so light-eyed and light-haired that the self-same rays appeared to draw out of him what little colour be ever possessed. His cold eyes would hardly have been eyes, but for the short ends of lashes which, by bringing them into immediate contrast with something paler than themselves, expressed their form. His short-cropped hair might have been a mere continuation of the sandy freckles on his forehead and face. His skin was so unwholesomely deficient in the natural tinge, that he looked as though, if he were cut, he would bleed white."

There is no need to insist on the force—representative of Dickens's art in general in *Hard Times*—with which the moral and spiritual differences are rendered here in terms of sensation, so that the symbolic intention emerges out of metaphor and the vivid evocation of the concrete. What may, perhaps, be emphasized is that Sissy stands for vitality as well as goodness—they are seen, in fact, as one; she is generous, impulsive life, finding self-fulfilment in self-forgetfulness—all that is the antithesis of calculating self-interest. There is an essentially Laurentian suggestion about the way in which 'the dark-eyed and dark-haired' girl, contrasting with Bitzer, seemed to receive a 'deeper and more lustrous colour from the sun', so opposing the life that is lived freely and richly from the deep instinctive and emotional springs to the thin-blooded, quasi-mechanical product of Gradgrindery.

Sissy's symbolic significance is bound up with that of Sleary's Horse-riding where human kindness is very insistently associated with vitality.

The way in which the Horse-riding takes on its significance illustrates beautifully the poetic-dramatic nature of Dickens's art. From the utilitarian schoolroom Mr. Gradgrind walks towards his utilitarian abode, Stone Lodge, which, as Dickens evokes it, brings home to us concretely the model regime that for the little Gradgrinds (among whom are Malthus and Adam Smith) is an inescapable prison. But before he gets there he passes the back of a circus booth, and is pulled up by the sight of two palpable offenders. Looking more closely, 'what did he behold but his own metallurgical Louisa peeping through a hole in a deal board, and his own mathematical Thomas abasing himself on the ground to catch but a hoof of the graceful equestrian Tyrolean flower act!' The chapter is called 'A Loophole', and Thomas 'gave himself up to be taken home like a machine'.

Representing human spontaneity, the circus-athletes represent at the same time highly-developed skill and deftness of kinds that bring poise, pride and confident ease—they are always buoyant, and ballet-dancer-like, in training:

> 'There were two or three handsome young women among them, with two or three husbands, and their two or three mothers, and their eight or nine little children, who did the fairy business when required. The father of one of the families was in the habit of balancing the father of another of the families on the top of a great pole; the father of the third family often made a pyramid of both those fathers, with Master Kidderminster for the apex, and himself for the base; all the fathers could dance upon rolling casks, stand upon bottles, catch knives and balls, twirl band-basins, ride upon anything, jump over everything, and stick at nothing. All the mothers could (and did) dance upon the slack wire and tight-rope, and perform rapid acts on bare-backed steeds; none of them were at all particular in respect of showing their legs; and one of them, alone in a Greek chariot, drove six-in-hand into every town they came to. They all assumed to be mighty rakish and knowing, they were not very tidy in their private dresses, they were not at all orderly in their domestic arrangements, and the combined literature of the whole company would have produced but a poor letter on any subject. Yet there was a remarkable gentleness and childishness about these people, a special inaptitude for any kind of sharp practice, and an untiring readiness to help and pity one another, deserving often of as much respect, and always of as much generous construction, as the every-day virtues of any class of people in the world.'

Their skills have no value for the Utilitarian calculus, but they express vital human impulse, and they minister to vital human needs. The Horse-riding, frowned upon as frivolous and wasteful by Gradgrind and malignantly scorned by Bounderby, brings the machine-hands of Coketown (the spirit-quenching hideousness of which is hauntingly evoked) what they are starved of. It brings to them, not merely amusement, but art, and the spectacle of triumphant activity that, seeming to contain its end within itself, is, in its easy mastery, joyously self-justified. In investing a travelling circus with this kind of symbolic value Dickens expresses a profounder reaction to industrialism than might have been expected of him. It is not only pleasure and relaxation the Coketowners stand in need of; he feels the dreadful degradation of life that would remain even if they were to be given a forty-four hour week, comfort, security and fun. We recall a characteristic passage from D.H. Lawrence.

'The car ploughed uphill through the long squalid straggle of Tevershall, the blackened brick dwellings, the black slate roofs, glistening their sharp edges, the mud black with coal-dust, the pavements wet and black. It was as if dismalness had soaked through and through everything. The utter negation of natural beauty, the utter negation of the gladness of life, the utter absence of the instinct for shapely beauty which every bird and beast has, the utter death of the human intuitive faculty was appalling. The stacks of soap in the grocers' shops, the rhubarb and lemons in the greengrocers'! the awful hats in the milliners all went by ugly, ugly, ugly, followed by the plaster and gilt horror of the cinema with its wet picture anouncements, "A Woman's Love," and the new big Primitive chapel, primitive enough in its stark brick and big panes of greenish and raspberry glass in the windows. The Wesleyan chapel, higher up, was of blackened brick and stood behind iron railings and blackened shrubs. The Congregational chapel, which thought itself superior, was built of rusticated sandstone and had a steeple, but not a very high one. Just beyond were the new school buildings, expensive pink brick, and gravelled playground inside iron railings, all very imposing, and mixing the suggestion of a chapel and a prison. Standard Five girls were having a singing lesson, just finishing the la-me-do-la exercises and beginning a "sweet children's song." Anything more unlike song, spontaneous song, would be impossible to imagine: a strange bawling yell followed the outlines of a tune. It was not like animals: animals *mean* something when they yell. It was like nothing on earth, and it was called singing. Connie sat and listened with her heart in her boots, as Field was filling petrol. What could possibly become of such a people, a people in whom the living intuitive faculty was dead as nails, and only queer mechanical yells and uncanny will-power remained?'

Dickens couldn't have put it in just those terms, but the way in which his vision of the Horse-riders insists on their gracious vitality implies that reaction.

SENTIMENTAL FALSITY

Here an objection may be anticipated—as a way of making a point. Coketown, like Gradgrind and Bounderby, is real enough; but it can't be contended that the Horse-riding is real in the same sense. There would have been some athletic skill and perhaps some bodily grace among the people of a Victorian travelling circus, but surely so much squalor, grossness and vulgarity that we must find Dickens's symbolism sentimentally false? And 'there was a remarkable gentleness and childishness about these people, a special inaptitude for any kind of sharp practice'—that, surely, is going ludicrously too far?

If Dickens, intent on an emotional effect, or drunk with moral enthusiasm, had been deceiving himself (it couldn't have been innocently) about the nature of the actuality, he would then indeed have been guilty of sentimental falsity, and the adverse criticism would have held. But the Horse-riding presents no such case. The virtues and qualities that Dickens prizes do indeed exist, and it is necessary for his critique of Utilitarianism and industrialism, and for (what is the same thing) his creative purpose, to evoke them vividly. The book can't, in my judgment, be fairly charged with giving a misleading representation of human nature. And it would plainly not be intelligent criticism to suggest that anyone could be misled about the nature of circuses by *Hard Times*. The critical question is merely one of tact: was it well-judged of Dickens to try to do *that*—which had to be done somehow—with a travelling circus?

Or, rather, the question is: by what means has be succeeded? For the success is complete. It is conditioned partly by the fact that, from the opening chapters, we have been tuned for the reception of a highly conventional art—though it is a tuning that has no narrowly limiting effect. To describe at all cogently the means by which this responsiveness is set up would take a good deal of 'practical criticism' analysis—analysis that would reveal an extraordinary flexibility in the art of *Hard Times*. This can be seen very obviously in the dialogue. Some passages might come from an ordinary novel. Others have the ironic pointedness of the school-room scene in so insistent a form that we might be reading a work as stylized as Jonsonian comedy: Gradgrind's final exchange with Bitzer (quoted below) is a supreme instance. Others again are 'literary', like the conversation between Gradgrind and Louisa on her flight home for refuge from Mr. James Harthouse's attentions.

GENIUS OF VERBAL EXPRESSION

To the question how the reconciling is done—there is much more diversity in *Hard Times* than these references to dialogue suggest—the answer can be given by pointing to the astonishing and irresistible richness of life that characterizes the book everywhere. It meets us everywhere, unstrained and natural, in the prose. Out of such prose a great variety of presentations can arise congenially with equal vividness. There they are, unquestionably 'real'. It goes back to an extraordinary energy of perception and registration in Dickens. 'When people say that Dickens exaggerates', says Santayana, 'it seems to me that they can have no eyes and no ears. They probably only have *notions* of what things and people are; they accept them conventionally, at their diplomatic value'. Settling down as we read to an implicit recognition of this truth, we don't readily and confidently apply any criterion we suppose ourselves to hold for distinguishing varieties of relation between what Dickens gives us and a normal 'real'. His flexibility is that of a richly poetic art of the word. He doesn't write 'poetic prose'; he writes with a poetic force of evocation, registering with the responsiveness of a genius of verbal expression what he so sharply sees and feels. In fact, by texture, imaginative mode, symbolic method, and the resulting concentration, *Hard Times* affects us as belonging with formally poetic works.

There is, however, more to be said about the success that attends Dickens's symbolic intention in the Horse-riding; there is an essential quality of his genius to be emphasized. There is no Hamlet in him, and he is quite unlike Mr. Eliot.

The red-eyed scavengers are creeping

From Kentish Town and Golders Green

—there is nothing of that in Dickens's reaction to life. He observes with gusto the humanness of humanity as exhibited in the urban (and suburban) scene. When he sees, as he sees so readily, the common manifestations of human kindness, and

the essential virtues, asserting themselves in the midst of ugliness, squalor and banality, his warmly sympathetic response has no disgust to overcome. There is no suggestion for
instance, of recoil—or of distance-keeping—from the game-
eyed, brandy-soaked, flabby-surfaced Mr. Sleary, who is suc
cessfully made to figure for us a humane, anti-Utilitarian
positive. This is not sentimentality in Dickens, but genius,
and a genius that should be found peculiarly worth attention
in an age when, as D.H. Lawrence (with, as I remember,
Wyndham Lewis immediately in view) says, 'My God! they
stink' tends to be an insuperable and final reaction.

SENTIMENTALITY

Dickens, as everyone knows, is very capable of sentimentality. We have it in *Hard Times* (though not to any seriously
damaging effect) in Stephen Blackpool, the good, victimized
working-man, whose perfect patience under infliction we are
expected to find supremely edifying and irresistibly touching
as the agonies are piled on for his martyrdom. But Sissy Jupe
is another matter. A general description of her part in the fable might suggest the worst, but actually she has nothing in
common with Little Nell: she shares in the strength of the
Horse-riding. She is wholly convincing in the function Dickens assigns to her. The working of her influence in the Utilitarian home is conveyed with a fine tact, and we do really feel
her as a growing potency. Dickens can even, with complete
success, give her the stage for a victorious *tête-à-tête* with the
well-bred and languid elegant, Mr. James Harthouse, in
which she tells him that his duty is to leave Coketown and
cease troubling Louisa with his attentions:

> 'She was not afraid of him, or in any way disconcerted; she
> seemed to have her mind entirely preoccupied with the oc-
> casion of her visit, and to have substituted that consideration
> for herself.'

The quiet victory of disinterested goodness is wholly convincing.

At the opening of the book Sissy establishes the essential
distinction between Gradgrind and Bounderby. Gradgrind, by
taking her home, however ungraciously, shows himself capable of humane feeling, however unacknowledged. We are reminded, in the previous school-room scene, of the Jonsonian
affinities of Dickens's art, and Bounderby turns out to be consistently a Jonsonian character in the sense that he is inca-

pable of change. He remains the blustering egotist and brag-gart, and responds in character to the collapse of his marriage:

> "'I'll give *you* to understand, in reply to that, that there un-questionably is an incompatibility of the first magnitude—to be summed up in this—that your daughter don't properly know her husband's merits, and is not impressed with such a sense as would become her, by George! of the honour of his alliance. That's plain speaking, I hope.'"

He remains Jonsonianly consistent in his last testament and death. But Gradgrind, in the nature of the fable, has to *experience* the confutation of his philosophy, and to be capable of the change involved in admitting that life has proved him wrong. (Dickens's art in *Hard Times* differs from Ben Jonson's not in being inconsistent, but in being so very much more flexible and inclusive—a point that seemed to be worth making because the relation between Dickens and Jonson has been stressed of late, and I have known unfair conclusions to be drawn from the comparison, notably in respect of *Hard Times*.)

The confutation of Utilitarianism by life is conducted with great subtlety. That the conditions for it are there in Mr. Gradgrind he betrays by his initial kindness, ungenial enough, but properly rebuked by Bounderby, to Sissy. 'Mr. Gradgrind', we are told, 'though hard enough, was by no means so rough a man as Mr. Bounderby. His character was not unkind, all things considered; it might have been very kind indeed if only he had made some mistake in the arithmetic that balanced it years ago'. . . .

LOUISA AND TOM

The psychology of Louisa's development and of her brother Tom's is sound. Having no outlet for her emotional life except in her love for her brother, she lives for him, and marries Bounderby—under pressure from Tom—for Tom's sake ('What does it matter?'). Thus, by the constrictions and starvations of the Gradgrind *régime*, are natural affection and capacity for disinterested devotion turned to ill. As for Tom, the *régime* has made of him a bored and sullen whelp, and 'he was becoming that not unprecedented triumph of calculation which is usually at work on number one'—the Utilitarian philosophy has done that for him. He declares that when he goes to live with Bounderby as having a post in the bank, 'he'll have his revenge'.—'I mean, I'll enjoy myself a little, and go about and see something and hear something.

I'll recompense myself for the way in which I've been brought up'. His descent into debt and bank-robbery is natural. And it is natural that Louisa, having sacrificed herself for this unrepaying object of affection, should be found not altogether unresponsive when Mr. James Harthouse, having sized up the situation, pursues his opportunity with well-bred and calculating tact. His apologia for genteel cynicism is a shrewd thrust at the Gradgrind philosophy:

> '"The only difference between us and the professors of virtue or benevolence, or philanthropy—never mind the name—is, that we know it is all meaningless, and say so; while they know it equally, and will never say so."
>
> 'Why should she be shocked or warned by this reiteration? It was not so unlike her father's principles, and her early training, that it need startle her.'

When, fleeing from temptation, she arrives back at her father's house, tells him her plight, and, crying, 'All I know is, your philosophy and your teachings will not save me', collapses, he sees 'the pride of his heart and the triumph of his system lying an insensible heap at his feet'. The fallacy now calamitously demonstrated can be seen focused in that 'pride', which brings together in an illusory oneness the pride of his system and his love for his child. What that love is Gradgrind now knows, and he knows that it matters to him more than the system, which is thus confuted (the educational failure as such being a lesser matter). There is nothing sentimental here; the demonstration is impressive, because we are convinced of the love, and because Gradgrind has been made to exist for us as a man who has 'meant to do right'. . . .

CRITICISM

Criticism, of course, has its points to make against *Hard Times*. It can be said of Stephen Blackpool, not only that he is too good and qualifies too consistently for the martyr's halo, but that he invites an adaptation of the objection brought, from the negro point of view, against Uncle Tom, which was to the effect that he was a white man's good nigger. And certainly it doesn't need a working-class bias to produce the comment that when Dickens comes to the Trade Unions his understanding of the world he offers to deal with betrays a marked limitation. There were undoubtedly professional agitators, and Trade Union solidarity was undoubtedly often asserted at the expense of the individual's rights, but it is a score against a work so insistently typical in intention that it should give the representative rôle to the agitator, Slackbridge, and make Trade Unionism nothing better than the pardonable error of the misguided and oppressed, and, as such, an agent in the martyrdom of the good working man. (But to be fair we must remember the conversation between Bitzer and Mrs. Sparsit:

> "'It is much to be regretted,' said Mrs. Sparsit, making her nose more Roman and her eyebrows more Coriolanian in the strength of her severity, "that the united masters allow of any such class combination.'"
>
> "'Yes, ma'am,' said Bitzer.
>
> "'Being united themselves, they ought one and all to set their faces against employing any man who is united with any other man,' said Mrs. Sparsit.
>
> "'They have done that, ma'am,' returned Bitzer; "but it rather fell through, ma'am.'"
>
> "'I do not pretend to understand these things,' said Mrs. Sparsit with dignity. ". . . I only know that those people must be conquered, and that it's high time it was done, once and for all.'")

Just as Dickens has no glimpse of the part to be played by Trade Unionism in bettering the conditions he deplores, so, though he sees there are many places of worship in Coketown, of various kinds of ugliness, he has no notion of the part played by religion in the life of nineteenth-century industrial England. The kind of self-respecting steadiness and conscientious restraint that he represents in Stephen did certainly exist on a large scale among the working-classes, and this is an important historical fact. But there would have been no such fact if those chapels described by Dickens had had no more relation to the life of Coketown than he shows them to have.

Again, his attitude to Trade Unionism is not the only expression of a lack of political understanding. Parliament for him is merely the 'national dust-yard', where the 'national dustmen' entertain one another 'with a great many noisy little fights among themselves', and appoint commissions which fill blue-books with dreary facts and futile statistics— of a kind that helps Gradgrind to 'prove that the Good Samaritan was a bad economist'.

Yet Dickens's understanding of Victorian civilization is adequate for his purpose; the justice and penetration of his criticism are unaffected. And his moral perception works in alliance with a clear insight into the English social structure. Mr. James Harthouse is necessary for the plot; but he too has his representative function. He has come to Coketown as a prospective parliamentary candidate, for 'the Gradgrind party wanted assistance in cutting the throats of the Graces', and they 'liked fine gentlemen; they pretended that they did not, but they did'. And so the alliance between the old ruling class and the 'hard' men figures duly in the fable. This economy is typical. There is Mrs. Sparsit, for instance, who might seem to be there merely for the plot. But her 'husband was a Powler', a fact she reverts to as often as Bounderby to his mythical birth in a ditch; and the two complementary opposites, when Mr. James Harthouse, who in his languid assurance of class-superiority doesn't need to boast, is added, form a trio that suggests the whole system of British snobbery.

But the packed richness of *Hard Times* is almost incredibly varied, and not all the quoting I have indulged in suggests it adequately. The final stress may fall on Dickens's command of word, phrase, rhythm and image: in ease and range there is surely no greater master of English except Shakespeare. This comes back to saying that Dickens is a great poet: his endless resource in felicitously varied expression is an extraordinary responsiveness to life. His senses are charged with emotional energy, and his intelligence plays and flashes in the quickest and sharpest perception. That is, his mastery of 'style' is of the only kind that matters—which is not to say that he hasn't a conscious interest in what can be done with words; many of his felicities could plainly not have come if there had not been, in the background, a habit of such interest.

Hard Times Once More

Malcolm Pittock

In his 1998 reading of *Hard Times,* scholar Malcolm
Pittock disputes critics, most notably F.R. Leavis, who
overvalued the novel. Although Pittock acknowledges
Dickens's creative genius, he finds that *Hard Times*
falls short of greatness on several counts. Foremost,
Dickens's manipulation of plot and character is strikingly conspicuous, revealing a slew of discrepancies
and highlighting the author's own prejudices. In this
vein, Dickens's rigid portrait of Gradgrindism is
strikingly biased while the countervailing ideal of
the circus as warm and humane is overly sentimental. Pittock's recent publications have discussed
George Orwell and Leo Tolstoy.

There appears to me to be something worrying about the way
an extremely high valuation of Dickens's achievement is assumed as a matter of course: a long tradition of adverse criticism has not been answered so much as quietly silenced. . . .

If one is to continue to make the claims for Dickens that
are currently made, one really has to answer, not ignore or
face down, the views of older critics. It is, indeed, a sobering
experience to read through Heinz Reinhold's seven hundred
page study, *Charles Dickens und das Zeitalter des Naturalis-
mus und der Ästhetischen Bewegung,* where, with the sys-
tematic thoroughness characteristic of German scholarship,
he shows that, in the later nineteenth and earlier twentieth
century, there was virtual transcontinental consensus that
Dickens had severe limitations and that there were many
things essential for a great novelist that he couldn't or didn't
do well.

The case made by such critics was still basically accepted
up to the mid-century. It is there in Humphry House, in the
Leavis of the *Great Tradition,* and in Marius Bewley's comparison of Dickens to a vintage car: 'The deceptive tone of

Excerpted from "Taking Dickens to Task," by Malcolm Pittock, *The Cambridge Quarterly,* vol. 27, no. 2 (1998), pp. 107–128. Reprinted by permission of Oxford University
Press Journals.

the motor at the beginning of the journey lulls us from thinking of the breakdown that will almost certainly occur a few miles down the road'. That seems to me admirably put and corresponds to my own response to Dickens and, as Reinhold shows, that of thousands of readers before me. Because Bewley wrote that in 1952 doesn't make it old hat.

GENIUS VERSUS PERFORMANCE

Dickens's genius is not in question, merely his actual performance. It is that we must scrutinise closely, not taking intention for achievement. And so, in the rest of this article, I want, in the spirit of that older criticism, to examine in detail the first novel of Dickens for which what appear to me inflated claims were made: *Hard Times*. Not that F.R. Leavis's view persuaded everybody. Critics like John Holloway and Douglas Jefferson felt that the novel did not adequately depict the historical reality it claimed to represent. But it was easy in the current climate to dismiss such evaluations as reflecting an irrelevant and simple-minded historicism. John Peck in the relevant volume in the New Casebook series criticises Jefferson's allegedly 'old fashioned approach' for example. But even if the consensus was not complete, with whichever minor disagreements and emphases Leavis's high valuation of *Hard Times* is still dominant.

In looking again at that novel, I want, of course, to raise issues that are more general. My purpose being to reinstate a way of looking at Dickens which has been lost sight of precludes my attempting a balanced general appraisal of his achievement. Though I believe, and shall try to show, that the attempt to see Dickens as a radical novelist profoundly critical of his society is mistaken, I think a serious case can be made out for him on quite different grounds. We need now to see Dickens in the context of his immense influence on the European novel and to try to isolate those characteristics which were to lead to Kafka and even Beckett (cf. the opening paragraphs of *Murphy*). But that is not my concern here.

Rereading Leavis's essay on *Hard Times*, I wondered why it had proved so persuasive. His long analytic exposition implicitly assumed that the novel was in need of interpretation. But there is no evidence that *Hard Times* had ever been seriously misunderstood. Those who thought little of it—and they were in the majority—knew well enough what Dickens was about but, none the less, wrote the novel off as a didactic tract. Leavis, however, came to meet Dickens more than half-way; like Ruskin and Shaw before him (the great exceptions), he agreed with what the Victorians would have called Dickens's message to such an extent that he thought that if the official meaning of the novel were expounded at length with periodical pats on the back for its author, others would accept his valuation of it. Unfortunately he was right.

It should have been obvious, however, that Leavis's critical acumen was beginning to desert him. This was unmistakable in his extravagant praise for Mrs Gradgrind's death-bed scene ('With this kind of thing before us, we talk not of style but of dramatic creation and imaginative genius.'). Admittedly, the scene contains one brilliant touch ('"I think there's a pain somewhere in the room, . . . but I couldn't positively say that I have got it"') but, otherwise, it has Dickens's all-too-familiar easy, quasi-humorous sentimentality, with touches of religious unction. And, though Leavis realised that Slackbridge and Blackpool would not do, he was uncritical about Sissy, a weakness which heralds his equally uncritical view of Amy Dorrit, while his wife's favourable view of Esther Summerson, contrasts with Charlotte Brontë's unfavourable one. Leavis, for example, has only praise for the tableau-like contrast between Sissy and Bitzer in Book One, Chapter 2 (stage-lighting courtesy of the sun). But physical appearance is not the expression of moral character and it is a degenerate form of neo-Platonism to pretend that it is. Bitzer is unfortunate enough to be an albino: that is all. (Compare Turgenev: 'Basistov was of robust build, with a simple face, and large nose, thick lips, and *small porcine eyes*, ugly and awkward, but kind-hearted, honest, and direct.' [my italics].)

OPPORTUNISM

As a novelist, Dickens is limited not only by a disabling sentimentality but by his refusal (or inability?) to imagine a situation in the round if it cuts across an effect he wants at the moment. He cannot allow himself to consider that, though it might be in order to represent Mrs Clennam's hysterical paralysis as being terminated by shock, muscle wastage would have effectively prevented her from running out of the room. However, the damage done by such opportunism is not confined to isolated incidents, but can bring into question Dickens's fundamental seriousness. Thus in *Bleak House*, he wants the law to be the inhuman agency of self-interested inefficiency which causes heartbreak and wastes not only material resources but life itself by its endless delays. By *Little Dorrit,* like the editor of a tabloid newspaper, he has switched off yesterday's campaign and switched on today's. The Circumlocution Office, a rather fuzzy alliance between Civil Servants and Ministers, has become the new *bête noire,* which is pilloried in much the same terms as the old. Meanwhile, the law, for no good reason, appears to have mysteriously pulled its socks up. It only requires the efforts of a rent-collector, the son of a turnkey, and some professional help from a solicitor to secure for Mr Dorrit 'a great estate that had long lain unknown of, unclaimed, and accumulating'. Whatever happened to Jarndyce v. Jarndyce? There is something close to effrontery, too, in such a barefaced plot device (naturally we hear no more of this providential estate, which appears, moreover, to run itself).

In *Hard Times,* there are several minor examples of Dickens's opportunism, which I shall mention first before showing more significant examples of it and, more generally, how Dickens's attempts to impose a merely rhetorical unity on much that is contradictory, incoherent and prejudiced. Thus the reader is cheated into believing that Tom has murdered Blackpool; but in order to do this Dickens has to represent Tom as being sure that Blackpool will not return, a certainty which, since he *hasn't* murdered Blackpool, he couldn't possibly have. Dickens resorts to a similar dodge when he tricks the reader at the end of Bk. 2, Chap. 12, into thinking that Louisa has eloped with Harthouse, or that in Bk. 3, Chap. 5, the title, 'Found', refers to Stephen Blackpool and not Mrs Pegler. Then there is the stale melodrama whereby Blackpool's apparent willingness to allow his wife to poison herself is frustrated by Rachael in the nick of time: and the creative irresponsibility of introducing Adam Smith and Malthus Gradgrind to make a broad satirical point, only apparently to terminate their existence at once: real children do not disappear so conveniently. Even Coketown despite having '. . . streets still more like another . . .' can suddenly change into a place 'where the chimneys . . . were built into an immense variety of stunted and crooked shapes . . .', while any shop at all like the squalid one, which, I take it, is meant to be representative, could hardly have provided the new and crusty bread, fresh butter and lump sugar with which Blackpool regales his guests. . . .

DISCREPANCIES

If one begins to question *Hard Times*, the structure which sustains the didactic message . . . begins to buckle. Let me take, as a start, a glaring discrepancy in the presentation of Stephen Blackpool which no one seems to have noticed (an oxymoron which could be true only of Dickens). For Blackpool, keeping a promise is a matter of fundamental integrity ("". . . he'd die a hundred deaths, ere ever he'd break his word""). So important is it to him that no one can release him from a promise once given—not even the person to whom he made it (""'Tis gone fro' me, for ever""). And so he is prevented from joining the union merely because he has promised not to: nothing else. And he did so in response to Rachael's concern lest he get into trouble, though, ironically, it is the promise *not* to join which does just that. None the less, because of his principles, Rachael cannot release him from his undertaking even in the light of changed circumstances. There is something heroic in such integrity, but also something perverse, as it is unreasonable to maintain that even the person to whom a promise was made cannot release you from it. None the less, Blackpool's behaviour is quite conceivable: such excessive scrupulosity does exist. However, when Blackpool married he didn't make a promise to a human being, he swore an oath to God, from which he could not have even the offer of release, that his union with his wife would be dissolved only by death: 'in sickness and in health . . . till death us do part. . .'. That he wants to be released from this oath, if the law allows it, is, of course, the *raison d'être* of his visit to Bounderby. There is an obvious contradiction here: for Blackpool, a promise is sacred but an oath is not, and a great novelist like, say, Tolstoy, would have been interested in the kind of personality, itself a perfectly credible one, which is a stickler for the lesser commitment while wanting to escape from the greater. But Dickens—and this alone tells us why with all his gifts he falls short as a novelist—shows no awareness that he has created such a character or even that there is an inconsistency, although he actually makes Bounderby remark to Stephen that he did not take his wife "". . . for fast and for loose; but for better for worse.""

Again, this inconsistency in Blackpool's character arises from opportunism. Dickens, probably from self-interested reasons, wanted to criticise the then state of the law relating to divorce, and saw that he could use Stephen as a vehicle for this. However, at the same time, he wanted Blackpool to be rejected both by his fellow-workers and by management in the shape of Bounderby: but if he had refused to join the union for political or religious reasons, it would probably have been a little more difficult to engineer his repudiation by Bounderby, who would surely have been inclined to regard him favourably. And so he devised The Promise that Must Be Kept. But such opportunism causes further damage; in order that Blackpool (and the reader) may learn what the current state of the law relating to divorce is, Dickens devised Stephen's visit to Bounderby. But this involves Bounderby's agreeing to see him over lunch in private and without notice, a privilege which the most liberal of Vice-Chancellors is unlikely to grant to a student even today when, as with Stephen, there is no immediate emergency. And yet Bounderby is supposed to be a monster of insensitive egotism! One has only to read Mrs Gaskell's account of Nicholas Higgins's attempts to see Thornton to realise what price Dickens paid for some of his effects. ('To catch him in the street was his only chance of seeing "the measter"; if he had rung the lodge bell, or even gone up to the house to ask for him, he would have been referred to the overlooker.)

SELF-INTEREST

This opportunism is, as I have already suggested, connected with a more general failure to think things through; so that, at one crucial point, Dickens's attack on the ethos of Gradgrindism is vitiated. It was a belief of vulgar utilitarians and the political economists with whom they were associated that by pursuing one's own interests, one would be serving those of society as a whole. It is clearly a very dubious belief, but it is still a mainstream one—indeed, however qualified, it is fundamental to the assumptions of a market economy and so it was reasonable that in a BBC TV adaptation of the novel for schools, Mr Gradgrind should have been identified with the modern Conservative Party. But it certainly could not have been any part of Dickens's intention to justify it. Yet that is what he has done in a sequence which, with only minor alterations and ending in victory rather than defeat, could have been devised by Harriet Martineau herself.

Bitzer covets Tom Gradgrind's position at Bounderby's bank: activated by such a self-interested motive, he pursues the escaping Tom and makes a citizen's arrest on him, for by such an action he knows he will recommend himself to Bounderby. Now, it is in the interests of society that criminals should be brought to justice and so Bitzer, in pursuing his own interests, is pursuing those of society. Further, without apparently realising it, Dickens shows that self-interest can produce actions which are indistinguishable in their effects from those actuated by moral beliefs. Bitzer, in refusing from self-interest to be bribed by Mr Gradgrind to compound a felony, actually behaves as a person of integrity would. Nothing shows Dickens's ability to mesmerise his readers more clearly than the fact that even a Leavis can be pushed into thinking that there are circumstances under which it is justifiable for the middle class to evade justice and protect their own. But if it is right to protect the Tom Gradgrinds of the world against the consequences of their crimes, then justice will be class justice. In an ironic coda to the tableau in the schoolroom, it proves to be Sissy, not Bitzer, who is willing to compound a felony.

In the presentation of Mr Gradgrind there is again a discrepancy between what Dickens wants us to think about him and what he actually shows him doing. But once more Dickens's rhetoric appears to carry all before it and readers even appear to swallow his prejudice against Gradgrind's house, Stone Lodge, the description of which ends:

> Gas and ventilation, drainage and water-service, all of the primest quality. Iron clamps and girders, fireproof from top to bottom; mechanical lifts for the housemaids, with all their brushes and brooms. . . .

Perhaps only Dickens could make such admirable features redound to the discredit of the person who devised them. I would certainly have liked to hear the opinions of the housemaids on the subject, though for some obscure reason, they appear to have been given notice, as both the Gradgrind and Bounderby households appear oddly servantless by the standards of the time.

GRADGRINDISM

The bias against Gradgrind evident here—and so far I have only sounded the keynote—further damages the claims of the novel to be taken seriously and justifies the traditional judgement. As Gradgrind is the linchpin in Dickens's scheme, however, it is necessary, before proceeding further, to outline what I take Dickens to be trying to say.

Gradgrind's philosophic materialism is seen as the expression of an inadequate view of human nature in its concentration on the rational and the useful at the expense of the emotional and imaginative, and on the egotistical (self-interest) instead of sympathy and altruism (love). Gradgrind has, in fact, no awareness of the existence, let alone the significance, of what one might call, in modern parlance, the deep structure of human experience. And so, particularly through his educational practices, he is seen as the propagandist ideologue or an oppressive society. It is Gradgrindism that makes Coketown possible.

It is not merely that Gradgrindian ideology can be used to justify the depredations of a Northern-based industrial and finance capitalism (personified by Bounderby); it is in symbiotic hegemony with other social and national groupings. It is in alliance, for example, with a futile and heartless Parliament and its bureaucratic cult of meaningless social surveys, and with the selfish egotism of a still powerful but increasingly effete aristocratic class, which is shown as capable of entering into formal partnership with it. It can be associated, too, with the architectural ugliness and, no doubt, other kinds of ugliness of organised religion, particularly nonconformism, and the oppressive exploitation of the situation and good feeling of the working class by power-seeking trade union demagogues.

Further, not only is Gradgrindism somehow responsible for, or associated with, virtually all society's ills, but its inadequate comprehension of human need leads it to wreak havoc in family life as well. As a direct result of his education and upbringing, Gradgrind's son becomes a heartless egotist, a gambler and a thief, who dies prematurely, while his daughter develops a protective armour of apathy to contain a sensitive feminine nature deeply aware of its own deformation. This makes it possible for her to contract a disastrous marriage to a much older man whom she hates and despises, which excludes her permanently from the joys of conjugal love and parenthood. (I will, however, be returning to the question of her motivation later.) Even Gradgrind is led by his philosophy to repress a basically kind nature.

The only countervalues to Gradgrindism are represented by the personal integrity and decency of ordinary working people, like Stephen and Rachael, (and their fellows, who can be led astray but who show their human worth at the scene of Stephen's rescue). And, of course, the circus. For the circus has as its *raison d'être* the development of 'useless' and 'unproductive' acrobatic skills, the dramatic enactment of highly coloured fictions, and a mode of fanciful, and fancifully advertised, play. In direct contrast to the selfish individualism promoted by Gradgrindism, its members show a generous solidarity and human directness of response. But the bearers of human value in working class and circus alike are marginalised and despised. Only Sissy Jupe, the finest flower of the circus way of life, has influence where it matters and becomes a beacon of effective light and goodness—a model for all of us to aspire to.

That in *Hard Times* we are dealing with a *Tendenzroman* which enforces unity on disparate materials is, I think, obvious. The spirit that informs it, moreover, is shown quite clearly in the way that Dickens uses the Gradgrind children as exemplificatory material. Dickens may mock the Coketown tracts 'showing how the good grown-up baby invariably got to the Savings-bank, and the bad grown-up baby invariably got transported', but his treatment of the Gradgrind children is merely a somewhat more sophisticated version of the same method with a different message.

With his usual rhetorical brio and through a repetition of key words, images and motifs, Dickens seeks to impose the illusion of unity and inevitability. There is, for example, the motif of the barren harvest carried by the titles of the three books, 'Sowing', 'Reaping', 'Garnering'. There is also an intermittent religious motif. Gradgrind is cast as an antichrist. His '. . . One Thing Needful' (Book I, Chap. I) is the obvious antithesis of the 'one thing needful' of *Luke*, ch. 10 v. 42. And in the title of the following chapter, 'Murdering the Innocents', he is identified with Herod. His political ally, James Harthouse, is, moreover, even associated with the devil himself. Representing the other side of the House, Blackpool is buoyed up at the bottom of the significantly named 'Old Hell Shaft' by the star which had shown him 'where to find the God of the poor . . .'. And Sissy, despite being brought up in an unchristian household, has an innate knowledge of the truths and even the phrasing of the New Testament ('"To do unto others as I would that they should do unto me"'), which survives all Mr McChoakumchild's attempts at suppression.

But for all the brio, tendencies which Dickens in other

novels sees as antagonistic here exhibit a unity of purpose which is specious. Thus Rouncewell in *Bleak House* and Doyce in *Little Dorrit*, both belong to Gradgrind's and Bounderby's world, the world of entrepreneurial capitalism, but the forces to which Doyce and Rouncewell are opposed—the traditional aristocracy, obstructive bureaucracy, the vested interests of powerful institutions (including Parliament) in so far as they are represented in *Hard Times*—are seen as Gradgrind's and Bounderby's associates. James Harthouse's alliance with Gradgrind is about as plausible as one between Daniel Doyce and Tite Barnacle.

SLACKBRIDGE

But there is one point where Dickens's attempt to forge a specious unity from conflicting social tendencies is more flagrant than elsewhere, and that is his presentation of Slackbridge. For the difficulty for Dickens is that Slackbridge is even more opposed to Gradgrind and Bounderby than he is. Despite Dickens's attempt to discredit him he still has to allow him to speak in the name of a common humanity; the chapter title, 'Men and Brothers', echoing the slogan used in the emancipation campaign, 'a man and a brother', while the 'United Aggregate Tribunal' inevitably suggests the idealistic and revolutionary general unionism of the 1830s typified by Owens's attempt to form the Grand National Consolidated Trades Union. Like Dickens, Slackbridge maintains that the workers are oppressed, though he differs from him in thinking that they should do something about it for themselves. For Dickens believed—and puts the belief into Blackpool's mouth—that something should be done for them "'by them as is put over [us]'", though he doesn't seem to realise that he has already put this out of court by the terms of his own analysis. The only way forward in the world of *Hard Times* must, on Dickens's showing elsewhere in the novel, be Slackbridge's, as he is a spokesman for that part of the population which, though oppressed, retains its human decency and therefore the only one which is likely to act collectively on humane principles. To try to discredit Slackbridge by identifying him with his opponents and assimilating him to Bounderby is too much even for Dickens's rhetoric to accomplish without alerting the reader.

It is not surprising, therefore, that there is a consensus that Slackbridge is a failure, but there is an attempt to isolate that failure by attributing it simply to middle class prejudice against trade unions, rather than to Dickens's attempts to impose a simple design on disparate material. Moreover, prejudice against trade unionism as such was already beginning to break down. In *North and South,* which succeeded *Hard Times* as a serial in *Household Words,* unions are already given recognition as an inevitable social fact with a definite role to play. And even when in the earlier *Mary Barton,* Mrs Gaskell had introduced 'a gentleman from London', whom she appears to present in a way analogous to Slackbridge, the effect is ultimately different; for she cannot withhold some respect from him and those who had chosen him:

> After a burst of eloquence, in which he blended the deeds of the elder and the younger Brutus, and magnified the resistless might of the 'millions of Manchester, the Londoner descended to a matter-of-fact business, and *in his capacity this way he did not belie the good judgement of those who had sent him as a delegate.* Masses of people when left to their own free choice, seem to have discretion in distinguishing men of natural talent . . . [my italics]

The dialectic between Gradgrindism and the circus, which is at the heart of the novel's system, is also factitious. For one thing, Sissy, like all Dickens's A-side heroines of humble birth, is not realistically related to the environment from which she comes. Whatever Dickens wants us to think, she is in behaviour, lexis, diction, syntax and phonology a thoroughly middle class girl from a world which is not otherwise represented in the novel at all. Of even more significance is that, almost from the start, Dickens vitiates the contrast between Gradgrind's allegedly soulless philosophy and the human warmth of the circus. It is a representative of that human warmth, who suddenly and cruelly abandons his daughter (though not his dog) and never communicates with her again; and it is the soulless philosopher, the antichrist of 'The One Thing Needful' and the Herod of 'Murdering the Innocents' who adopts the abandoned girl and who treats her like a daughter—even if he does insist that she is called Jupe. Dickens works very hard to obscure the significance of what he has done by trying to exonerate 'Signor' Jupe, but he has to put in a good word however grudgingly for Gradgrind, which hardly marches with the opening presentation of him: 'His character was not unkind, all things considered; it might have been a very kind one indeed, if he had only made some round mistake in the arithmetic that balanced it, years ago.' But in relation to Sissy there are no 'mights' about it: it is the act of 'a very kind one indeed'. In *Little Dorrit*, Mr Meagles's decision to bring Tattycoram into his household appears to be viewed favourably (see I, 2)—but he makes her into a lady's maid to wait on his daughter. Mr Gradgrind shows an altogether superior sensitivity and, unlike Meagles, never patronises his protégée. I doubt whether even Tattycoram would have run away to join Miss Wade under such circumstances.

The implied reason for 'Signor' Jupe's abandonment of his daughter was that he was being hissed on a nightly basis and could not stand it. This, in itself, suggests a darker side to circus life, which undermines Dickens's attempt to portray it positively. One aspect of the operation of Fancy is the extravagant advertisements which accompany the advent of the circus. According to one of them, 'Signor Jupe was . . . to exhibit his astounding feat of throwing seventy-five hundredweight in rapid succession back-handed over his head, thus forming a fountain of solid iron in mid-air. . .'. But the fact of the matter was that '"his joints [were] turning stiff and he [was] getting used up . . ."': '"he [had] his points as a Cackler still, but he [couldn't] get a living out of them."' Jupe suffers doubly: in addition to the financial insecurity which relates him to an industrial worker, he endures humiliation at the hands of audiences who have been led by fanciful advertising to believe that he can perform impossible feats.

That Dickens's commitment to the circus as a countervailing ideal is unreal and sentimental emerges almost inadvertently when Mr Sleary disguises Tom as a clown to facilitate his escape:

> In a preposterous coat like a beadle's, with cuffs and flaps exaggerated to an unspeakable extent; in an immense waistcoat, knee-breeches, buckled shoes, and a mad cocked hat; with nothing fitting him, and everything of coarse material, moth-eaten and full of holes; with seams in his black face, where fear and heat had started through the greasy composition daubed all over it; anything so grimly, detestably, ridiculously shameful as the whelp in his comic livery, Mr Gradgrind never could by any other means have believed in. . . .

But if such a garb is 'grimly, detestably, ridiculously shameful' for Tom (and it is obviously not merely because of his guilt or the registering consciousness being that of Mr Gradgrind), why not for anybody? The circus is all very well in its place (where it can be patronised), but it will not do as an occupation for the middle class.

And, though Gradgrind is identified with the egotistical orthodoxies of political economy, except in his marriage to Mrs Gradgrind, who 'was most satisfactory as a question of figures. . .', he is never shown, quite apart from his treatment of Sissy, as behaving in a self-interested way. In his public capacity he is a philanthropist. He has established and maintains a school, presumably at his own expense, made sure that the schoolmaster in charge has the best qualifications available, and, apparently, charges fees so low that even Bitzer, whose widowed mother we later hear of in the workhouse can attend ('"my schooling was cheap"). It is true that under the influence of Bounderby he proposes to exclude Sissy from his school, but he had admitted her presumably with the knowledge that not only could she attend for only a few days but that she came from the circus. Further, Gradgrind's view of education is progressive in several ways. It is not class based: the education of Tom and Louisa is more advanced than that of the pupils at the school, but it is of the same kind. His educational ideal is also gender-inclusive: he does not believe in a separate curriculum for girls. Tom and Louisa are taught together. And corporal punishment, to use the old but still convenient cliché, is conspicuous by its absence both at home and school. There is nothing whatsoever of Dotheboys Hall or Salem House about Mr Gradgrind's school. The children are not terrorised and the 'corpulent slow boy', who says he would not paper the room but paint it shows that even under a regime which Dickens wants to represent as completely oppressive, the spirit of childhood can survive. In three lines characteristic of his genius, Dickens has created an unforgettable character as an involuntary witness against himself.

As regards the curriculum and teaching methods, whether at home or at school, since Dickens's aim is to prejudice us against them, it is not surprising that they are presented scantily and patchily and only a vague impression emerges. At school they appear to involve the inculcation of a variety of facts, possibly by rote learning (though Dickens does not actually say that Bitzer had *learned* his definition of a horse) but there is an attempt to inculcate principles through a pseudo-Socratic method of question and answer—but one in which pupils are guided to what is the 'right' answer. It is also implied that there is an exclusive emphasis on the empirically verifiable, the practical and the useful. But the school is clearly not as bad as Dickens wants us to think it is. Literacy and numeracy appear to be assumed and some rather advanced secondary school subjects, political economy and statistics, appear to be introduced. Bitzer may first appear as a probable rote learner, but in his argument with Mr Gradgrind he shows a capacity to relate general principles to particular instances and to express himself cogently, which is the mark of a trained mind. He had certainly learned to do more than regurgitate facts.

The education of the young Gradgrinds, which is supposed to have such momentous consequences, has about as much imagined reality as Adam Smith Gradgrind and Malthus Gradgrind. All we can, in fact, say is that it appears to have laid stress on the natural sciences (collections of conchological, metallurgical and mineralogical specimens are mentioned), mathematics (which does not of course deal with facts as such), and statistics. Nothing is said about political economy, but we must assume it was part of the curriculum.

One may readily admit that a system of education which frowned on leisure and play and neglected and even repressed the imaginative and emotional development of the child would be oppressive. Thus far, Dickens is clearly right. But he is unfair to represent Gradgrindian ideas of education as wholly negative and dehumanising and, in the case of Tom and Louisa, leading to personal disaster. At no time are they permitted to show any interest in the subject matter of their studies or, unlike Bitzer, display any of the skills that education had given them. There is an obvious bias here: the facts of the natural world and of the cosmos can themselves be a source of wonder or, at least, of interest both to children and adults and can survive unattractive presentation (even Bitzer's definition of a horse contains some genuinely interesting facts). As for mathematics, Bertrand Russell's response to being introduced to geometry at eleven, 'I had not imagined that there was anything so delicious in the world . . .', while obviously not typical is a rebuke to the rigid simplifications and dichotomies that Dickens is dealing in. That Dickens should represent a scientific and factual education as necessarily stultifying hardly marches with his knowledge—a knowledge shared with Mrs Gaskell in her depiction of Job Legh—that among the more gifted workers, reaction to their environment often took the form of a strong interest in science: ('[Blackpool] took no place among those remarkable "Hands" who, piecing together their broken intervals of leisure through many years, had mastered difficult sciences, and acquired a knowledge of most unlikely things').

TREATMENT OF WOMEN

Behind Dickens's distrust of Gradgrindian education lurks, moreover, a reactionary attitude to the education of women, which it is amazing that Dickens can still get away with in an age when Gradgrind's sexual egalitarianism has long since triumphed. Particularly as even a contemporary, like John Stuart Mill, knew perfectly well what really underlay all the fun at Mrs Jellyby's expense in *Bleak House*. In a letter to Harriet Taylor he explodes:

> . . . That creature Dickens . . . has the vulgar impudence in this thing to ridicule rights of women. It is done in the very vulgarest way—just the style in which vulgar men used to ridicule 'learned ladies' as neglecting their children and household etc . . .

Well, it *was* a private letter. But Mill's comments, despite their intemperateness, illuminate *Hard Times*. For it is the contrasting effects of Gradgrindism on the two girls, Sissy and Louisa, which reveal the strength of Dickens's prejudices. Tom, on the other hand, is so crudely done that he can't be taken seriously even on a diagnostic level. His gambling, dishonesty, selfishness towards his sister, and his attempt to incriminate Blackpool have nothing to do with his education and upbringing except by the most special of special pleadings. The Toms of this world come from a variety of social and educational backgrounds.

In Sissy, Dickens embodies a conventional Victorian ideal of womanhood: a true woman would have patience, sympathy, an innate knowledge of the good and a capacity for self-sacrifice, but though she might be intelligent she was not fitted for intellectual pursuits. That Sissy is a dunce is a sign of her merit as a woman. It is her unintellectual femininity which protects her against the ethos underpinning Gradgrindian education: she is even made rather implausibly to stumble over the word, statistics, as a sign of her implicit rejection of *hoc genus omne*. But it is quite possible for a person to benefit from an education whose ethos (s)he rejects. Marxist revolutionaries have profited from capitalist seminaries. Mill was himself critical of his own education in ways which commentators have regarded as relevant to *Hard Times*. But that education, none the less, produced a mind of formidable power, originality and humanity, which enabled Mill in *The Subjection of Women* to show an enlightenment far ahead of his time and in an area, too, where Dickens merely reflected contemporary prejudices.

THE DEVELOPMENT OF LOUISA

For Dickens, Louisa, though feminine, is not feminine enough. She has too much intellectual capacity. She is clearly an apt pupil and, for purposes of the plot, Dickens has even had to make her cleverer than her brother. She is Gradgrind's favourite child and he even appears to have boasted to Harthouse about her accomplishments. But she is feminine enough to resent her education as denaturing her (she regrets that she does not know what other girls know and can't play and sing to Tom). She does not, however, have the intellectual incapacity to be unaffected by its ethos and does not encourage Sissy in her implicit rejection of that ethos either.

So far, if one accepts Dickens's period *parti pris* about the nature of women, Louisa's development is at least consistent. But in making her accept Bounderby as a husband, Dickens enters deeper waters than he can allow himself consciously to negotiate, while still not being wholly unaware of their depth. For although Dickens often contrives to write about marriage as if it did not involve intimate physical relations (think of David Copperfield and Agnes), he naturally knew differently and however much he tried to block it out, he must have been in some sort aware that Louisa had agreed to a life of marital prostitution. That he was so is illuminated by the partly analogous situation in *Nicholas Nickleby*. There Madeline Bray shows herself willing to sacrifice herself to her father by marrying Arthur Gride, who is even older and more repulsive than Bounderby. But it is I think precisely because Madeline does not, in fact, marry Gride (he dies in the nick of time) that Dickens can afford to show a limited realisation of the prostitution involved: Madeline's health is represented as seriously deteriorating at the repulsive prospect before her. But even here Dickens, in trying to present Madeline's decision as morally commendable if mistaken, attempts to see it as merely an extreme example of the feminine capacity for self-sacrifice, and in so doing does not allow himself to contemplate how really disgusting physical relations with Gride would be—though the cop out through death acts as a kind of substitute.

Louisa, however, actually marries Bounderby and does so voluntarily—it is clear that her father would not try to compel her to accept him. Why then does she do so? In the scene where Gradgrind passes on Bounderby's proposal, it is implied that she does so as a result of the moral apathy resulting from the repression of her feminine nature. But a woman who is willing to prostitute herself because she thinks that nothing matters must in Dickens's world have become so defeminised as to be past hope along with the father who is seen as responsible for her state. So Dickens bolts on a second motive: her self-sacrificial love for Tom, which feminises her decision.

But, unfortunately, Louisa's love-for-Tom motive reacts with the repression—apathy motive to take Dickens quite out of his depth. For a sister to prostitute herself for a brother implies a serious displacement of feeling and the presence of incestuous elements (these have already been noted). Dickens tries to counteract this (of which he would have to repress conscious awareness) by involving Louisa in a commonplace seduction intrigue: but not only does this bring the question of her moral apathy to the fore again, it also involves turning Tom into a sort of involuntary pander—so the confusion is worse confounded. It is perhaps a sign that Dickens was not quite oblivious to these unwelcome implications that even after Louisa and her father's rehabilitation, he seems to take his revenge on her: she may be a victim; she may have sacrificed herself for her brother; but she must be permanently shut out from the possibility of a second marriage and of motherhood. It is this sense of something going on under the surface which makes Louisa by far the most interesting character in the novel, despite the bias in which she was conceived.

I have tried to show that the traditional view of *Hard Times* is justified. But, though it doesn't affect the final evaluation of the novel, there is one short sequence in Book I, Chapter 2, where Dickens shows himself capable of developing aspects of his theme much more interestingly than he does elsewhere. What happens in this sequence is that Dickens shows that Gradgrind's attachment to facts is ultimately ideological: he is not interested in facts *per se,* only in those which are socially admissible. The existence of the circus is an undoubted fact but "'We don't want to know anything about that here'". Further, if for Gradgrind facts have to be socially admissible, then the result will be that he will devise admissible fictions as a substitute for real facts considered inadmissible to which, none the less, reference in some sort has to be made. So Sissy Jupe's father is transformed into what he is not: "'a veterinary surgeon, a farrier and horse-breaker'", because what he is, a circus employee, can't be admitted. But, by so transforming him, Gradgrind is indulging in a flight of fancy: he has crossed the floor of the House: the traitor is within the gates. Again Dickens shows that Gradgrind and the 'third gentleman' can't even be relied upon to make crucial distinctions. Neither of them realises that there is a fundamental difference between an object and the representation of an object. It is Sissy, interestingly, who puts her finger on the fallacy by arguing that there is a crucial distinction between treading on actual flowers and treading on pictures of flowers:

'It wouldn't hurt them . . . They wouldn't crush and wither . . . They would be the pictures of what was very pretty and pleasant . . .'.

It is a pity that Dickens didn't allow Sissy to become the intellectually capable girl she is shown to be here.

Judging *Hard Times*

Earle Davis

Dickensian critic Earle Davis describes why he
judges *Hard Times* as "something less than a great
novel," citing, for example, constrictions in the
weekly format, lack of humor, and faulty caricature.
Yet despite its imperfections, Davis finds that the
novel retains force because of its purpose—Dickens's
attack on an inhumane economic system. The following essay is excerpted from Davis's book *The
Flint and the Flame: The Artistry of Charles Dickens.*

The second novel in Dickens' dark period continues his indictment of Victorian society. Since *Hard Times* is—of all his
books—the clearest in its statement of his economic beliefs,
it naturally holds the attention of all those readers who find
this phase of Dickens' fiction to be the most stimulating in
our times. Yet for years this was the novel most easily dismissed by traditional Dickensians, since it represents few of
the narrative qualities they were accustomed to praise. It is
tempting for the modern critic to say that the traditional
Dickensian has been wrong and that *Hard Times* is an un-
derrated novel. Its thesis is challenging, it contributes materially to Dickens' total study of the social microcosm, but it
is something less than a great novel for several reasons.
Since it has been enthusiastically praised by George Bernard
Shaw, and since a critic of the stature of F.R. Leavis thinks it
is Dickens' greatest book—"a completely serious work of
art"—one needs to look closely at the reasons for finding it
less effective than *Bleak House* or *Little Dorrit.*

JUDGING *HARD TIMES*

Several factors must be taken into account in judging *Hard
Times.* It was not meticulously planned; it was written some-
what hurriedly to fill a blank in the schedule of *Household
Words;* and it was constructed in the weekly and constricted

Reprinted from *The Flint and the Flame: The Artistry of Charles Dickens,* by Earle
Davis, with permission from the University of Missouri Press. Copyright © 1963 by the
Curators of the University of Missouri.

installments with which Dickens had last contended in *The Old Curiosity Shop* and *Barnaby Rudge.* Despite the fact that the thesis of *Hard Times* is an integral part of his narrative intentions in this creative period, he found less room for developing his contrasting plot sequences. He also had difficulty in focusing all his narrative technical resources on his subject, so that the novel does not call upon many of his best devices. One needs a relatively large scope for many contrasting plots in action. The sequences which interlocked the large monthly parts of *Bleak House* had no similar opportunity in the smaller pieces which were required by the magazine's weekly issues. The novel sometimes gives the effect of choppy episodes, of undeveloped contrasts, of unfinished business, and this kind of effect is not exactly characteristic of Dickens' last period of creation.

Dickens was hampered by several other considerations in writing this novel. He evidently intended to discuss unions and strikes at more length, but he had contracted to print a novel by Mrs. Gaskell immediately after his own. He had read her manuscript before he began *Hard Times.* She was using the same subject matter, as anyone who wishes to examine *North and South* can see. Mrs. Gaskell read the installments of *Hard Times* with growing uneasiness, and even seems to have been suspicious (apparently with good reason) that Dickens was stealing her thunder as well as appropriating her material. Her protests must have bothered Dickens.

Hard Times retains force because of its purpose. It is influenced materially by Carlyle's economic ideas; it follows naturally Dickens' attack on legal and social maleficence in *Bleak House,* since economic exploitation was another phase of his case against Victorian society.

As the novel stands, its thesis is a satire on utilitarian economy. Dickens felt that a dependence upon capitalistic *practicality* without reference to *sympathy* and *brotherly understanding* causes continued difficulties in the relations of capital and labor. His scene was Manchester or Leeds or some such center of England's industrial revolution, and he called the place Coketown.

THOMAS GRADGRIND

Dickens planned three separate plot sequences for his novel, each of them presenting opportunities for development and contrast. His main action was to center around Thomas

Gradgrind, a retired wholesale hardware merchant who had become a member of Parliament. Gradgrind is Mr. Utilitarian, "a man of realities; a man of facts and calculations; a man who proceeds upon the principle that two and two are four, and nothing over." Mathematically speaking, with no allowances for the tender or susceptible emotions, Mr. Gradgrind conducts all the business of life *practically*, because this is the way one gets ahead, makes money, and becomes financially and socially successful according to Victorian standards. Mr. Gradgrind bows to Carlyle's God of Cash-Payment, and he intends to conduct his life and bring up his children according to his philosophy.

The plot divisions show how this utilitarian philosophy works out. There are four children in the family, plus the adopted Sissy Jupe. Two of the children (named Adam Smith and Malthus) are mentioned, then dismissed from the tale. But Louisa, Tom, and Sissy carry the main action. Louisa is given in marriage to the capitalist, Mr. Bounderby, and is tempted to escape from her resulting unhappiness by an affair or elopement with Mr. Harthouse, a handsome dilettante who offers her admiration and some degree of excitement. The temptation of Louisa is the first complication in the Gradgrind plot; Dickens handles it as he had occasionally done in the past, by showing his heroine on the verge of succumbing to temptation, but successfully resisting it at the last moment. Certainly Louisa's upbringing and her father's philosophy are of no help to her. This sequence is a typical intrigue borrowed from the tradition of sentimental drama.

In contrast, young Tom is ruined by his environment. He is presented as selfish, ill-natured, sensual, and completely mercenary. He is employed as a clerk in a bank owned by his sister's husband, Mr. Bounderby, and eventually steals money from the bank in order to cover his debts contracted in dissipation and idleness. He contrives a scheme to throw the blame on Stephen, a workman in Mr. Bounderby's factory, and the resulting action which establishes Stephen's innocence and fixes the blame properly on Tom brings the novel to its conclusion.

Sissy Jupe is the daughter of a clown, who deserts her and runs off from the circus which is playing in Coketown. The father had grown so old and stiff that he had lost his ability to amuse his audiences. Thinking his daughter well-situated at the Gradgrind school, he disappears, and Mr. Gradgrind decides to provide for her. Sissy, like a character in a morality play, illustrates all the ideas opposite from the utilitarian philosophy taught at school. If any special intrigue was to have been developed around her, it never finds place in the novel. However, she does shame Mr. Harthouse into leaving the neighborhood just as Louisa seems on the verge of joining him, and she helps Tom escape when he is about to be arrested for stealing, sending him to the circus where Mr. Sleary, the owner, conceals him and gets him safely abroad.

MR. BOUNDERBY

The second division of action centers about Mr. Bounderby, who is an even more vicious portrait of the hardhearted capitalist than was Scrooge or Mr. Dombey. Mr. Bounderby is part of the Louisa-Harthouse triangle, but he also has a separate course of action, based upon his relationship to his housekeeper, Mrs. Sparsit. This lady is from a higher caste and presumably brings social distinction to the home of a man who had made his own money. Since she is destitute, she accepts money from Mr. Bounderby. She nurses an unrequited affection for him which shows itself in jealousy of the young wife he brings home. Bounderby also has a mother he is ashamed of, and there is a small intrigue which shows her visiting Coketown on occasion just to look at her son from a distance. Bounderby thus illustrates false pride as well as a lack of filial affection. He is exposed at the end as having fabricated much of the story he tells about his youth and the lack of opportunities afforded him in his climb to fortune and power.

STEPHEN BLACKPOOL

The third division of action concerns the power-loom weaver, Stephen Blackpool. Stephen is tied to an impossible wife who has drunk herself into a state which defies marital happiness. Stephen loves another woman, Rachael, wants a divorce from his wife, but finding it impossible to secure one, he and Rachael live in a state of frustration. Since it is Stephen who is used by Tom Gradgrind in his scheme to shift responsibility for the theft from the bank, Stephen is connected with the Gradgrind sequence. He refuses to join the union of workingmen, suffering ostracism because of this, but he insists on defending his fellow workers when Mr. Bounderby asks him about the union. He is accordingly fired and blacklisted. Dickens then shows him leaving Coketown at the time when he is coincidentally suspected of stealing. He tries to return to defend himself, but falls into an abandoned mine shaft on the way back. He is discovered just before he dies.

DICKENS'S THESIS

These three plot sequences illustrate Dickens' general plan for revolving his action around his thesis. The thesis is broader than the attack on utilitarian economy, since it also encompasses criticism of the educational system, the caste system, and divorce laws. Mr. Gradgrind's school, conducted by M'Choakumchild, stresses hard facts and resembles in many respects the forcing school of Dr. Blimber in *Dombey and Son*. Mr. M'Choakumchild knows a little about everything, but has never learned how to communicate anything but knowledge for its own sake. Sissy reports to Louisa her difficulties in understanding him in a particularly suggestive pass age:

> "And he said, Now, this school room is a Nation. And in this nation there are fifty millions of money. Isn't this a prosperous nation? Girl number twenty, isn't this a prosperous nation, and an't you in a thriving state?"
>
> "What did you say?" asked Louisa.
>
> "Miss Louisa, I said I didn't know. I thought I couldn't know whether it was a prosperous nation or not, and whether I was in a thriving state or not, unless I knew who had got the money, and whether any of it was mine. But that had nothing to do with it. It was not in the figures at all," said Sissy, wiping her eyes.

The caste system finds satiric emphasis through the story of Mrs. Sparsit, whose ambition and position in the social scheme are at variance. Mr. Harthouse shows the decay which comes from rank without character. The criticism of the divorce law is quite modern, because it is obvious that one cannot get a divorce in England without luck, influence, or money. Since Stephen's wife is an impossible matrimonial companion, since she has not even enough personality to give him reason for divorcing her according to the law which fixes adultery as the only legal excuse, and since Stephen has not enough money to circumvent the law, happiness is out of reach. Dickens had some feelings about his own marital unhappiness which related to the opinions expressed in the novel.

The plot sequences of *Hard Times* are not so complex as those of *Bleak House,* nor are they so fully developed. There is a reasonable amount of motivation in the details of Louisa's abortive attraction for Harthouse, and there is careful preparation for Tom's theft. Mr. Gradgrind is shown as a man with a heart underneath his philosophy, for he aids Sissy, and he sees the error of his ways after his children experience unhappiness or ruin because of his utilitarian philosophy. Louisa is studied with care, and the reader is likely to sympathize with her difficulties. There is mystery and suspense in the circumstances of Tom's theft, and there is sensation in Stephen's death in the mine pit.

But the humor is absent; the caricature technique fights a losing battle; the speech devices are less effective than usual. The shadowy ghost of caricature shows itself in the early description of Gradgrind and of M'Choakumchild. Mrs. Sparsit has a Coriolanian nose and dense black eyebrows. Her great-aunt, Lady Scadgers, is an immensely gross woman who loves meat and possesses a leg which has refused to get out of bed for fourteen years. Probably the best characters in what is usually an effective Dickensian technique are the circus people. Mr. Sleary, the proprietor, is a fat man with one fixed and one loose eye, a voice like a broken bellows, a head which is never either completely sober or sufficiently drunk, and a manner of speaking which is affected by his asthma and comes out in a lisp which makes his speeches difficult to read. Mr. E.W.B. Childers is a horseman with the troupe and is described extravagantly as resembling a centaur "compounded of the stable and the playhouse. Where the one began, and the other ended, nobody could have told with any precision." Master Kidderminster is a dwarf who assists Childers, being carried on the palm of Childers' hand, feet upward, while the daring vaulting act goes on.

The best speech device is given to Slackbridge, the union organizer. He talks in an oratorical manner which capitalizes on all the rhetoric and elocution usually accompanying hypocrisy. He addresses the Coketown hands in this manner:

"But, oh, my friends and brothers! Oh, men and Englishmen, the downtrodden operatives of Coketown! What shall we say of the man—that working-man, that I should find it necessary so to libel the glorious name—who, being practically and well acquainted with the grievances and wrongs of you, the injured pith and marrow of this land, and having heard you, with a noble and majestic unanimity that will make

Tyrants tremble, resolve for to subscribe to the Funds of the United Aggregate Tribunal, and to abide by the injunctions issued by that body for your benefit, whatever they may be—what, I ask you, will you say of that working-man, since such I must acknowledge him to be, who, at such a time, deserts his post and sells his flag; who, at such a time, is not ashamed to make to you the dastardly and humiliating avowal that he will hold himself aloof, and will *not* be one of those associated in the gallant stand for freedom and for Right?"

The symbolic atmosphere which distinguishes the total effect of *Bleak House* is much less important in *Hard Times.* In its place is the rhetorical, exclamatory manner of Carlyle, explaining Dickens' effects instead of implying them. It is true

CRITICAL RESPONSE

Even critics who praise Hard Times *concede that the novel has some faults. Robert Giddings describes some of the flaws commonly cited by modern critics.*

A failure of a documentary kind is the presentation of the demagogue Slackbridge—'a mere figment of the middle-class imagination. No such man would be listened to by a meeting of English factory hands' (George Bernard Shaw). Similarly, the use of a professional circus to represent Fancy as opposed to Fact has been faulted on the grounds that Dickens might have found Fancy in the native recreations of working people (David Craig). A more 'ideological' criticism would allege that Dickens's *concept* of Fancy was, judging from the symbols by which he represented it, too trivial to weigh effectively against the Fact of Utilitarian economic theory and philosophy of education (John Holloway, David Lodge). Other critics have admitted faults of characterization—the girl Sissy is sentimentally presented and emerges as inadequate: her childhood attributes do not ground her later strength on Louisa's behalf. Again, Stephen and Rachael are said to be too good to be true; Stephen's martyrdom to a drunken wife is a cliché; his refusal to join the union is not motivated and therefore puts him into a weak, contradictory position in relation to his fellow-workers. Now these allegations of faults of construction are not naïve 'Dickensian' complaints. There is real evidence that many things are not quite right with the book, for whatever reason: because of the unfamiliar constraints of small-scale writing for weekly parts, because of the secondhand nature of Dickens's experience?

Robert Giddings, *The Changing World of Charles Dickens.* New York: Vision, 1983.

that a smoky haze hovers over Coketown, and elsewhere the workers are described as rising in protest and falling in defeat like the sea. Stephen falls into a pit, and Dickens explains the significance of the pit in Stephen's dying speech:

> "I ha' fell into th' pit, my dear, as have cost wi'in the knowledge o' old fok now livin', hundreds and hundreds o' men's lives—fathers, sons, brothers, dear to thousands an' thousands, an' keepin' 'em fro' want and hunger. I ha' fell into a pit that ha' been wi' th' Fire-damp crueler than battle. I ha' read on 't in the public petition, as onny one may read, fro' the men that works in pits, on which they ha' pray'n the lawmakers for Christ's sake not to let their work be murder to 'em, but to spare 'em for th' wives and children that they loves as well as gentlefok loves theirs. When it were in work, it killed wi'out need; when 'tis let alone, it kills wi'out need. See how we die an' no need, one way an' another—in a muddle—every day."

Edgar Johnson and several other critics have found effective symbolism in *Hard Times,* but it is difficult to rank this symbolism in the same class with the fog, mist, rain, and spontaneous combustion of *Bleak House,* or with the prison atmosphere of the following novel, *Little Dorrit.* Surely *Hard Times* should be judged on its artistic merits, a statement which means that it should not be underestimated because of its narrative insufficiency, nor overestimated because its thesis appeals to the reader who is concerned with weaknesses in the capitalistic system. Even George Bernard Shaw descends to a judgment which he would normally ridicule in the writings of anyone else. He says:

> Here he begins at last to exercise quite recklessly his power of presenting a character to you in the most fantastic and outrageous terms, putting into its mouth from one end of the book to the other hardly a word which could conceivably be uttered by any sane human being, and yet leaving you with an unmistakable and exactly truthful portrait of a character that you recognize at once as not only real but typical.

The least one can say in response to this kind of praise is that it is special pleading. Furthermore, it does Dickens' case little good.

AN INHUMANE SYSTEM

Dickens' criticism of the economic system is quite plain. He is obviously opposed to the excesses of selfish capitalism; he knows that too many workers are underpaid. If something is not done to organize our economy so that laborers have a fair chance to make a reasonable living, he states, there will be trouble. These opinions he holds in common with Carlyle. He says:

> Utilitarian economists, skeletons of schoolmasters, Commissioners of Facts, genteel and used-up infidels, gabblers of many dog-eared creeds, the poor you will have always with you. Cultivate in them, while there is yet time, the utmost graces of the fancies and affections, to adorn their lives so much in need of ornament; or, in the day of your triumph, when romance is utterly driven out of their souls, and they and a bare existence stand face to face, Reality will take a wolfish turn, and make an end of you.

This comment indicates that Dickens is aware of the threat of revolution or other violence. Yet Stephen, a sympathetic character, does not join the union. The organizer Slackbridge, in *Hard Times,* is given a most offensive mannerism of speech, and the general impression of the union is that it forms because foolish capitalists will make no concessions to reality. Workers join a union in an effort to protect themselves. Dickens says, in describing the Coketown hands, that when they rise "like a sea," they do harm chiefly to themselves. This is their dilemma. The implication is that strikes and violence do not help in the long run.

Most of the critics who argue that Dickens is a conscious or unconscious radical either ignore Slackbridge or belittle his importance in relation to Dickens' economic views. Edgar Johnson apparently is one of this group:

> Such a description is a piece of sheer ignorance, not because union leaders cannot be windbags and humbugs as other politicians can, but because labor organizers are not like Slackbridge and do not talk like him, and did not do so in Dickens' day any more than in ours.

It would be possible for ministers to argue that no preacher talks like Chadband, or for servants to argue that no one talks like Sam Weller, or for Dickens' mother to insist that no woman talks like Mrs. Nickleby. It all depends on whose ox is being gored. One must either assume that Dickens did not mean what he was saying in heightened form, or else he was bowing to the opinions of his readers. If either is true, his entire picture of Victorian society loses force, and the reader might as well discount whatever part of the picture he disagrees with.

THE RIGHT TO ORGANIZE

There is some further evidence which bears upon the problem. In *Household Words* Dickens says that laborers have the same right to organize that their employers have. In another issue he asks workingmen to force reforms from the Government. On the occasion when he read *A Christmas Carol* to an audience composed entirely of workingmen and their wives, he made an introductory address in which he said that it was necessary and right for workers to take a share in the management of industry. Cooperation would make an end of exploitation. This view would not startle a Fabian Socialist or a member of England's Labour party, but it would hardly satisfy Lenin.

One last quotation from *Hard Times*. Stephen speaks for Dickens:

> Sir, I canna, wi' my little teaming an' my common way, tell the genelmen what will be better aw this—though some workingmen o' this town could, above my powers—but I can tell him what I know will never do 't. The strong hand will never do 't. Vict'ry and triumph will never do 't. Agreeing for to mak' one side unnat'rally awlus and forever right, and t'oother side unnat'rally and forever wrong, will never, never do 't. Nor yet lettin' alone will never do 't.

This is usually taken as an attack upon the laissez-faire system of letting business do what it pleases. But Dickens says that neither side can be always and forever right without reference to the other side. He is arguing for what he conceives to be justice to both capital and labor; he is arguing for cooperation; he is saying that Victorian society does not award justice to labor; he is saying that something drastic needs to be done, or revolution will erupt and ruin all.

This conclusion is also the moral of the later *Tale of Two Cities*. In what is perhaps the most rewarding essay written about Dickens, George Orwell says:

> Revolution, as he sees it, is merely a monster that is begotten by tyranny and always ends by devouring its own instruments. In Sidney Carton's vision at the foot of the guillotine, he foresees Defarge and the other leading spirits of the Terror all perishing under the same knife—which, in fact, was approximately what happened.

This novel, as well as *Hard Times*, contributes its evidence to show how deep was Dickens' "horror of revolutionary hysteria."

In the final analysis *Hard Times* has a kind of fictional importance which transcends its effect as a work of art. Reading it helps explain what Dickens did more subtly in *Bleak House, Little Dorrit,* and *Our Mutual Friend*. When Leavis

praises *Hard Times* in *The Great Tradition* as being the only
novel of Dickens which he is willing to put with the works of
the "greatest English novelists"—Jane Austen, George Eliot,
Henry James, and Joseph Conrad—he does so for deceptive
but perfectly genuine reasons.

> The Adult mind doesn't as a rule find in Dickens a challenge
> to an unusual and sustained seriousness. . . . It [*Hard Times*]
> has a kind of perfection as a work of art that we don't associ-
> ate with Dickens—a perfection that is one with the sustained
> and complete seriousness for which among his productions
> it is unique.

Further reasons for praising *Hard Times* are all based on
Leavis' interest in the kind of art which is significant because
it is profoundly serious. He finds in all the other novels too
much that is merely entertaining or falsely melodramatic.

In disputing this view one is placed in a peculiar position.
The critic may find himself in more or less complete agreement with Leavis' general premises and judgments, but for
what seem almost exactly the same reasons cited may find
Bleak House, Little Dorrit, and *Our Mutual Friend* to be better illustrations of all that Leavis praises in *Hard Times.* One
supposes that many modern readers besides this incisive
critic ought to be able to use *Hard Times* as a springboard to
enjoyment and appreciation of Dickens' other profoundly
serious and greater novels.

CHRONOLOGY

1812

Charles Dickens born February 7, to John and Elizabeth Dickens; War of 1812 begins with United States.

1814

John Dickens transferred to London.

1817

John Dickens transferred to Chatham.

1821

Charles Dickens starts school.

1822

John Dickens transferred to London.

1824

John Dickens arrested for debt and sent to Marshalsea Prison; Charles Dickens begins work at Warren's Blacking Factory.

1824–1826

Attends Wellington House Academy in London.

1827

Works as law clerk; improves his education at the British Museum Reading Room.

1830

Meets Maria Beadnell.

1831

Becomes reporter for the *Mirror of Parliament.*

1832

Becomes staff writer for the *True Sun.*

1833

First published piece appears in the *Monthly Magazine;* slavery abolished in British Empire.

1834

Becomes staff writer on the *Morning Chronicle;* street sketches published in the *Evening Chronicle;* meets Catherine Hogarth; Poor Law of 1834 enacted.

1836

Sketches by Boz published in book form; marries Catherine Hogarth; plays *The Strange Gentleman* and *The Village Coquettes* produced at St. James's Theater; meets John Forster, a lifelong friend and biographer; Ralph Waldo Emerson publishes *Nature.*

1836–1837

Pickwick Papers published in monthly installments.

1837

Pickwick Papers published in book form; begins installments of *Oliver Twist* in *Bentley's Miscellany;* play *Is She Your Wife?* produced at St. James's Theater; first child, Charles, born; Catherine's sister Mary Hogarth dies suddenly; Victoria becomes queen of England; Thomas Carlyle publishes *The French Revolution.*

1838

Nicholas Nickleby appears in installments; *Oliver Twist* published in book form; first daughter, Mary, born; first railroad train enters London.

1839

Nicholas Nickleby published in book form; second daughter, Kate, born; People's Charter, stating six demands for voting and representation for the poor; Chinese-British Opium Wars begin; end 1860.

1840

Dickens edits *Master Humphry's Clock,* a weekly; *The Old Curiosity Shop* appears in installments and in book form; England annexes New Zealand; Queen Victoria marries Prince Albert; James Fenimore Cooper publishes *The Pathfinder.*

1841

Barnaby Rudge appears in *Master Humphrey's Clock* and in book form; Dickens's second son, Walter, born; the magazine *Punch* founded; Ralph Waldo Emerson publishes *Essays.*

1842

Dickens tours America with Catherine; *American Notes* published; Alfred, Lord Tennyson publishes *Poems;* anesthesia first used in surgery.

1843

Martin Chuzzlewit appears in monthly installments; "A Christmas Carol" published for Christmas; William Wordsworth becomes poet laureate.

1844

Dickens tours Italy and Switzerland; *Martin Chuzzlewit* published in book form; "The Chimes" published for Christmas; Dickens's third son, Francis, born; first message by Morse's telegraph.

1845

Dickens produces the play *Every Man in His Humour;* "The Cricket on the Hearth" published for Christmas; Dickens's fourth son, Alfred, born; Edgar Allan Poe publishes *The Raven and Other Poems.*

1846

Dickens creates and edits the *Daily News; Dombey and Son* appears in monthly installments; *Pictures from Italy* published in book form; "The Battle of Life: A Love Story" published for Christmas; Irish potato famine results in mass immigration to United States; repeal of Corn Laws, which regulated grain trade and restricted imports; Elias Howe invents sewing machine.

1847

Dickens starts a theatrical company and takes *Every Man in His Humour* on a benefit tour; Dickens's fifth son, Sydney, born; Charlotte Brontë publishes *Jane Eyre;* Emily Brontë publishes *Wuthering Heights;* Henry Wadsworth Longfellow publishes *Evangeline.*

1848

Theatrical company performs for Queen Victoria; theatrical company performs *The Merry Wives of Windsor* to raise money for preservation of Shakespeare's birthplace; *Dombey and Son* published in book form; "The Haunted Man" published for Christmas; Dickens's sister Fanny dies.

1849

David Copperfield appears in monthly installments; Dickens's sixth son, Henry, born; Henry David Thoreau publishes "Civil Disobedience."

1850

David Copperfield published in book form; Dickens establishes and edits *Household Words;* Dickens's third daughter, Dora Annie, born, dies in infancy; Elizabeth Barrett Browning publishes *Sonnets from the Portuguese;* Tennyson becomes poet laureate; Nathaniel Hawthorne publishes *The Scarlet Letter.*

1851

Dickens and theatrical company perform charity plays; Dickens's father, John, dies; Nathaniel Hawthorne publishes *The House of the Seven Gables;* Herman Melville publishes *Moby Dick.*

1852

Bleak House appears in monthly installments; *A Child's History of England* published in book form; Dickens's seventh son, Edward, born; Harriet Beecher Stowe publishes *Uncle Tom's Cabin.*

1853

Bleak House published in book form; Dickens gives first public reading from the Christmas books; travels to France and Italy.

1854

Dickens travels to Preston, England, to observe industrial workers on strike and later chronicles events in article "On Strike" for *Household Words; Hard Times* appears in installments in *Household Words; Hard Times* published in book form; Henry David Thoreau publishes *Walden;* Crimean War begins; ends 1856.

1855

Little Dorrit appears in monthly installments; Dickens and family travel to Paris; Walt Whitman publishes *Leaves of Grass.*

1856

Dickens purchases Gad's Hill.

1857

Little Dorrit published in book form; Dickens spends year on theatrical productions.

1858

Dickens separates from Catherine; Dickens gives public readings; Henry Wadsworth Longfellow publishes *The Courtship of Miles Standish.*

1859

Dickens ends *Household Words;* begins *All the Year Round; A Tale of Two Cities* appears in *All the Year Round* and in book form.

1860

Great Expectations appears in weekly installments.

1861

Great Expectations published in book form; *The Uncommercial Traveller,* a collection, published; George Eliot publishes *Silas Marner;* U.S. Civil War begins; ends 1865.

1862

Dickens gives many public readings; travels to Paris; Victor Hugo publishes *Les Misérables;* Lincoln issues Emancipation Proclamation, freeing slaves.

1863

Dickens gives public readings in London and Paris; mother, Elizabeth, dies; Lincoln delivers Gettysburg Address.

1864

Our Mutual Friend appears in monthly installments.

1865

Dickens suffers a stroke, leaving him lame; *Our Mutual Friend* published in book form; *The Uncommercial Traveller,* a second collection, published; Lewis Carroll publishes *Alice in Wonderland;* Leo Tolstoy publishes *War and Peace;* rapid postwar industrialization in United States.

1866

Dickens gives public readings in Scotland and Ireland; Fyodor Dostoyevsky publishes *Crime and Punishment.*

1867

Dickens travels to America to give public readings; England grants dominion status for Canada.

1868

Dickens gives public readings in England; Louisa May Alcott publishes *Little Women.*

1869

Dickens begins *The Mystery of Edwin Drood;* Mark Twain publishes *Innocents Abroad;* imprisonment for debt abolished; Suez Canal opened.

1870

Dickens gives farewell public reading in London; *The Mystery of Edwin Drood* appears in monthly installments; becomes seriously ill, June 8; dies, June 9; buried in Poet's Corner, Westminster Abbey, June 14.

FOR FURTHER RESEARCH

ABOUT CHARLES DICKENS AND *HARD TIMES*

Peter Ackroyd, *Dickens.* New York: HarperCollins, 1990.

Harold Bloom, ed., *Charles Dickens's "Hard Times."* New York: Chelsea House, 1987.

Geoffrey Carnall, "Dickens, Mrs. Gaskell, and the Preston Strike," *Victorian Studies,* 1964.

G.K. Chesterton, *Charles Dickens: The Last of the Great Men.* New York: Readers Club, 1942.

Nicholas Coles, "The Politics of *Hard Times:* Dickens the Novelist Versus Dickens the Reformer," *Dickens Studies Annual,* 1986.

Philip Collins, ed., *Dickens: Interviews and Recollections.* London: Macmillan, 1981.

Monroe Engel, *The Maturity of Dickens.* Cambridge, MA: Harvard University Press, 1959.

George Harry Ford, *Dickens and His Readers.* Princeton, NJ: Princeton University Press, 1955.

John Forster, *The Life of Charles Dickens.* 2 vols. New York: E.P. Dutton, 1928.

Stanley Friedman, "Sad Stephen and Troubled Louisa: Paired Protagonists in *Hard Times,*" *Dickens Quarterly,* 1990.

Paul Edward Gray, *Twentieth Century Interpretations of "Hard Times": A Collection of Critical Essays.* Engelwood Cliffs, NJ: Prentice Hall, 1969.

Gerald Grubb, "Dickens's Pattern of Weekly Serialization," *English Literary History,* 1942.

Patricia Johnson, "*Hard Times* and the Structure of Industrialism: The Novel as Factory," *Studies in the Novel,* 1989.

Fred Kaplan, *Dickens: A Biography.* New York: William Morrow, 1988.

Stephen Leacock, *Charles Dickens: His Life and Work.* London: Peter Davies, 1933.

Sylvia Manning, *"Hard Times": An Annotated Bibliography.* New York: Garland, 1984.

J. Hillis Miller, *Charles Dickens: The World of His Novels.* Cambridge, MA: Harvard University Press, 1958.

Harlan S. Nelson, *Charles Dickens.* Boston: Twayne, 1981.

Ian Ousby, "Figurative Language in *Hard Times,*" *Durham University Journal,* 1981.

Hesketh Pearson, *Dickens: His Character, Comedy, and Career.* New York: Harper, 1949.

Allen Samuels, *"Hard Times": An Introduction to the Variety of Criticism.* New York: Macmillan, 1992.

John A. Stoler, "Dickens's Use of Names in *Hard Times,*" *Literary Onomastics Studies,* 1985.

Angus Wilson, *The World of Charles Dickens.* London: Martin Secker & Warburg, 1970.

WORKS BY THE AUTHOR

Charles Dickens, *Hard Times.* With an introduction by Dingle Foot. Oxford, England: Oxford University Press, 1989.

——, *Hard Times.* With an introduction by Christopher Hibbert. London: Folio Society, 1983.

——, *Hard Times.* Ed. Gwen Jose. Cambridge, England: Cambridge University Press, 1996.

——, *Hard Times.* With an introduction by John H. Middendorf. New York: Harper, 1960.

——, *Hard Times: An Authoritative Text, Contexts, Criticism.* Ed. Fred Kaplan and Sylvere Monod. New York: W.W. Norton, 2001.

——, *Hard Times for These Times.* Ed. Graham Law. Orchard Park, NY: Broadview, 1996.

——, *Hard Times for These Times.* With an introduction by John T. Winterich and illustrations by Charles Raymond. New York: Limited Editions Club, 1966.

ABOUT DICKENS'S TIMES

Arthur Bryant, *Spirit of England.* London: William Collins Sons, 1982.

Robert James Cruikshank, *Charles Dickens and Early Victorian England.* New York: Chanticleer, 1949.

John W. Cunliffe, *Leaders of the Victorian Revolution.* New York: Appleton-Century, 1934.

Valentine Cunningham, *Everywhere Spoken Against: Dissent in the Victorian Novel.* Oxford, England: Clarendon, 1975.

John W. Derry, *A Short History of Nineteenth-Century England.* London: Blandford, 1963.

John Foster, *Class Struggle and the Industrial Revolution.* London: Weidenfeld & Nicolson, 1974.

Jo Murtry, *Victorian Life and Victorian Fiction: A Companion for the American Reader.* Hamden, CT: Archon Books, 1979.

Philip A.M. Taylor, ed., *The Industrial Revolution in Britain: Triumph or Disaster?* Lexington, MA: D.C. Heath, 1970.

R.J. White, *The Horizon Concise History of England.* New York: American Heritage, 1971.

Index